OUR
BACKYARD
WAR West Merioneth
in World War II

OUR BACKYARD WAR

West Merioneth
in World War II

Les Darbyshire

Diolch i'm ffrindiau, cwmnïau a mudiadau lleol am
eu cymorth a'u cyfraniadau tuag at gostau'r cyhoeddi.

Hefyd i Dr Elin Angharad am ei gofal a'i chyngor
ar ran gwasg y Lolfa, Talybont, Ceredigion.

*Sincere thanks to all my friends, local businesses
and organisations who contributed towards the cost of publishing.*

*Also to Dr Elin Angharad for her advice and guidance
on behalf of Y Lolfa publishing house, Talybont, Ceredigion.*

First impression: 2015

Cover design: Y Lolfa
Cover photographs courtesy of Ian Corps and Eleanor Owen

ISBN: 978 1 78461 132 3

Published and printed in Wales
on paper from well-maintained forests by
Y Lolfa Cyf., Talybont, Ceredigion SY24 5HE
website www.ylolfa.com
e-mail ylolfa@ylolfa.com
tel 01970 832 304
fax 832 782

'There is many a boy here today who looks on war
as all glory, but, boys, it is all hell.'

General William T. Sherman 1820–91
Union General in the American Civil War

Western Merioneth

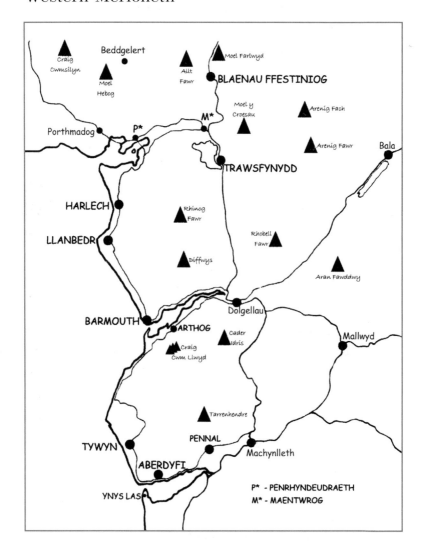

Contents

Rhagair

PAN FYDDWN NI'N arfer y gair 'rhyngwladol' rydym ni'n tueddu i feddwl am lefydd enwog, a phan feddyliwn ni am yr Ail Ryfel Byd mae'n debyg mai meddwl am ddinasoedd ym Mhrydain a fomiwyd a llefydd mewn gwahanol rannau o'r byd sydd wedi dod yn enwog mewn newyddion, llyfrau hanes, a ffilmiau rhyfel y byddwn ni. Ond y mae llefydd sy'n gyfarwydd iawn inni yn rhan o'r hyn sy'n 'rhyngwladol', ac y mae'r llyfr hwn yn dangos inni sut y bu i bobol gogledd-orllewin Cymru chwarae eu rhan yn y gwrthdaro mileinig yr ydym ni'n ei alw yn Ail Ryfel Byd.

A 'doedd eu rhan nhw ddim yn un ddibwys. Hogyn go ifanc oeddwn i yn ystod y rhyfel, a gallaf gofio am adroddiadau papurau newydd am yr ymladd, a chofnodion y 'Newyddion' – y 'British Pathé' a'r 'Gaumont British' – a ddangosid ymhob pictjiwrs ar y pryd. Gallaf gofio, hefyd, y dogni a fu, y catrodau 'Home Guard', y trychinebau achlysurol, fel achos yr awyren a ddaeth i lawr yn Nhrawsfynydd, yn ogystal â'r galar oedd yna am rai yn y lluoedd arfog a laddwyd neu a gollwyd yn y rhyfela. Ond 'doedd gen i ddim syniad am gymaint o ôl y rhyfel oedd yna yng ngogledd-orllewin Cymru. Y mae'r llyfr hwn o atgofion ac adroddiadau gan dystion sydd wedi eu cywain yn ddiwyd iawn a'u cyflwyno gan Les Darbyshire, a'u gosod yn aml yng nghyd-destun y rhyfela cyffredinol, yn agoriad llygad i mi.

I unrhyw un o'm cenhedlaeth i bydd y llyfr hwn yn deffro atgofion, rhai ohonyn nhw'n drist ac eraill yn eithaf doniol, ond y cwbwl yn dwyn i'r meddwl gyfnod tyngedfennol yn hanes y byd. I'r rhai hynny sy'n rhy ifanc i gofio, bydd y llyfr hwn yn gyfrwng i roi amcan iddynt o sut yr oedd hi'n teimlo i fod yn fyw yn ystod blynyddoedd y rhyfel.

Rydw i, yn un, yn dymuno diolch i Les am ei gamp, ac am ei ymroddiad yn rhoddi ar gof a chadw ran o fywyd, yn arbennig mewn un rhan o Gymru yn ystod yr Ail Ryfel Byd. Y mae ei lafur yn weithred o goffâd briodol a theilwng.

Diolch yn fawr.

Yr Athro Emeritws Gwyn Thomas, Bangor

Foreword

WHEN WE USE the word 'international' we tend to think of famous places, and when we think of the Second World War I suppose we tend to think of cities in Britain which were bombed and of places in various parts of the world which have been made famous in news reports, history books, and war films. But places that are familiar to us are part of the 'international' scene, and this book shows how people in north-west Wales played their part in the savage conflict known as World War II.

And the part they played was not insignificant. I was a boy during the war and can remember newspaper reports of action, and the British Pathé and British Gaumont News account of events which were shown in all cinemas at the time. I can also recall the rationing, the Home Guard outfits and patrols in Blaenau Ffestiniog, and the occasional disasters, such as a plane crash in Trawsfynydd, as well as the grief for servicemen killed or lost in action. But I had no idea of the extent of the impact of the war on north-west Wales. This book of reminiscences and reports by witnesses assiduously gathered and put together by Les Darbyshire, and often given a context within the larger conduct of the war, was a real revelation to me.

For anyone of my generation this book will kindle memories, some of them sad and some of them quite comic, but all of them evocative of a momentous period in the history of the world. For those too young to remember, this book will give them a feeling of what it was like to be alive during the years of the war.

I, for one, wish to thank Les for his accomplishment, and

for his dedication in putting on record a part of life, especially in one part of Wales during the Second World War. His work is an appropriate and worthy act of remembrance.

Diolch yn fawr.

Emeritus Professor Gwyn Thomas, Bangor

Introduction

LITTLE HAS BEEN written about the events and tribulations of west Merioneth during WWII, although the tranquillity of the area was shattered when war was declared on Germany. This part of the county became the nursery to produce troops ready for battle; its meagre manufacturing skills were harnessed to produce war materials and its natural resources of disused slate quarries used for the safekeeping of priceless national treasures and vital munitions.

This narrative is not a historical record of the period, but tries to convey the general atmosphere of the time, its people, their problems, and the changeover from civilian to wartime mode in a world where many items and basic foodstuffs were suddenly rationed. What had been a small close-knit community suddenly saw the upheaval of families being split up with relatives 'called up' or directed to work in industries far away from home. Additionally, there was always the risk of an air raid or the dread of receiving a telegram saying that a loved one was either missing or had been killed.

Official records are not always available, and by now there are very few of us left who remember that period. Moreover, our memories unfortunately are not always accurate in the finer details. Much information is second hand, what children of the time can remember or what they had been told – and many accounts have possibly 'grown' over the years!

It is not possible to record all the events of that era. Some may have been shrouded in the mists of time, and as we get older our memories fail, recollections fade, and even today there is a real possibility that some events remain 'classified'.

This volume hopefully chronicles the fact that Merioneth was not a quiet backwater during the war and shows how the area and its people contributed, in no small part, to the war effort.

I wish also to convey my grateful thanks to all those who have allowed the use of their stories, memories, documents and insight into that period of time from the dark days of 1939 to happier times in 1946. Without them much valuable and interesting information would have been lost.

Les Darbyshire
2015

This book is dedicated to my late wife
Gwyneth
1924–2013

About the Author

LES DARBYSHIRE WAS born at Manod, Blaenau Ffestiniog; he attended Manod Council School and then the Ffestiniog Grammar School. Owing to wartime restrictions, he was unable to proceed with his preferred option of a career in electrical engineering, and he was apprenticed to his father as a carpenter.

He worked on the construction of the Llanbedr Aerodrome, Trawsfynydd Artillery Camp, and also worked underground at Manod Slate Quarry building chambers to store and protect National Art Gallery pictures from London as well as treasures from other cities. He then became part of a team working at Morfa Conwy on a secret project to construct Mulberry Harbours ready for the invasion of France on D-Day. He also joined the Royal Navy and served on landing crafts.

After demobilisation, he returned to the family business before taking up an appointment as Resident Engineer with the Deudraeth Rural District Council and later with the Merioneth Water Board. He was later appointed to the staff of the Estate Department of the Forestry Commission, Aberystwyth and was based at Coed y Brenin and Dyfi Forest.

During his years at Blaenau Ffestiniog, he became involved with the Workers' Educational Association and was a delegate to their first post-war conference at Harrogate. He served for a period as a member of the old Ffestiniog Urban District Council and took a keen interest in local history.

It was whilst working with the Water Board that he met his future wife Gwyneth, and they enjoyed fifty years of married life in Barmouth before Gwyneth passed away in 2013. Les's interest in local history continued; he became a representative of Barmouth on the Merioneth Historical and Record Society and also an Elder at Caersalem Presbyterian Chapel, Barmouth – an office which he has held for over forty years.

Les's first book, *Barmouth Sea Heroes* (2012), quickly sold out, and a donation of £1,000 was given from its sale to the Barmouth District Nurses Equipment Fund.

Heroes

Don't speak to me of heroes until you've seen this tale
Of Britain's merchant seamen who sailed through storm and gale
To keep those lifelines open in our nation's hour of need
When a tyrant cast a shadow across our island creed.
Captains, greasers, cabin boys, mates and engineers
Heard the call to duty and cast aside their fears.
They stoked those hungry boilers and stood behind the wheel
While cooks and stewards manned the guns on coffins made of steel.
They moved in icy convoys from Scapa to Murmansk
And crossed the western ocean, never seeking thanks.
They sailed the South Atlantic where raiders lay in wait
And kept the food lines open from Malta to the Cape.
Tracked by silent U-boats which hunted from below,
Shelled by mighty cannons and fighters flying low,
They clung to burning lifeboats where the sea had turned to flame
And watched their shipmates disappear to everlasting fame.
I speak not of a handful but 30,000 plus,
Some whose names we'll never know in whom we placed our trust;
They never knew the honour of medals on their chests
Or marching bands and victory and glory and the rest.
The ocean is their resting place, their tombstone is the wind,
The seabirds' cry their last goodbye to family and friend.
Freighters, troopships, liners and tankers by the score,
Fishing boats and coasters, 2,000 ships and more
Flew the proud Red Duster as they sank beneath the waves
And took those countless heroes to lonely ocean graves.
Their legacy is freedom to those who hold it dear,
To walk with clear horizons and never to hide fear.
So when you speak of heroes, remember those at sea,
From Britain's Merchant Navy who died to keep us free.

Composed by David Partridge, Botany Bay, Australia
for Merchant Navy Day.

Recollections of Blaenau Ffestiniog

ON SUNDAY, 4 September 1939 we were at home at No. 4, Tyddyn Gwyn, Manod awaiting the radio announcement which had been promised for 11 a.m. that morning. Prime Minister Neville Chamberlain came over the air and said that a state of war existed between Britain and Germany. The news was not unexpected, but one realised that changes would occur to the way of life with which we had become accustomed, and our family of five would have to experience many changes. What were our thoughts then? My brother was a student at the University of Wales, Bangor whilst my sister and I were still at home. My father, an ex-serviceman from WWI, had been severely gassed and knew the horrors of war only too well; his thoughts were for us, the children, and what would be our destiny and that of the family.

My brother had already been involved with registration for military service as a militiaman and had had a deferment whilst in college. Many local lads had already being called up to the forces to do their six months training; work in the Blaenau area was getting scarce, the demand for slates had diminished, and numerous people had gone to work on building the army camp at Kinmel Bay, Rhyl. Eventually my father had to go and work in Marchwiel near Wrexham and came home at weekends on the GWR railway from Wrexham to Blaenau. Later, my sister was directed to work in a factory in Dowlais, south Wales, which only left my mother and me at home.

Evacuees from Liverpool and Birkenhead came to the

area; I was at the county school then, and we had an influx of girls from Birkenhead to the school. At the time, concern was expressed that with the influx of so many evacuees the Welsh language would suffer; in any event, English was the main language of the school, so it did not make a lot of difference. Local families received payment for each evacuee they took in and their plight was not lost on large companies. An 'interesting' advert appeared in the *Cymro* newspaper on 30 September 1939 concerning the feeding of evacuees:

> The Feeding of Evacuated Children
>
> The Government allowance of 10/6*d.* per week for one child and 8/6*d.* per week per child if more than one is taken is to cover not only feeding but fuel, lighting and other charges. This means that most careful planning is necessary to make sure that the children get the full nourishment that the allowance permits.
>
> A large cup of Bournville cocoa (6*d.* per quarter pound) made with half milk and water costs only 1*d.* and yet together with a slice of bread (preferably brown) and butter, it provides a satisfying supper for any child. This meal has the equivalent food value of four eggs.
>
> On account of its low cost and high food value, Bournville Cocoa is one of the most economical drinks for the children's breakfast or lunch.
>
> Issued By
> CADBURYS'
> of Bournville

The St John Ambulance played a vital part in our lives; as children we were already cadet members of the organisation. Blaenau had a worthy contingent of first aiders in the senior section and nearly all had signed on as reservists in the Army Medical Corps and went to the military hospital at Netley for their annual training. Throughout the pre-war period these men had given their time and service at all public functions. The cadets were trained by Mr Hugh Owen Jones of Cae Clyd, Manod, who, with all the others, was called up immediately when war was declared; they served in all theatres of war with distinction. Though most of the brigades were quarry men, very few returned to the quarries on completion of their service; some became ambulance drivers or joined the nursing profession whilst others became first aid men on large civil engineering works.

Everybody had to join some civil defence organisation, and I was directed to the Civil Defence Search and Rescue Group as I was in the building trade by now and had also been a cadet in the St John Ambulance. Our headquarters was the cellar below the then public library in Church Street; the floor above had been strengthened by solid tree trunks and beams to reinforce the cellar against air raids. The officer in charge was Robert Glyn Williams (Bob Glyn Dairy) and we were issued with blue overalls, a tin hat, and an Air Raid Precaution (ARP) badge. Fortunately, we were never called out, but we were on standby duties during the raids on Coventry. The Home Guard became part of the life of the town. Their commanding officer, Tom Williams, had been a sergeant in WWI; they conducted manoeuvres and the ARP were always on standby duties during those times.

During both world wars, quarry men's battalions were raised in Blaenau; during WWII, some 100 men enlisted under the command of Captain T. W. Owen, Caerblaidd Office, and they became part of the Royal Engineers. One notable person who joined them was schoolmaster and dramatist John Ellis Williams; he attained the rank of sergeant before moving on to the Army Educational Corps. The writer remembers seeing John, before he joined the battalion, walking to condition his feet to army-type boots – such was the spirit of the time. The Royal Engineers served in London during the Blitz and were responsible for defusing various bombs and land mines, and Sergeant Ieuan Emyr Jones was mentioned in dispatches for his work in defusing mines. Afterwards, the battalion served in North Africa.

Life continued as usual in the town, although various

restrictions prevailed: petrol was not available for private cars and was severely rationed for business purposes. The practice of queuing began which has carried on to the present time. All road signs and place names were removed by the authorities in the hope that this would impede the progress of an occupying army if an invasion took place. Windows had to be 'blacked out' using black cloth attached to a wooden frame and fitted inside each window – woe betide anyone if a chink of light was visible to the wardens. Car headlights were also adapted to regulate the beam, a measure that was supposed to prevent German aircraft from pinpointing their route. The police had changed; the young ones had joined the services and wartime police officers came into being. In Manod, we had an ex-quarry man, John Llewelyn Jones, as our local constable, a job which he carried out with pride.

Brian Paul of Penrhyndeudraeth recounts the experience of his father, John R. Paul, who had been born with a 'gammy' foot. In 1938 he had taken over a newsagent's business in the village, but like all others when war came he had to register for military service and in due course had his medical. His disability classed him as unfit for military duties, but he was then directed to join the fire service in Blaenau Ffestiniog as a full time fireman, thus relieving another able-bodied person for more arduous duties. The role also gave John, as a disabled person, the opportunity to show his capability. John served throughout the war in Blaenau, though fortunately the service was not called out to any major incidents. In all likelihood, however, there would have been many standby calls from nearby towns and cities. By the end of hostilities, he had attained the rank of leading fireman. Blaenau was busy with the influx of troops of all nationalities from Trawsfynydd Camp; lorries used to bring them to town for recreation, the cinemas did a roaring trade, and it was a boom time for many local businesses.

One incident has remained in my memory. One night there was a terrible noise as if there had been an explosion;

the house shook, windows rattled, and the general opinion was that something had happened at the Cooke's Factory in Penrhyndeudraeth. However, there was no news to that effect – in fact, there was a complete silence, no information whatsoever. It was only after the end of the war that we learnt that it had been a mild earthquake and it had not caused any damage. News was obviously censored and often delayed before being released to the public in case it might give useful information to the enemy.

During the war Germans used broadcasting for propaganda purposes; they had an Irishman named William Joyce who was at the forefront of their radio propaganda. In some way it was hilarious – his call sign 'Germany Calling, Germany Calling' was known to everybody. Uncannily, he seemed to possess knowledge of various local events in particular areas which seemed to be very accurate. When hostilities ended, William Joyce (Lord Haw-Haw) was tried in a British Court for treason, found guilty and hanged.

Somehow or other people did pass information to the enemy, and the writer had occasion to see the full implication of this type of espionage. Whilst based at Chichester and serving on a special duties flotilla squadron in the Royal Navy, we were completely 'in the dark' as to our purpose and destination, but over the radio Lord Haw-Haw gave an accurate résumé of our orders. We were not told officially until we were halfway across the English Channel, when our commanding officer opened his sealed orders and divulged our destination. Yes, Lord Haw-Haw had been right: he had correct information which only 'someone high up' could have divulged; the lives of the British Jack did not matter. During the various stops we had whilst transporting our crafts to the forward area we were continually shelled as soon as we arrived – our timetable had been well and truly divulged. Blaenau, like so many other places, suffered casualties , and the official telegrams came too often. To my knowledge, five were killed or died through war injuries in the Manod area alone.

Prior to joining the navy, my friend and neighbour Dick Jones was an assistant working in the Star Supply Stores in town; he was drafted to the submarine service and sailed to Murmansk, Russia with the Arctic convoys and was later sent to the Mediterranean on the submarine HMS *Trooper*. He was lost when the submarine was listed as 'missing'; it was assumed that she must have hit a mine. David Morris Jones was a butcher before joining the army; he was taken prisoner in North Africa. Tragically, whilst being transported across the Mediterranean to Italy, an Allied warship torpedoed the transport and all prisoners perished.

Gwynedd Lloyd Williams, a shop assistant at the Bells Store, Church Street, joined the navy and trained as a cook. He was drafted to HMS *Bon Adventure*, which was sunk in the Aegean Sea with all on board lost. Gwynedd was very close to his mother, and his father, a ship's carpenter, was away for long periods of time. One night, his mother woke up in a lather of sweat. She had heard Gwynedd shouting 'Mam, Mam', and she realised that something terrible had happened to him. In the morning, she told neighbours of her experience and that she knew her son was dead. A few weeks later, the official telegram came informing Mrs Williams that her son was missing, presumed dead. It affected her so much that she never recovered from the shock of her experience and died not long afterwards. It must be stressed that this incident was no fairy tale but a true account which cannot be explained – but as Shakespeare said, 'There are more things in heaven and earth, Horatio, / Than are dreamt of in your philosophy.' Similar incidents have been recorded elsewhere.

By now my brother had completed his studies at Bangor and had been directed to work at a scientific establishment in Hammersmith, undertaking research on radio valves. He was offered a post in the Admiralty Scientific Group at Teddington to conduct research on tides and waves – the birth really of oceanography. Their prime work was to evaluate waves and tides for the opening of the second front – the D-Day landings.

I, for my part, was apprenticed to my father as a carpenter and joiner and had employment in the army artillery camp at Bronaber, Trawsfynydd. We were part of the maintenance team responsible for the upkeep of the camp and building additional accommodation for the troops. When our work at Bronaber was finished, the Llanbedr Aerodrome project started; we had to leave Blaenau at about 6.30 a.m. and a fleet of small buses took us to Llanbedr. The contractors were that well-known firm William Mowlems Ltd of London. The main site was just south of the village; this was the site for the accommodation and administration. Work was also proceeding on clearing the sand dunes to make way for the massive runways needed, and thousands of wild rabbits who inhabited the dunes perished. One could see them running, but the big caterpillar machines held no pity.

During this period, as I did not want to be conscripted into a service that I did not like, my friend Hughie Hughes and I volunteered for the Royal Air Force. We had medicals at Chester and passed A1. Unfortunately, there were no vacancies for anything in my line whilst Hughie opted for what was offered. He became an air gunner and served on bombers. He was wounded but survived the war.

Whilst at Llanbedr, all the tradesmen from Blaenau were transferred to work in the caverns of the Bwlch y Slaters Quarry, as it was known locally. At the completion of the conversion work, I was directed to work at Morfa Conwy, where we had to work on massive concrete structures. Their purpose was not known at the time, but they were designed to be sunk somewhere as they were fitted with valves internally. Much later it became known that we had been working on the Mulberry Harbours ready for the second front, a project which was unique in its conception. My work entailed designing and positioning the slipway down to the mouth of the Conwy river – 18" × 18" baulks of timber were bolted together in threes to form the slipway. The work had to be done in conjunction with the tide, so our hours of work varied from day to day.

Whilst at Conwy, I had to register for military service and noted a preference for the Royal Engineers as my father had been in that regiment. Eventually I had my medical at Caernarfon, passing A1, and waited for my 'call-up papers'. An official letter arrived one morning and I thought this is it, but no, it was a notification that I had to attend another medical at Caernarfon, but this time for the Royal Navy. I again passed A1 and had an interview with a naval officer who stated, with gusto, that I had been accepted for duties in the service. I think he was a little shocked when I said that I did not want to join the navy, but I was told quite curtly that I had no choice – the navy wanted joiners, and that was that! Three weeks later I was on my way to Devonport Barracks with my toolbox in hand – odd as it may seem, we had to supply our own tools in those days!

St John Ambulance Brigade, Blaenau Ffestiniog taken at Chirk Castle, 1938.
All senior members had volunteered to be reservists in the Army Medical Corps. Unfortunately only some names are now to hand.
Standing (Cadets): L to R Isaac Davies and Gwilym Lewis
Seated Front Row: L to R Bob Roberts, Les Darbyshire (first and third from left respectively.)
Second Row: L to R Robert Griffith Roberts (with arms folded), Hughie Pierce (with right hand raised), Emyr Stoddart (seated and smiling).

Arnhem/Rhine Crossing
662 Flottila, P Squadron, U Force, Royal Navy, April 1945, based at Nijmegen, Holland. The first time ever for a Royal Navy force to operate so far inland. Landing craft transported from Antwerp to Nijmegen by army tank carriers.

A railway bridge demolished during a night raid by the Germans on Nijmegen.

Crew of 662 Flotilla. Author – centre front row.

Final meal at Huissen prior to zero hour to land at Arnhem, 13 April 1945.
Author – second from left.

Homeward bound after a successful mission, Firth of Forth Bridge, making our way to base at Queensferry (south).

Loading the Landing Craft at the Power House Basin, Nijmegen, 12 April 1945. British Army personnel from the Lincoln, Wellington and Leicester Regiments of the British 49th Polar Bear Division landed successfully at Arnhem at 4 a.m. on Friday 13 April.

D-Day Money.
Here are two examples of cash given to soldiers prior to embarking for the D-Day invasion of Europe – a French 5 Franc note and a German 2 Rentenmark note. The money supplied was 'part' of the soldier's normal wage and would be recorded in his pay book.

A Mulberry Harbour at Morfa Conwy being floated out into the river.

Memories of WWII

THE LATE MISS Dilys Davies, on the occasion of celebrating her 100th birthday in 2007, gave an interview in which she recounted her life and experiences in Barmouth. Dilys was born in room No. 11 of the Royal Station Hotel as it was then called; her mother was the hotel manageress, running it single-handed, whilst her father had a bookshop under the Arches in town. Dilys was brought up by a nanny, her mother dying at the early age of 55. Her father, concerned about Dilys's welfare, thought that the best way to keep her from mischief would be if she had a small business, so he provided her with a shop selling stationery and leather goods. She kept the shop going until she retired at the age of 62 in 1969.

Dilys saw quite a few changes in the town, including many peaks and troughs; she remembered the slump and depression of the 1930s which affected every local business, though possibly not as much as in the industrialised areas of the county. However, the Second World War saw a revival in Barmouth's fortunes. Tonfannau Army Camp was being built, providing work for many locals. Eventually, on completion, members of the armed forces came and stayed, patronising hotels and private homes in the town. As the war progressed, Barmouth became a boom town almost, serving as the hub of an economic wheel extending across south-west Merioneth and in particular along the county's coastal belt.

***

Various military installations were established; hotels, boarding houses and private houses were commandeered for military use. After Dunkirk, Barmouth saw an influx of returning soldiers, all in a pitiful condition and in a state of distress. Then came the birth of the Home Guard, originally named the Local Defence Volunteers. To the north of Barmouth, at Llanbedr, an aerodrome was being built with the sand dunes being flattened to make room for the massive runways required; these later played a vital part in the defence of the realm. Further north at Blaenau Ffestiniog, the existing slate caverns at Bwlch y Slaters, as it was called locally (the more imposing official name was Manod Slate Quarry, now Cwt y Bugail Quarry), were taken over and adapted to store valuable and irreplaceable pictures and art work from the National Art Gallery in London. There had been an artillery camp at Bron Aber, Trawsfynydd since the early 1900s, and this had the reputation of having the best ranges in the country. With the advent of war, an overflow camp and training facilities were established at Morfa in Harlech; this had a small firing range which had its own railway track to move the targets. This camp was also linked to the GWR railway and the spur line was called the Harlech Military Railway.

Penrhyndeudraeth had an existing explosives factory (Cooke's Explosives) which increased its capacity and provided employment to many in the area, especially women. To the south, Tonfannau Camp trained troops in anti-aircraft defence, and to complement their work a small grass runway was built at Morfa Tywyn so that aircraft could tow targets for shooting practice. However, the runway was not always operative as it was found to get waterlogged easily.

Camps were based at Llwyngwril, Arthog, Friog, the Royal Marines at the Fegla, and Barmouth, with the 164th Officers Cadet Training Unit (OCTU) being the town's largest contingent. There were also POW camps in the area – Coed y Brenin, Trawsfynydd, Harlech and Tywyn. The WRVS gave unstinting service to the troops by manning canteens and undertaking various other voluntary work, though they were not always appreciated for what they did. The Local Defence Force comprised the Red Cross, St John Ambulance, air raid wardens, the fire service, and, last but not least, the lifeboat service, and all gave sterling service as required of them.

Virtually every town, village and hamlet was affected by the war, with men being called up for military service and families being split up and directed to work away from home, for instance, in munitions factories. Some men were also directed to work in the coal mines. Fundraising for various causes was instigated – a popular one was raising money to buy a Spitfire – and they were very successful. Food rationing was very severe, but as always many people were able to procure materials and goods and sell them on at a higher price on the black market. The term 'spiv' came into vogue to refer to individuals who were able to obtain goods in short supply, and needless to say they made a thriving business.

A local businessman recounted his experience of dealing with the shortages. He was able to buy a half side of pig from a farmer, but he had to take it home in his van. The journey was fraught with trepidation and the fear of being stopped by the police. Being a person of substance, the consequences to him would have been dire had he been found dealing in black market goods. He reached home safely, and next time he saw the farmer who had sold him the pig, told him about his journey home and his misgivings. The farmer laughed and said, 'Do you know who had the other half?' Yes, it was a high-ranking police officer, so there was no need to worry – the black market was big business! Farms produced butter for the market, and if you had the money anything was available. All goods were rationed in some form or other: food, clothes and furniture were all in short supply; petrol was only available for urgent and essential services. Most private cars had been laid up owing to the shortage of fuel.

Before going into the history of various places and their

contributions, it should be noted that although some of the text is written by people who were there at the time, the veracity of their accounts cannot always be verified. Nearly seventy-five years have elapsed since the events, and memories tend to become clouded. Unfortunately, the number of people still alive from that period is now limited, and we are fortunate in those who have volunteered to give their recollections in this book.

To understand the conditions prevailing at the time, it is helpful to have a chronicle or diary of events noting the peaks and troughs of the war. We should also not forget that every area had the onerous task of coping with the loss of a dear husband or son, and the anguish, pain and uncertainty of waiting for news of loved ones who had either been taken prisoner or had been reported missing after their ships had been sunk. Were they alive or dead? Would they ever come home?

Though the war did not begin until September 1939, life in general before this time was very strained. From 1938 it was obvious to all that the 'powers that be' were preparing for war, and in some way the announcement of war on that Sunday in September came not as a surprise but as a relief. People had been conditioned by the newspapers to the possibilities of war, and as always there was a firm belief that it would not last long and that the status quo would be restored between the nations quickly.

On 26 May 1939, parliament passed the Military Training Act, which required all males aged 20 and 21 to register for military service and to be called to the colours for a period of six months. The 'militiamen', as they were called, registered on Saturday 3 June and were then called up. Needless to say, these men had to serve for a period exceeding six years and quite a few of them were taken prisoners at the fall of France.

The RWF Territorial Battalion held a massive parade in Blaenau. Quite a few local boys were serving in it, and they held the final parade in the field opposite Tanrhos Cottages, Manod. To us children, it was a glorious sight. Blaenau at the time had several local weekly papers – *Y Glorian*, *Y Gloch* and *Y Rhedegydd* – all with a good circulation. The town could also boast three cinemas: the Forum, the Empire and the Park Cinema, the latter being an old renovated army hut that had taken over showing films previously screened at the Market Hall. The hall itself saw many changes. In its heyday, it contained on the ground floor all the commodities you could want: a second-hand bookshop, a homemade toffee stall, and a Co-operative store which dedicated a large section of the floor to the selling of groceries. The main area was taken by a Mr Kahn, a Turkish Armenian Jew who had had to flee his country. He ran a veritable treasure trove, selling everything from hobnails and tools to leather and hardware – something for everyone, in fact. However, the hall was taken over for war production, and a Mr Ackett set up a business producing camouflage nets for the use of the armed forces, an enterprise which gave employment to quite a number of local people. Mr Kahn was able to keep a small ironmongery stall on the ground floor partitioned from the factory area.

The town itself was changing. There was a dearth of local young men, who had been replaced by soldiers from the Trawsfynydd camp coming into town for enjoyment and relaxation. There were also a few local lads home on leave and tired of being asked, 'When are you going back?' A few girls had joined the Women's Land Army, and they looked very smart in their uniforms. Church bells were ordered to be silent, only to be rung to warn people of an imminent invasion by the enemy. There a few conscientious objectors, but fortunately they were not harassed as those in the First World War had been; they were mostly directed to work on farms and in other non-combatant duties.

Diary of Events

1938

| | Car manufacturers switch to aircraft production. |
| September | Prime Minister Neville Chamberlain agrees to the Munich Agreement, which is signed by Britain, France, Italy and Germany. During this period, men and women volunteer for civil defence. |

1939

March	Germany invades Czechoslovakia.
April	Compulsory conscription for men aged 20 and 21.
August	Germany signs a non-aggression pact with Russia. United Kingdom signs a treaty of alliance with Poland.
September	German troops enter Poland. War declared between Britain and Germany. France declares war on Germany. Instructions for gas masks issued to civilians, to be carried at all times. Identity cards issued. Registration for ration cards.

1940

January	Food rationing begins: 4oz ham, 4oz bacon, 12oz sugar and 4oz butter per adult per week.
March	Meat rationed to 1s. 10d. worth a week (about 1lb in weight) and 11d. for children (old money).
April	Germany invades Denmark.
May	Mr Neville Chamberlain resigns as prime minister. Germany invades Belgium, Luxembourg and Holland. Mr Winston Churchill appointed prime minister. Holland surrenders. Emergency Powers Act passed. Belgium surrenders.

29 May–3 June	British and Allied troops evacuated from Dunkirk.
June	Germans enter Paris.
July	Tea, cooking fats and margarine rationed to 2oz a week; cheese rationed to 2–8oz a week depending on supply.
	Purchase tax imposed.
August	Battle of Britain.
September	Blitz begins on London.
	Battle of Britain won by the Royal Air Force
Sept.–Nov.	London bombed every night. Over one million houses damaged or destroyed, with an estimated 30,000 dead from the bombing.
October	Bombing at its peak, with an estimated average of 200 tons of explosives dropped every 24 hours on Britain.

1941

March	Battle of the Atlantic begins.
	Registration of Employment Order for women aged 20 and 21 extended to women up to the age of 30 and for men over 40 years of age.
	Income tax raised to 6s. 6d. in the pound.
	Jams, margarine, treacle etc. rationed to a maximum of 8oz per month.
	700,000 tons of British shipping are sunk.
	Women's Services become part of the armed forces and subject to military discipline.
	Cheese rations down to 1oz a week.
	Clothes prices at least 150% higher than during the pre-war period.
	Clothes rationing introduced.
	Egg distribution controlled.
	William Beveridge appointed to oversee the introduction of social insurance schemes.
	Germany invades Russia.
	Ernest Bevin directs 30,000 men (dubbed the Bevin Boys) to work in the mines.

Japanese forces bomb Pearl Harbour.

Conscription for single women aged between 20 and 30 introduced. Eligible women are liable for military service or other work of national importance.

Call-up for men lowered to 18 years of age.

HMS *Prince of Wales* and HMS *Repulse* (battleships) sunk by Japanese planes.

America declares war on Germany and Italy.

1942

February

American troops arrive in Britain.

Soap rationed to 3oz a month.

Members of the Home Guard recruited to man ack-ack batteries (anti-aircraft).

Clothing rations reduced to 48 coupons per year.

Singapore falls to the Japanese.

April — White bread discontinued.

Oct.–Nov. — Battle of El Alamein.

1943

Wages 35% higher than during the pre-war period.

Wings for Victory, a civilian campaign to raise money for aircraft.

March–Sept. — Bomber Command offensive on German towns.

April — Cigarettes on average cost 1*s*. 9*d*. for every packet of twenty.

July — Food, drinks and fuel in short supply.

Allied forces land in Sicily.

September — Italy surrenders.

1944

Salute the Soldier Week to encourage civilians to save money in government accounts.

Average wage for men in engineering £7 and for women £3.10*s*.

Coal rationed to 4 cwt per month.

January — Anzio (Italy) landings.

140,000 members of the Home Guard serving on anti-aircraft guns.

1,400,000 non-British troops stationed in the UK, the majority of whom are American GIs.

June   D-Day landings in Normandy, France.

The first flying bombs hit London.

Liberation of Paris.

First V-2 rocket lands in Britain.

Arnhem airborne attack fails.

1oz extra tea for 70 year olds.

1945

Yalta Conference, at which Churchill, Roosevelt and Stalin meet.

Dresden in Germany devastated by Bomber Command.

April   Russian forces take Berlin.

Hitler commits suicide.

May   Germany surrenders.

VE Day (Victory in Europe).

August   America drops an atomic bomb on Hiroshima.

Second atomic bomb dropped on Nagasaki.

Japan surrenders.

VJ Day (Victory in Japan).

With the end of the war, life returned to normal, though some things would never be the same again. Values had altered, class distinctions had been eroded, and women, following their wartime contributions, were now demanding and increasingly attaining equality. However, all this was in the future. The immediate reaction after the war was one of rejoicing, with prisoners of war returning home to their loved ones, though the festive atmosphere was marred somewhat by knowledge of German and Japanese atrocities.

But it is time to resume our history of Merioneth during the war and the contribution of the county to the war effort. The narrative in this book is based on the coastal area from Penrhyndeudraeth to Aberdyfi and includes Blaenau

Ffestiniog, Trawsfynydd, Dolgellau and Corris, which were the main areas of activity during the war in Merioneth. It should be emphasised that this narrative is based only on information currently available, as well as on the goodwill of those whose memories are still active. There is still much information that has not come to light, and perhaps this book will inspire others to recount and record their own war experiences.

The Home Guard

THE YEAR 1940 was when major changes took place; it represented the end of an era and a new beginning. The events and decisions of that year still remain with us today. In the later part of the year, after untold military disasters, the country woke up to its dangers and the Dunkirk spirit came through, showing that Britain could face any adversity and still win through.

Winston Churchill had become prime minister and installed a new spirit and determination in the nation, and in May 1940 the then Foreign Secretary Anthony Eden announced the formation of an unpaid Local Defence Volunteer force (LDV) and asked all able-bodied men to answer the call to defend their country. Their prime role was to safeguard waterways, railway stations, bridges and factories, to clear rubble, and man the anti-aircraft batteries. By the end of the first day, 250,000 men had volunteered, equal in number to the peacetime regular army; this figure increased, exceeding 350,000 by the end of May and 1,400,000 by the end of June. The scale of this response had not been expected by the authorities, who were forced to restrict volunteers to those of between 17 and 65 years of age. Nevertheless, this was not strictly enforced initially, and a few old soldiers still managed to join up. In the Barmouth area, one old soldier, Joe Finnegan, who had seen service in the Boer War and WWI, volunteered even though he was 68 at the time.

Not only had the numbers responding to their call caught the authorities by surprise, but the LDV was launched without any staff, funds or premises of its own. Officialdom had been caught napping, and insufficient enrolling forms meant the police had to resort to making a list of volunteers' names.

The War Office could not supply uniforms, so arm bands were issued with LDV printed on them; some were made by the Women's Voluntary Service (WVS). Weapons were in short supply, and volunteers were ordered to find any weapons which they could use; many men had to drill using broomsticks instead of rifles. It was said that in June 1940 there was only one rifle to every six men in the force. Churchill insisted that the force be renamed the Home Guard. They trained in the evenings, being instructed in weapon handling, unarmed combat, and basic sabotage. The dearth of weapons was serious and the War Office issued 250,000 pikes – bayonets welded on metal poles. Local commanders received no training and it was up to them to develop tactics suited to their area.

Dad's Army, a television series based on the Home Guard, depicts a rather rosy picture of the force; no doubt there was a happy comradeship among the volunteers, but the reality was they did valuable work under severe circumstances. They relieved the army of many mundane duties – acting as sentries, patrolling the countryside, and guarding vital bridges – which meant the army was able to concentrate on more vital roles. The Home Guard also manned anti-aircraft guns and rocket launchers. In the London area, a heavy anti-aircraft gun would require at least ten men to operate it. The Home Guards supplied the men, thus relieving the regular army for other duties. It was estimated that 100,000 Home Guards worked on anti-aircraft (AA) batteries and one of their main tasks was to shoot down V-1s. It has been estimated that guns placed along the channel coast and manned by the Guards managed to destroy 60% of the V-1s aimed at London.

A *Home Guard Handbook* was issued in 1940 which stated that the main duties of the Home Guard were as follows:

Guarding important points.
Observation and reporting – prompt and precise.

Immediate attack against small lightly armed parties of the enemies.

The defence of roads, villages, factories and vital points in towns to block enemy movements.

Every member of the Home Guard is expected to know the whole ground in his own district; the personnel of his own detachment; the headquarters of the detachment and where he is to report for duties in the event of an alarm; what the alarm signal is and the form of reports concerning enemy landings or approaches; what the reports should contain; and to whom they should be sent.

Many people did not realise that under the National Service (Number 2) Act of December 1941 male civilians could be ordered to join the Home Guard and attend up to 48 hours training a month. Whether this was enforced is not known, since the number of volunteers had, anyway, far exceeded expectations. However, it might have been necessary to order those with specialist or particular skills to enlist.

An interesting document was seen at the Merioneth Archives: a carbon copy of a letter sent to a farmer in the Harlech district. The letter has the heading 'Ministry of Labour and National Service' and was sent by the Harlech Local Office on 1 February 1942:

Compulsory Enrolment in the Home Guard

After giving careful consideration to your explanation of your failure to comply with the directions issued to you to enrol in the Home Guard, you are hereby directed to report for enrolment at the Glyn, Home Guard Headquarters, Talsarnau on 5/2/42 at 7 p.m. Failure to do so will be immediately reported under the Defence [Home Guard] Regulation 1940.

[signed] E. Humphreys for National Service

In this particular case, the appellant had had his case reviewed and a final decision had been reached. Looking back and knowing some of the people who sat on these various tribunals, one does question how impartial their ruling was. To a large extent, these tribunals were composed of people who favoured the establishment, and as such their rulings would be predictable and tend to be biased towards the establishment. The national papers at the time emphasised that work had to come first; if the work was not done, everything else failed.

A press report in April stated that General John Vaughan of Nannau, Dolgellau, had been appointed Local Defence Volunteers Organiser for Merioneth and Montgomeryshire. In fact, the 70-year-old general had been appointed Zone Commander for Merioneth. General Vaughan, a product of Eton and Sandhurst, had joined the army in 1891 and had seen action in various fields of battle. He was badly wounded during the second Boer War, was mentioned thrice in dispatches, and was awarded the Distinguished Service Order (DSO) in 1902. During WWI, he had command of the Third Cavalry Brigade. He was again mentioned in dispatches and was appointed a Companion of the Order of the Bath (CB) in 1915; a bar was added to his DSO in 1919. That year, he commanded the First Cavalry Brigade but retired from military life the following year, in 1920. He died in 1956 after falling from his horse – a sad end to a very distinguished soldier.

It was reported that the response to Eden's appeal in both counties had been very satisfactory, but a further appeal was made to farmers to enrol with the Volunteers. It seems that the Home Guard came under the jurisdiction of the Western Command, and the various districts incorporated in different battalions and with the tradition of their local regiments the Royal Welch Fusiliers.

The main north Wales districts were divided into seven different areas, and they consisted of:

Mid-West District No 2 Snowdon Sector
Cambrian Sub District
2nd Batt. Caernarvonshire   [Bangor]
3rd Batt. Caernarvon   [Caernarvon]
4th Batt. Caernarvon   [Criccieth]

1st Batt. Merioneth   [Blaenau Ffestiniog]

Mid West District No 6 Corwen Sector
Cambrian Sub District
4th Batt. Merioneth   [Corwen]

Mid-West District No7 Dolgelley Sector
Welsh Border Sub Section
2nd Batt. Merioneth   [Dolgelley]
3rd Batt. Merioneth   [Machynlleth]

It seems that the main headquarters of the 2nd Battalion was at Newtown, whereas the 1st would be at Caernarfon. Barmouth District came under the 2nd Battalion, and the identity pass of platoon commander Captain John Parry of Bryn Mynach Lodge was issued at Newtown. There was quite a lot of correspondence between various units and the colonel of the regiment with regards to the right to wear the distinctive black flash at the back of the neck. The colonel gave his permission for the Home Guard to wear the distinguished flash of the Royal Welch Fusiliers on their uniform.

At Blaenau, one of the platoon commanders was Captain Tom Williams, a carpenter who was also the Schools Maintenance Officer; his second in command was William Osborne Thomas, a local businessman. At Barmouth, Captain John Parry had been a gardener employed at Bryn Mynach and had also served as a sergeant in WWI; his second in command was Harry Jeffs. The command of the company was eventually taken over by Lewis Williams, a local businessman who had served as an officer in the RWF in WWI and had seen action in France.

The 1st Battalion RWF [Home Guard] seems to have operated in the Blaenau Ffestiniog, Trawsfynydd, Penrhyn and Harlech areas, whilst the 2nd Battalion operated in Barmouth, Dolgellau, Tywyn and Corris.

Information about the activities of the various platoons is scarce. The Merioneth Archives hold only the details of the

Penrhyndeudraeth platoons, though this in itself gives an insight into the working of the force which would have been repeated in practice in all other districts. Penrhyn, owing to its industrial capabilities (Cooke's Explosives, Gwaith Powdwr), had a large workforce which had joined the Home Guard. It was part of C Company and had five platoons, namely numbers 6, 7, 8, 9 and 10, with each platoon on average containing around forty men under the command of two officers and two sergeants.

E Company was based in the Harlech district with its headquarters at the 'Glyn', Talsarnau; Penrhyn HQ was at 'Treflyn'; and the Blaenau HQ at the British Legion/ United Service Club. C. J. Cooke (Llanbedr) was the officer commanding No. 7 Platoon.

Major W. Wyn Kirkby, DSO, RWF, was the officer in charge of C Company and, according to notes, he resided at the Fishing Club, Trawsfynydd, but his HQ was at Maentwrog. Captain R. W. Jones (Erfyl Fychan), the battalion adjutant, was based at Plas Talwaenydd, Blaenau Ffestiniog, and a Lieutenant T. W. Hughes was the lieutenant quartermaster of C Company. Listed in a diary by an unknown author are names and numbers of prominent persons. Some of the names are familiar and were probably the names of contacts if there was ever a need to muster:

Colonel Williams Ellis, Blaenau Ffestiniog
Major W. Wyn Kirkby
Capt. Kitching RN., Plas Penrhyn
Lieut Cooke, Penrhyn Powder Works
Lieut Forward, Penrhyn
Lieut R. Richard Evans, Penrhyn
Lieut Wil Jones, Talsarnau
Owain Jones, Company Sergeant Major, Electric Sub Station
Sergeant Jennings, Grapes Hotel, Maentwrog
Capt. R. W. Jones, Adjutant

Another interesting copy of orders given in July 1942 is headed:

HOME GUARD
Name _____   Your Post is _____
   You will attend HOME GUARD DUTIES with full equipment etc., cup, plate, knife, fork and spoon at your Platoon Headquarters at 19.30 hrs. on July 18th 1942.
   The only excuse for absence will be the production of a Medical Certificate from Capt. Pritchard, Company Medical Officer.
   Action will be taken against defaulters
   [signed] W. W. Kirkby
   Major Officer Commanding, C Company.

Later on, Major Kirkby was promoted to lieutenant colonel and left for a new appointment.

As in all things, wear and tear paid its toll on the force, and a letter of 21 May 1942 from Lieutenant Quartermaster names Mr William Griffith of Cambrian View, Penrhyn, as the official boot repairer to the 1st Merioneth Battalion's C Company.

Another interesting piece of information that came to light is a duplicate list referring to a member of the Home Guard joining the services. The list refers to a David Roberts, who on 21 May 1942 was joining the Royal Army Service Corps (RASC) at Tidworth and taking with him the following:

1 Battle Dress Blouse
1 Battle Dress Trousers
1 pair Boots ankle
1 Field Dressing
1 Cap F. S.
1 Great Coat
1 Respirator

Also a D. Evans joining the RAF on 30 June 1942, it is noted that he has not taken nothing with him, all handed in [signed] Lieut C. S. Cooke.

However, in some instances where lads had joined the services and not returned equipment, the quartermaster would contact their new CO with the cost of the equipment, which would then be deducted from their pay. In another case, a mother brought back a pair of boots which belonged to her son. However, the boots were not army boots and so not accepted, and a charge was made against the person by a deduction from his service pay. Notes in the diary refer to the programme of E Company:

Sept 2nd 1942	Drill at Castle with Gas Masks
4th	Field Exercise
5th	Road Patrols from Castle
	Firing Practice on the beach
	Members to bring their own rifle and in
	No. 4 Platoon on February 6th Inspection
	of Rifles and Bayonets
May 10th	Company Parade, Maentwrog
Sunday June 21st	Parade Inspection by General Vaughan,
	14.00 to 18.00 hrs.

There were shortages of rifles, but a shipment of old Ross rifles was sent from the United States. One enterprising teacher at Ffestiniog Grammar School (B. Hawes – a metalwork and woodwork master who was also the quartermaster sergeant at Penrhyn) made quite a few dummy wooden rifles so that the lads could drill. Some friction did arise between the Home Guard and other voluntary services, especially over the use of buildings, but common sense prevailed and they worked together amicably. A few Home Guard officers were full-time, paid staff and their duties were to oversee the organisation. The Blaenau Ffestiniog platoons used the old disused Soar Chapel at Rhiw as their base.

Basil Evans, headmaster of the Ffestiniog Central School, became a full time captain; he had served in the Flying Corps in WWI and was proud to wear his wings. Jack Davies from Trawsfynydd became sergeant major and, in Barmouth, John

Parry was appointed platoon commander. Lewis Williams of Ceylon Café became the company commander with the rank of captain; he was promoted to major in 1944 and at the end of hostilities to lieutenant colonel. Lewis Williams had been commissioned 2nd lieutenant in 1916 in the 7th Battalion Royal Welch Fusiliers (RWF) and promoted to lieutenant six months later. He saw action in France and remained with his unit until restored to establishment at the end of hostilities.

No records have been found appertaining to the Barmouth Home Guard. They met and trained in the old Arrowe Hall at the end of Jubilee Road, which was subsequently destroyed by fire. By browsing through records and asking various people, I have acquired the names of some of the personnel, which have been made available through the courtesy of the *Barmouth Advertiser*. In May 1943, there is a column extolling their virtues under the heading 'Home Guard ready for War's most vital phase'. The article states:

> The Home Guard, now trained and efficient, grows in importance as Britain's bodyguard against counter attack whether by airborne troops, parachutist, saboteurs or sea borne invasion. May 14th 1943 was the 3rd anniversary of its foundation, May 16th celebrated throughout the country as Home Guard Sunday, when there were staged parades and demonstrations designed to illustrate the efficiency of this force both in the use of weapons and in tactics.

The article goes on to cover a demonstration by the Barmouth Company (under the command of Captain Lewis Williams) on the Recreation Ground on Sunday week:

> Following a most effective display of field craft the Company then took part in a mock attack upon a detachment of 'German troops' in charge of Lieutenant Harry Jeffs (who is 2nd in command of the Barmouth Company). The crowd was greatly impressed with the thoroughness and efficiency of all who took part and the demonstration throughout reflected much credit upon those in charge of this company.

From the Hugh Roberts 'Henddol' collection of photographs, we have pictures of the concrete blocks on Fairbourne beach, the concrete pillbox in the sand dunes at Rowen, Dyffryn, a brick-built pillbox not far from Wayside, an Anderson shelter in Tal-y-bont, and a stone-built pillbox built into the rock face opposite Aberamffra which has two peep holes effectively covering Barmouth Bridge.

Very few names in the company have come to light. Some names have appeared in the *Advertiser*, and we also have names of Home Guard personnel who played billiards at the Sailors' Institute. There was an A- and B-team, with the A-team as follows:

E. Tank (Marine Gardens) Sergeant; W. E. Clark (Wine Stores); Harry Jeffs (Balmoral); J. Jones; W. J. Morris (Cambrian Stores); Morris Jones with other names mentioned: H. G. Williams and H. J. Rowlands. It is hoped that the records may come to light and that the full names of those who served in the Barmouth Company can be listed.

There are quite a few stories about the force which have now passed into Home Guard folklore, and the Barmouth Company was no exception. The Battle of the Peak was one such incident. An officer cadet training unit (OCTU) was based in Barmouth, and it was not unusual for both forces to exercise together and have mock battles to test their efficiency. During one of these exercises, held on a Sunday, the cadets had to defend and hold the 'Peak', the highest point above Barmouth with a full view of the town. The Home Guard, on the other hand, were given the orders to take the 'Peak' – a simple enough order – with battle to commence at 10 a.m. This, however, created a problem for the Home Guard – being a Sunday, there were other things to attend to, especially as the CO was also the church organist. They resolved the problem by deciding that they would commence battle at 12 noon after local duties had been met. The cadets guarded the Peak all morning without any sign of the enemy. At twelve, the Home Guard commandeered a local coal wagon and took it up Panorama Road and on to Gellfawr Farm, which lay directly behind the Peak. The adjudicators stationed at the farm adjudged the Home Guards to be the victors, as the Cadets had not reckoned on being overwhelmed from their rear. The authenticity of these stories cannot be verified, and there is no doubt that over the years they have grown with the telling. Nevertheless, the essence of these stories is probably true and provided the basis for the popular TV series *Dad's Army*. Be that as it may, there should be no doubt that the Home Guard was a force to be reckoned with, with official figures putting the total number of men in the force throughout the war at around 1,750,000. By 1942, some 140,000 men of the Home Guard had been recruited to and served at ack-ack batteries.

From photographs acquired of the Ffestiniog area, it seems that Tanygrisiau and Manod had their own platoons, whilst at Llan Ffestiniog there were about fifty Home Guard members. Archibald Smart (manager of the local Co-op store) was lieutenant here and Eddie Owen the sergeant. However, later on in the war Eddie lost his life whilst serving in the RAF, and his name is commemorated on the Blaenau Ffestiniog War Memorial.

A farmer from outside Newtown recalls joining the Home Guard in December 1940. Their task was to guard the roads around Newtown at night. There were eight men on duty, and they took turns in two groups of four to keep watch for a few hours at a time. They also went to Barmouth with the Home Guards from Newtown and Kerry on the pretence that the Germans had landed there. In a recent TV broadcast, it was stated that, had there been an invasion, the Home Guard would have been deployed on guerrilla activities. With the end of the war in 1945, the Home Guard was disbanded.

Major Humphrey Lloyd Jones

THE AUTHOR'S FIRST recollection of the major dates from before the war, when walking in the street in Blaenau he saw a very young person in uniform making his way towards the Territorial Army Drill Hall. It was obvious from his demeanour that he was very self-conscious of being in army uniform with the black flash hanging down from the back of his jacket collar. (A 'flash' is the name given to the five black ribbons on the back of the collar and is a link with the days when soldiers wore pigtails. An officer's flash is nine inches long and a fusilier's seven.) There was one pip on the shoulder epaulette to denote that he was a 2nd lieutenant and on his peaked cap was the distinctive badge of the Royal Welch Fusiliers.

In those days he was known locally as 'Wmff Lord' and his brother as 'Tom Lord'. It is not known how the appellation 'Lord' came into being; one assumes that the family had some connection with the local Diffwys Quarry, known locally as 'Chwarel y Lord' (the road leading to it was also called Lord Street). Both Wmff and Tom worked for the local Yale Electrical Company which supplied the town with its electricity.

The Terriers (short for Territorials) were quite popular at the time, and many had joined up to get what they considered a free fortnight's training holiday by going to the various Terrier camps in the country. However, with the declaration of war, all Terriers were mobilised, and the local contingent made their way to the Hay-on-Wye area to await further orders and placement.

As far as is known, Lloyd Jones's battalion did not join the British force sent to France and was not therefore in the Dunkirk retreat but was on duty in the UK. In August 1942, the 10th Battalion RWF was converted to the 6th (Royal Welch) Parachute Regiment. All members of the battalion had to undergo a twelve-day parachute training course at No. 1 Parachute Training School, RAF Ringway (Manchester). The course began with parachute jumps from a converted barrage balloon and finished with five parachute jumps from an aircraft. Anyone failing to complete the course descents was returned to his old unit; those who successfully completed the parachute course were presented with their maroon berets and parachute wings.

The battalion had to have the ability to cover long distances at speed; airborne platoons were required to cover a distance of fifty miles in twenty-four hours and a battalion in thirty-two hours. It is worth noting that the commanding officer of the 6th (Royal Welch) Parachute Regiment was Lieutenant Colonel Charles Hilary Vaughan Pritchard (later better known to us as Brigadier Vaughan of Nannau, Dolgellau. (The brigadier changed his name by deed poll from Pritchard to Vaughan on inheriting the Nannau Estate in 1956.)

Lloyd Jones commanded the B Company of the battalion, and they embarked for North Africa on 10 May 1943, where they saw service in Algiers and Tunisia. He was mentioned twice in dispatches and was also awarded the Military Cross. The company did a parachute drop in Sicily and made an amphibious landing in Italy in September 1943. The Allied landings were successful, but the transport ship HMS *Abdial* struck a mine in Taranto Harbour on 10 September killing fifty members of the battalion (fifty-seven officers and men are commemorated on the memorial in the Free Church, Taranto). They also took part in the battle of Monte Casino.

Lloyd Jones also led his men on a parachute drop into southern France before returning to Italy. It was said that,

'His inspiration in battle was legendary; he led from the front, he chose to disregard the presence of the enemy, and exposed himself to enemy fire.' It is also said that when he did a drop he carried a walking stick tied to his wrist by a piece of string and taped his rimless glasses to his ears.

During fighting in the mountainous regions of Italy, it was discovered that the Germans were able to pick up radio signals between the battalion's companies and were thus acquiring information and plans of movements. To counteract this, Major Lloyd Jones got Welsh speakers to man the radio transmitters in the 6th (Royal Welch) Parachute Regiment. It proved a successful move, denying the Germans any information and leaving them extremely puzzled.

The company also took part in a parachute drop in Greece; the brigade spent three months there following the retreating German army and maintaining law and order in the country. At the end of hostilities, the battalion became part of the 6th Airborne Division and served in Palestine from 1945–7 before amalgamating with the 4th Parachute Regiment.

During their sojourn in Palestine, the regiment had to enforce law and order as part of their peacekeeping mission and were the targets of a vicious and cruel terrorist organisation that had no respect for human lives. Though the major's duties were onerous, he still had time to remember his folks at home, and a junior officer, Grafton Maggs, recalls how the major called him over one time to ask for a favour. He understood Maggs was a keen photographer and he wanted some photos taken of the graves of those Royal Welch Soldiers who had fallen during the First World War when General Allenby had liberated Palestine from the Turks. This military cemetery was at Gaza, which was under Arab control, so there would be no difficulty in visiting it, unmolested from the terrorists. The major had a list of all the Blaenau men who were buried there, and he explained to Maggs that, as the wages of slate workers were not very high, few of their relatives could afford to make the visit in person. His cousin was the chairman of the local

British Legion branch, and he would see that the relations got the photos.

Sometime later, the major showed Maggs a letter; it was from the people of Blaenau and it gave thanks for the photographs of their loved ones' graves. It said that this was the first time anyone in the Blaenau area had seen the last resting place of their dear boys, which they had waited twenty-five years for, and that they now had something concrete by which to remember them by.

Maggs said: 'It was moving in the extreme, and thanks to the major I had played a small part in helping to alleviate the grief felt in those cottages in Blaenau.'

The letter was handed back, and the major said, 'I think you will agree, our long day was worthwhile and you have helped bring comfort to a lot of people. Now, before we go in for dinner, let me buy you a drink.'

The Bradley Boys

IN THE 1881 census, John Bradley and his family are recorded as residing at 3 Albert Street, Rhuddlan, Flintshire. John was originally from Clent in Worcestershire, where records indicate that he was born in 1844, and he gave his occupation as an engineer and fitter at works. His wife, Helen, born at St Asaph, was twelve months his junior. By the time of the 1891 census, the family – John, Helen, and their four children – had moved to Blaenau Ffestiniog, where John's occupation was recorded as a fish and game dealer. They lived at No. 9, High Street, which was the shop opposite the current post office. At that time, Blaenau was a boom town and a good place to open a business – more than likely they had the fishmonger's shop at No. 9. Thus began the Bradley family connection with the town.

Their son Oswald married Winifred Deed of Ormskirk, Lancashire, in 1914. They in turn had five children: Oswald John, Francis (Frank), Joseph, Winifred Eleanor (who died at the age of four), and Frances Eileen. All the children attended the local school and eventually gained places at the county school as it was then called. Very little is known of their childhood, only that they lived in Tirionfa, No. 3, The Square. With the advent of war, the three brothers joined the services – Oswald and Joseph in the Royal Air Force and Frank in the Royal Navy.

Oswald John Bradley

Very little is known about Oswald's career in the RAF except that he served in North Africa. Thankfully, he survived and came home, where in due course he was appointed history master at the local grammar school. He was a very popular teacher but died in 1965 aged only 50. In *Blodau'r Grug*, the school magazine, the headmaster Mr A. O. Morris wrote a eulogy in which he stated:

> One of the greatest tragedies in the history of the school has been the death of Mr O. J. Bradley. There are no words to describe the great loss felt by the staff and pupils alike and indeed by all those who knew and respected him. His popularity was not confined within Ysgol Sir; there was hardly a person in Blaenau who did not know him. Our deepest sympathies are extended to his family; we are proud to have been his pupils and his friends.

A sixth-former wrote (in Welsh): 'I clearly remember like it was yesterday how he recounted in a very lively manner his life and tribulations in the RAF, and many of his pupils loved their history lessons as they could listen to his stories.'

Mention is also made of a silver cup presented by Toc H in memory of Oswald Bradley to be given to the best swimmer of the year. The year after Oswald's death, the first recipient of the award, Peter Marwood, was presented the cup by Oswald's brother Frank. Peter, though not a native of Blaenau, joined the army and attained the rank of brigadier before retirement.

Frank Bradley

Frank joined the Royal Navy and became a petty officer. Here he experienced the realities of war, serving on HMS *Edinburgh*, a very fast modern cruiser launched in 1938 and commissioned in July 1939. She had seen combat service in the North Sea and Arctic Ocean, which was where she was eventually sunk.

In 1941, HMS *Edinburgh* escorted convoy WS10 to Simonstown, South Africa. She then escorted convoy WS9B to the Middle East, returning to Gibraltar in July. She had a close call when a German torpedo bomber attacked her, but fortunately no damage was sustained and she was able to resume her course to the Clyde.

She again provided cover for the Arctic convoys carrying aid to Russia in December 1941. After being refitted on the Tyne, she returned to duties in March 1942 in the Iceland/ Faroes area, escorting two convoys, QP4 and PQ13. In April she left Scapa Flow to escort PQ14 to Murmansk, but because of bad weather sixteen ships were forced to return to Iceland; one ship was sunk by a U-boat. HMS *Edinburgh* and the rest of the vessels (nine in total) arrived safely in Murmansk.

In her final voyage, HMS *Edinburgh* was also the flagship of Rear Admiral Bonham Carter. He was commanding the escort of returning convoy QP11, comprising seventeen ships; they left Murmansk on 28 April 1942. En route, a U-boat (U-456) fired a torpedo into her starboard side. The ship listed but good seamanship and quick reactions in closing watertight bulkheads prevented her from sinking. U-456 fired another torpedo into her stern, wrecking her steering equipment and effectively crippling her. *Edinburgh* was taken in tow with the intention of returning to Murmansk, but she was harassed by German torpedo bombers, and although she progressed at a snail's pace under her own power, she was attacked by three German destroyers off Bear Island. HMS *Edinburgh* slipped her tow and started to sail in circles. She was able to fire her guns at the destroyers, sinking one of them, but unfortunately she was struck again by a stray torpedo, which effectively sealed her fate. The crew had to abandon ship, and HMS *Gossamer* took off 440 men and HMS *Harrier* about 400. Two officers and fifty-six other ranks were killed in the attack. HMS *Foresight* used her last torpedo to ensure that HMS *Edinburgh* sank so as not to be a danger to shipping, but was that the only reason?

Unbeknown to the crew, HMS *Edinburgh* had, whilst at Murmansk, been loaded with sealed wooden boxes, which had been placed in the armoured torpedo room on the starboard side. This was in fact a consignment of gold bullion weighing approximately 4½ tons which the Russian government had made as a partial payment for the military supplies received. According to reports, there were 465 gold ingots which had been placed in ninety-three wooden boxes, and at that time its value was around one and a half million pounds. It was vital that the *Edinburgh* did not fall into enemy hands or even those of the Soviet government, who could then claim the gold. Frank was amongst the lucky survivors. He continued his career and served on various ships before being demobilised at the end of the war. He became an agent for the Prudential Assurance Company Limited and was also elected as a town councillor. He became a veteran in the true sense of the word.

In 1954, salvage rights were offered to British salvage companies, but owing to political tensions between Britain and the Soviet Union the project was delayed. In 1957, the wreck of the *Edinburgh* was designated a war grave, complicating plans for any future salvage attempts.

The British government was anxious to reclaim the gold, and by 1970 there were fears that saboteurs might loot the wreck or that the Soviets might instigate a salvage attempt as their coast was nearby. In 1980, salvage rights were granted to Jessop Marine, on the grounds that their method of salvage – which did not deploy explosives – was deemed more appropriate for a war grave. In 1981, they located the wreck lying in less than 800 feet of water in the Barents Sea. Fortunately for the team, they were able to assess the layout of the *Edinburgh* by inspecting her sister ship HMS *Belfast*, which had survived the war.

In August of that year, divers were able to penetrate the torpedo room and recover a bar of gold. Subsequently, 431 of the 465 ingots were recovered, and a further twenty-nine bars were recovered in a salvage operation in 1986. A total of 460 ingots were recovered, leaving five unaccounted for, the total recovered value then being in excess of £43 million. Yes, HMS *Edinburgh* had to be finished off and sunk to safeguard her treasures.

Joseph Bradley

The author remembers Joseph Bradley in 1938 when he was a sixth-former at the Ffestiniog Grammar School. He was a keen athlete at this time. There is very little information about the period prior to his joining the Royal Air Force, though needless to say, like all youngsters, he would have considered the period before joining the services to be a waste of time. Again, there is no record of his early days in the RAF or of what training he received; the first record available is the official reports of his time stationed at Lossiemouth. Although these reports are very brief, they give a glimpse of what these lads had to endure in the course of their duties, and an understanding of how grateful they must have been to survive.

By March 1942, Joe had become a flight sergeant and was classified as a wireless operator/air gunner. He was stationed at Lossiemouth on the north coast of Scotland and was part of the crew of a Halifax bomber, W1039 ZA-C from the 10th Squadron. On 30 March 1942, he took part in attacks on the German battleship *Tirpitz*, which was moored in Fættenfjord, Norway. The *Tirpitz* was a thorn in the side of the Royal Navy as it was a perpetual threat to all convoys taking supplies to Russia. Convoys generally operated between Iceland and Murmansk, in the extreme north-west of Russia. They were generally provided with a strong escort, as the presence of the *Tirpitz* in the vicinity was sufficient to make any seaman shudder and pray.

The official report for 30 March names all the crew, their rank, and their respective roles. Sergeant Bradley was listed as W/Op Air Gunner and a comment after the sortie reads 'Returned'. The report states that it was impossible to see the fjord and valley in the Trondheim area owing to bad visibility; they had failed to locate the *Tirpitz* and had to jettison their load of mines with their position noted.

The second report, dated 27 April 1942, records another attack on the *Tirpitz*. This time visibility was good, with *Tirpitz* and other escort vessels deploying smoke screens to obscure themselves. Flak was intense from both sides of the fjord. The aileron control was shot away and the starboard flap control damaged, but Bradley's bomber managed to drop its mines, and the captain was able to fly the aircraft safely back to Lossiemouth.

The following day, a further attack was made on the *Tirpitz*, but Flight Sergeant Bradley did not take part in that particular sortie. The perils and dangers encountered by these Halifax bomber crews are listed, rather tersely perhaps, but in sufficient detail for us to know the risks which they had to face and endure. The crew saw the *Tirpitz* from about 300 feet altitude, and they saw one of their mines burst beneath the stern of the ship. Visibility had been excellent, but again the flak from both sides of the fjord was intense. The leads to the petrol cocks were shot away, leaving the starboard engine failing; an 18-inch square hole was blown in the tail plane; and the navigator, after releasing the mines, had a narrow escape when he returned to his position in the aircraft to find a gaping hole a foot long below his seat caused by flak. The shrapnel from the hit had been caught up in his navigation bag and had torn all the maps to pieces. On the return flight, he had to sit in position with a howling gale blowing through the hole, through which the North Sea was visible.

The damage to the fuel supply was of deep concern to the flight engineer, and in setting a course for home they had to think in terms of ditching the aircraft. With prudent engine handling, however, they managed to land at RAF Sumburgh. The pilot was awarded an immediate Distinguished Flying Cross (DFC). As the aircraft was too badly damaged to fly again, the crew was flown back to Lossiemouth the following day to join the other members of the squadron who had returned from the *Tirpitz* sortie. The official report on the flight simply states 'Returned'.

In midsummer 1942, the squadron appears to have been deployed in North Africa. Crete had been invaded in May 1940, and spasmodic bombing continued on military installations there. Fierce fighting was taking place around Tobruk and adjoining areas, so there was a need for Bomber Command to help and augment the ground troops.

Crete had been a thorn in the side of the German military. Unlike many other European countries, which had fallen within days, German forces were compelled to fight for weeks before they could say they had conquered the island. Standard military vehicles struggled to adapt to the mountainous terrain and the winding mountain tracks that threaded their way across the island. Distances in Crete are based more on time than physical distance, so, for instance, the distance from 'A' to 'B' would be given as perhaps two hours rather than a couple of miles, as the length of the winding tracks was not easy to calculate. The Germans had not previously encountered the type of fighting they saw in Crete, whose resistance movement had surprised them with its skill and ferocity. The Cretan was a skilful, independent fighter used to the mountainous terrain and was more than capable of outwitting the Germans at their own game.

On 5 September 1942, the Halifax bomber in which Sergeant Bradley was part of the crew left North Africa on a bombing mission to Crete. After completing the bomb run on Heraklion Aerodrome, their aircraft was hit by flak, caught fire, and later crashed at Kastelli Pediada, Crete. Three of the six crew members were killed, but Sergeant Bradley and Sergeant MacFarlane were able to bale out, along with Pilot Officer Turner. While Turner was taken prisoner, Bradley and MacFarlane were able to evade capture, helped by the Cretan Resistance.

British supplies were being dropped to the Resistance whilst British agents were still on the island. Officers had been landed to direct and lead the resistance, marking the beginning of the British mission to occupied Crete: the secret infiltration of the island by men in small boats and submarines, including perilous journeys through areas under German control. Major Paddy Leigh-Fermor, Major Xan Fielding and Major Bill Moss were the principal leaders. After the war, Paddy Leigh-Fermor translated George Psychoundakis's book *The Cretan Runner* into English. The book is a worthwhile account of life under German occupation and as a runner for the British agents in Crete. Psychoundakis states in the book:

> Flight Sergeant Joe Bradley DFM, MM, from Blaenau Ffestiniog, Merioneth. A charming man, who sang beautifully in Welsh, to the delight of the Cretans. When my operator Mamoli was captured and later executed, he became my operator till he was evacuated by MTB next year. After he and his comrade bailed out SE of Heraklion, they were hidden and led to safety by Grigori Khnarakis of Threpsana.

As a wireless operator for Paddy Leigh-Fermor, Joe Bradley had to be on the move constantly to avoid capture by the Germans; they lived mostly in caves on the outskirts of small villages and depended for food on the generosity of the villagers who shared their own meagre supplies.

It was an onerous job being hunted from place to place not knowing who their friends or foes were. From their caves, they could often see German patrols prowling in the villages, searching house to house for them, as somebody could have told them about the British presence in the village, and often it was only by pure luck that they were not captured. Eventually Joe was evacuated back by boat to Egypt to rejoin his squadron.

During his time in Crete, Joe learnt Greek and became quite fluent. It is interesting to note that the British Resistance group in Crete, shortly after Joe's departure, kidnapped the commander of the 22nd Panzer Division, General Karl Kreipe. He was sent to Cairo and onwards to Canada and then brought back to the UK and lodged as a POW at Island Farm Special Camp X1, Bridgend, Wales. General Kreipe was a bachelor, a long-serving soldier who had also served in WWI. His father was a pastor in Noiederspier. Karl Kreipe died in June 1976 in Northeim, Lower Saxony.

Very little information has been found regarding Joe Bradley's life in the RAF after Crete, although it is known that he continued in the service and attained the rank of warrant officer. In April 1949, he was given a temporary commission as a pilot officer, and in October of that year became a flying officer and progressed to the rank of flight lieutenant. The June 1949 issue of the supplement to the *London Gazette* notes that his rank as a flight lieutenant had been made permanent, indicating that he was making the RAF his full-time career.

In May 1949, he was transferred to the Secretarial Branch of the service, which effectively blocked all information about his work. He was again promoted in January 1956, this time to squadron leader, and then to the senior rank of wing commander in July 1963. He retired from the RAF in 1973, at which time he was stationed at RAF Brampton having completed some thirty-three years in the service.

Joseph Deed Bradley (it seems he added his mother's maiden name to his) died in May 1996 and was cremated at Cambridge Crematorium. His decorations and campaign medals were sold in April 2006 at Bonhams, London, for the price (including premium) of £6,815. It can also be said that Joe attained the highest ever military rank of any person from the Blaenau Ffestiniog area who served in WWII.

Joe's nephew, Mr Paul (Paddy) Middleton (the son of Joe's youngest sister Eileen was brought up in Northern Ireland but now resides in Northumbria) was able to add a little extra information about his Uncle Joe.

Memories of Uncle Joe by Paddy Middleton

After leaving school, Joe aspired to become a trainee accountant but had to join the RAF before completing the course.

He remembered some of the stories his uncle told him, but

Joe was very reticent to talk about his service career. With the naturally inquisitive mind of a youngster, Paddy probed Joe and was able to extract a few reminiscences of the time when he was virtually on the run from the German forces in Crete.

Joe's plane having been hit and the crew forced to bale out over Crete, it was some years later when Paddy spoke with the pilot of another plane which had taken part in the bombing of the airfield at Heraklion. He saw Joe's plane being attacked by two German Messerschmitts and saw some of the crew baling out, though very possibly the plane had also been hit by flak.

Joe's experience with the Resistance Movement was horrendous; to a large extent they were dependant on the goodwill of the Cretans for food, and they themselves did not have much. In fact, Joe admitted that at times they had to eat grasshoppers and locusts to sustain themselves.

School photograph of Joe Bradley.

Joe Bradley's War Medals.
Left to right: Military Medal, 1939–45 Star, Air Crew Europe Star, North Africa Star with RAF Clasp 1942–43, Defence Medal, War Medal, General Service Medal with South Arabia Clasp.

The Flight Engineer's Log from another plane taking part in the bombing of Heraklion Drome with Joe Bradley

Joe recounted why, to the end of his days, he hated hearing the carol 'Silent Night' being sung as it brought back unpleasant memories of a particular Christmas. They were hiding in a house when a German patrol entered. They were looking for Resistance fighters – Patriots – and it was their duty to exterminate them. Whilst there they started singing the carol. Joe and his group were hiding upstairs and had to listen to the carol knowing that, if found, they would be executed immediately without trial.

After returning from Crete to Egypt and then back to the UK, Joe had become very emaciated owing to the rigours of his Cretan experience, but he was well enough to attend his Military Medal award ceremony in the presence of King George VI.

When the author asked Paddy why the Greek government award of the Distinguished Flying Medal to Joe had not been sold with the rest of his medals at Bonhams, he answered that Joe had been awarded the medal but never received it, as the records appertaining to the award had been destroyed.

Joe did not undertake any operational duties after being shot down; it was said that there was a policy of not using personnel who had been shot down for further operational duties. Joe was promoted to officer rank and was appointed the officer in charge of the Officer Cadet Unit (OCU) at Manchester University. There he met his future wife, who was studying pharmacy at the university. Whilst serving as the CO of the OCU, Joe was able to continue studying for his accountancy examinations, the RAF funding the cost of the course, and he later became a qualified accountant.

However, it seems that Joe was better employed giving lectures and instructions on how to survive and run insurgency operations behind enemy lines. He travelled extensively and visited both America and Aden. He also served in Germany at the end of the war, and it is said that, once again, as in Crete, he learnt the language and became a fluent German speaker.

Paddy also stated that at one period there were some of

Joe's artefacts from Crete – a signalling lamp, a tin hat with a dent in it where a bullet or shrapnel had hit it, and Joe's flying boots – at home in Blaenau Ffestiniog, but Paddy did not know what had become of them. He added that Joe never lost his Welsh accent.

On 30th March 1942, the crew of Halifax W1039 ZA-C from 10 Squadron took off at 1840 hrs from RAF Lossiemouth on the North East Coast of Scotland to participate in an attack on the German Battleship Tirpitz which was moored at the time in Fættenfjord in Norway.

Due to their being 10/10th low cloud which made it impossible to see the fjords and valleys in the Trondheim area the crew were unable to locate the target. Mines were jettisoned at 2311 hrs from 8,000 feet at a position of 63.34 N 06.65 E.

The aircraft and crew returned safely to base landing at RAF Lossiemouth at 0247 hrs on 31st March.

Rank	Name	Force	Crew Position	Age	Home Town	Fate
F/L	HACKING		Pilot			Returned
P/O	DEMPSEY		2nd Pilot			Returned
F/Sgt	TURNER		Navigator			Returned
Sgt	BRADLEY		W/Op Air Gunner			Returned
Sgt	CARSON		W/Op Air Gunner			Returned
Sgt	PORRITT		Tail Gunner			Returned
Sgt	McFARLANE		Flight Engineer			Returned

On 27th April 1942, the crew of Halifax W1039 ZA-C from 10 Squadron took off at 2058 hrs from RAF Lossiemouth on the North East Coast of Scotland to participate in an attack on the German Battleship Tirpitz which was moored at the time in Fættenfjord in Norway.

The target was attacked at 0106 hrs from 350ft. The smoke screen being used to cover the target was deployed and two puffs of smoke were seen to come up. Visibility was good and flak was reported to be intense from both sides of the fjord. The aileron controls were shot away and the starboard flap controls damaged but the Captain, F/Lt Hacking, was able to fly the aircraft home.

The aircraft and crew returned safely to base landing at RAF Lossiemouth at 0555 hrs on 28th April 1942.

Rank	Name	Force	Crew Position	Age	Home Town	Fate
F/L	HACKING		Pilot			Returned
P/O	DEMPSEY		2nd Pilot			Returned
F/Sgt	TURNER		Navigator			Returned
Sgt	BRADLEY		W/Op Air Gunner			Returned
Sgt	CARSON		W/Op Air Gunner			Returned
Sgt	PORRITT		Tail Gunner			Returned
Sgt	McFARLANE		Flight Engineer			Returned

Ms Linzee Duncan (née Druce) of www.archieraf.co.uk has kindly allowed the use of her tabulated extracts from the 10 Squadron Operation Record Book (ORB) of the Tirpitz raids on 30 March and 27 April 1942 of Halifax A1039 ZA-C. Joe Bradley is mentioned as a crew member. The original documents can be viewed at the National Archives at Kew, London.

Edmund Morris

EDMUND (EMWNT) MORRIS, Blaenau Ffestiniog – the son of the local GP, Dr J. W. Morris – was a schoolboy when war was declared. However, he and his father joined the Home Guard when the call came, with Emwnt later volunteering for the army after he came of age.

His daughter Mrs Gwyneth Jack of Invergordon, Ross-shire, recounts his experiences. After undertaking his initial training at Aldershot, he later became part of the 1st Airborne Reconnaissance Squadron under the command of Major C. F. H. Gough. He left Edinburgh in spring 1943 on the MV *Staffordshire* for North Africa and saw service there. Later, he went on to Italy before coming back to the UK. In 1944, he was stationed at Ruskington where he trained for Operation Market Garden – a bold plan to take Arnhem in Holland by using paratroopers – which unfortunately was doomed to fail.

The squadron glider-borne force left Tarrant Rushton airfield on 17 September, but owing to a shortage of gliders, 160 men had to travel to Barkston Heath airfield to emplane for the drop at Arnhem. On landing, Emwnt was placed in charge of a group of men and provided with a jeep, but his luck ran out when he was ambushed at a place called Wolfheze.

John Fairley in his book *Remember Arnhem* mentions Emwnt by name and describes him as being wounded in the ambush. Attacked by overwhelming German forces, the party was taken prisoner. Emwnt had seen many of his comrades killed, and there was further horror after they had been rounded up together in a church. Fiddling with his radio, one of the lads was able to tune into a broadcast by the BBC. Taking hold of the lad, the Germans marched him outside, where he was reputedly shot. Another lad tweaked the radio again, this time tuning in to BBC Wales. The Germans did not recognise the Welsh language and left the radio alone; its sound heartened Emwnt when he most needed it. He was taken to a POW camp at Fallingbostel, Lower Saxony. As far as it is known, Emwnt was not recommended for any awards. His period as a POW affected his health, and on his release he weighed barely six stone.

It was said that the squadron lost twenty-nine men during the action, with around 140 men taken prisoner. The glider planes normally had seating for about thirty men plus equipment and carried modified jeeps and field guns.

The local Blaenau Ffestiniog British Legion branch honoured Emwnt by asking him to preside and take the salute at their annual remembrance service, a duty which he performed with pride and dignity for many years. He was an imposing figure and carried his bowler hat well. He also served in the Territorial Army after the war, in the Staffordshire area. On his release from the army, he had resumed his studies and trained at Bangor Normal College. He subsequently became a teacher of maths and music. He taught at Wolverhampton and later at Wrexham. He died in March 1991 at the age of 67.

The Backroom Boys

IT IS VIRTUALLY impossible to find contributors who are willing to disclose their activities during the last war. In most cases, the persons could not divulge what their work was owing to the Official Secrets Act. Many budding young scientists from this area were directed to various works of importance without thought to their future careers. These backroom boys deserve credit. Some had to suffer injustice because they did not wear a uniform, but in many instances their contribution to the war effort was far greater than many who did.

The names of two of Merioneth's backroom boys have survived: Jack Darbyshire and John Hughes Jones, both past pupils of Ffestiniog County School. Both graduated with first-class honours degrees in physics from the University of Wales, Bangor, around the beginning of WWII. Their exploits and work, fortunately for us, have been recorded in the press and magazines.[1]

Jack Darbyshire

Jack Darbyshire's contribution is unique, particularly when considering that he came from Blaenau Ffestiniog, a slate-mining district with no seafaring traditions, and became an expert on waves. In that period, the choice of careers was very limited. To a large extent, there were only two options available in order for a young student to acquire a university education: become a teacher or a minister of religion. Either

---

[1] It's a pity that no names have come forward from the southern area of the county. Appeals were made in the local press and radio for information regarding individuals who had backroom careers during WWII, but to no avail.

of these options would allow the student to access grants and financial assistance to support their studies.

During his period at the University of Wales, Bangor, the Military Service Act had come into being, and Jack had to apply to defer his call-up until he had finished his studies. His request for deferment was granted, and on gaining a first-class degree in physics and completing an MSc course, Jack was directed to work with a team of researchers at the Osram Radio Valve Unit in Hammersmith, where he undertook research on radio valves. At that time, the RAF were having problems with the radios fitted in their aircraft. The vibrations in the planes caused the very delicate valve filaments to fail as they could not withstand the constant shaking, which caused them to malfunction. This led to problems for the crew, as without radio they were not able to find their bearings or receive any instructions. Luckily, the team were able to find a solution to the problem.

Jack was invited in 1943 to join a team at the Admiralty Research Laboratory in Teddington, Middlesex. At that time, Britain's supply lines were threatened by U-boats, and the laboratory's focus was on the field of anti-submarine warfare. As part of their work, the laboratory developed a method for detecting iron objects underwater involving the placement of big loops of cable on the sea floor. The magnetic effect of metal objects sent an electrical current through each loop, which could then be detected. A similar principle was adapted to combat the threat of the magnetic mine, with a system of electrical cables installed around the circumference of a ship's hull, running from bow to stern on both sides. A measured electrical current was then passed through the cables to cancel out the ship's magnetic field, and thus many ships and lives were saved from destruction. The method was referred to as degaussing.

In 1944, it was realised that the technique could be adapted to measure the size of waves. With the Allied invasion of Europe being planned, there was an urgent requirement to learn the properties of waves in the English Channel and to correlate them with local wind conditions. The idea was to assist the military beach landings by producing better forecasts of wave conditions.

One humorous story from that period involves Jack and a colleague, Fritz Ursell (a German refugee and technically an 'enemy alien'). Fritz, who was a renowned mathematician and later became Professor of Mathematics at Manchester University, was conducting research with Jack on an area of beach off limits to the public near Padstow, Cornwall, when they were both detained by local police on suspicion of being German spies. Ursell's thick German accent and Jack's Welsh accent aroused police suspicions, and although Ursell was soon freed, Jack was forced to spend the night at the station before being released! Another colleague on the team, who later became an assistant director of MI5, was Peter Wright, the author of *Spycatcher* (1987), a controversial memoir which the then government tried to ban. Both he and Jack came to be principal scientific officers.

After the war in 1953, the group moved from Teddington to Wormley near Godalming, where the National Institute of Oceanography was established. The head of the group, Dr G. E. R. Deacon, became director of the institute; he was later knighted for his services to the field of oceanography. Whilst at Wormley, Jack acquired a doctorate in science from the University of Wales, Bangor.

In June 1963, Jack was appointed the first Professor of Oceanography at the University of Wales, Bangor. He built the department up from scratch and was able to acquire the research vessel *Prince Madog*. He retired in 1986 with the title of emeritus professor, and during his time had the satisfaction of seeing the Menai Bridge Laboratory recognised by the University Grants Committee as one of only two centres of excellence in oceanography in the UK. Jack died in 2004 at the age of 85 and retained his interest in oceanography to the end.

John Hughes Jones

John Hughes Jones, a native of Penrhyndeudraeth, was born and bred at Pen Cefn. Familiar with country life and fond of shooting, he was a star pupil at the old Ffestiniog County School and gained a distinction in physics in the Higher examination. He was awarded two scholarships to the University of Wales, Bangor, where, in 1939, he gained a first-class honours degree in physics – the only student that year to do so. In September 1939, he started on a teacher training course, which had to be abandoned owing to the declaration of war.

John volunteered for the forces and went to a recruitment centre, where he was recommended to be interviewed for a post with the Royal Aircraft Establishment (RAE). It was felt that, as a physicist, his knowledge, expertise and research ability would make him a far more valuable asset to his country here than by being drafted into one of the services.

He was successful in his interview and worked initially at Farnborough, where his work involved bomb dynamics. His work presumably involved investigating how time of fall would be affected by aircraft speed, wind speed and direction, atmospheric pressure, and temperature.

John was later recruited by the Ministry of Aircraft Production and was based at a research station at Orford Ness in Suffolk. This was a military-controlled area comprising a vast shingle spit some twelve miles long by two miles wide lying just north of the Suffolk coast. The spit had a desolate, desert-like appearance and had become a prohibited zone to all civilians. Indeed, Orford Ness was regarded as a top-secret establishment, and the public were unaware of its existence. The similarity between Orford Ness and the establishment at Ynyslas, Ceredigion, is uncanny, but it seems that research of the same nature was being carried out at both places. However, it is not known whether there were any formal links between the two sites.

The work at Ness was conducted by some of the greatest boffins of their generation, and they played a crucial part in winning the war. Secret experiments were made on a vast range of weapons, on the effects of bombing, and on the development of the radar system before the project was moved to Bawdsey Manor. Radar played a prominent part in the Battle of Britain, and it has been said that, but for the work done at Orford Ness, the outcome of the Battle of Britain could very well have been different.

John conducted research work on the comparable construction of German and British planes, and in 1943 he had the responsibility of deciding the merits of various metals for their strength and composition for use in Allied aircraft. His work also involved research into self-sealing aircraft fuel tanks. His team were invited to compare the relative effectiveness of US and British 0.5" incendiary ammunition in attacking German bomber self-sealing fuel tanks. They constructed replicas of the bombers' wings and their tanks, and in one case used a genuine Heinkel He 111 bomber wing. They fired 175 rounds of each type of ammunition into almost completely filled tanks and filmed the impact of every one. The report concluded that some seventeen 'variables' had to be taken into account, including the size and volume of fuel in the tank, the angle of attack, and the atmospheric conditions at the time. It then supplied a detailed analysis of every single bullet's performance. This was painstaking work, and with high-octane fuel involved, not without its dangers. The conclusion was that US ammunition was significantly more effective. Equally, the report drew attention to an earlier Ness trial, when in November 1941, German 7.92-millimetre nose-fused incendiary ammunition was fired into British fuel tanks. The issue here was the importance of preventing fires from becoming lethal before the self-sealing chemical process could kick in. The research team had to decide on the relative value of the 'soft and flexible bag type' of tank as opposed to the 'rigid metal-covered type'. John Hughes Jones was specially commended by the British Air Commission for his 'excellent work'. He returned to his homeland and became a physics master at his old school and also became its deputy headmaster. He died in February 2002.

There is no detailed list of John Hughes Jones's work at Orford Ness during the period from 1940 to 1944. After his death, his son Timothy discovered papers at his father's home relating to his wartime work at Orford Ness. These comprised a complete report on a special project under John's charge. These papers were initially donated to the National Trust Archives at Orford Ness, but they were found to be of such national historical importance that they are now lodged at the National Archives at Kew.

In his book *Most Secret: The Hidden Secrets of Orford Ness*, Paddy Heazell refers to the work of John Hughes Jones and also comments on the wartime papers donated by his son: 'Very few such reports have survived from the Second World War.' Today, the site at Orford Ness is an internationally renowned nature reserve, bought by the National Trust from the Ministry of Defence in 1993, and its natural and historic features are carefully protected.

Only two of the backroom boys are listed, though there were many more. Their achievements today have perhaps become dimmed with the passage of time, but it should be remembered that these boffins saved countless lives by their devotion and dedication to their research.

Reflections of a Home Guard

BELOW IS A summary of part of a conversation transcript recorded between the author and John Iscoed Williams.

John Iscoed Williams MBE was a young lad when the LDV/Home Guard came into being. At the time, John, a native of Trawsfynydd, was working at Messrs Jacob Jones and Sons, Woollen Mill, Tanygrisiau, and was already an ARP Warden in Blaenau Ffestiniog. He volunteered to join the Home Guard despite being slightly underage, but during that period age was not a crucial factor. He trained at the disused Soar Chapel in Rhiw, Blaenau, which was the HQ of the local Home Guards. The drilling and square-bashing took place on the open ground in front of the building and below the old Baltic Hotel. Their training covered the practice and use of a Lewis machine gun. All recruits were blindfolded with a scarf and had to dismantle and reassemble the gun, so they would be conversant with it in the dark. A convenient and safe place had been secured for firing the guns at Llechwedd Quarry.

One of their duties was to take a 3-inch artillery gun from Blaenau to Croesor Quarry; the gun was kept in a shed behind the Band Room by Bryn Bowydd Chapel and was towed to the site by a Canadian Buick car owned by the woollen factory. The squad had the arduous job of hauling it up to the firing area. Another detachment of Home Guards from that area actually undertook the firing, with the Blaenau squad being forced to wait while the firing practice was in progress. On completion, they had to take the gun back and secure it in its shed. John was unable to account for why the gun was kept at Blaenau when suitable storage might have been found closer to the quarry at Penrhyndeudraeth.

The Blaenau Brigade consisted of roughly 400 men. Among the officers were W. O. Thomas (Bryn) and L. F. Davies, headmaster at Glan-y-pwll School. Gwynfryn Williams, who had seen service in WWI, was the sergeant. The adjutant was R. W. Jones (Erfyl Fychan) from Welshpool, who had also had war service; he finished his stint in the Home Guard as a major. His son, the late Canon Geraint Vaughan Jones, was at one time a curate in Barmouth before taking up the post of rector in Mallwyd.

The Blaenau Home Guard came under Western Command and was part of Mid-West District, No. 2, Snowdon Sector, Cambrian Sub Division, which comprised:

1st Batt. Merioneth (Blaenau Ffestiniog)
2nd Batt. Caernarfon (Bangor)
3rd Batt. Caernarfon (Caernarfon)
4th Batt. Caernarfon (Criccieth)

Dolgellau and the southern part of Merioneth were also in the Mid-West District:

2nd Batt. Merioneth (Dolgellau)
3rd Batt. Merioneth (Machynlleth)

The 'top brass' visited Blaenau periodically to carry out inspections etc.; later, they would address the whole brigade from the gallery of the Market Hall, the only place large enough to accommodate them all. On one occasion, the brigade had been given an outline of proposed manoeuvres by staff officers resplendent in their gold-braided uniforms. When they had finished, the adjutant R. W. Jones rose and said in Welsh: 'Now, lads, let us understand what we have to do in this circus.'

John remembers a weekend manoeuvre in which they assembled on a Friday evening. Their objective was to secure the Blaenau Post Office, Maentwrog Power Station and the Tan y Bwlch Railway Station; the opposing force was the Royal Welsh Commandos. Needless to say, the post office and power station were taken fairly quickly by the commandos, although they failed to take the railway station. The Home Guard had entrenched themselves in various nooks and crannies around the railway bridge which spanned the road leading to Rhyd and were able to repel the attackers.

Playing soldiers is all right in fine weather, but on this occasion torrential rain was also their enemy. The cook, Dafydd Vaughan, struggled to prepare food in the field kitchen; the lads had gathered plenty of kindling, but, being so wet, it was nigh on impossible to get it going. It would not burn but gave out thick smoke which nearly suffocated him. They heard the sound of a vehicle crashing into a wall and then a battered car pulled up, minus its mudguards. The occupants were the local doctor, J. W. Morris, and his chauffer 'Scars'.

When the doctor saw how wet they were, he said to them: 'What the Hell are you doing here? Why don't you shelter in that shed?' On being told that it was locked, he grabbed an old railway bar lying on the ground and with a vicious swing he hit the padlock away from the door and they were able to enter the old engine shed. To their amazement, the floor of the shed was full of swedes and turnips and they had to squat on top of them.

By late Sunday afternoon, the weather had changed and the sun came out. Sergeant Gwynfryn Williams gave orders to pack up and to make their way home, which they did by walking along the rail track from Tan y Bwlch to Blaenau. By the time they reached their destination, their clothes had dried, and fortunately no one in the brigade suffered any colds or other ill effects after their arduous weekend manoeuvres.

John enjoyed his time in the Home Guards and delighted in meeting the many different characters which were part of the unit – even if, at times, they might have been a bit boisterous and frivolous. Had the call come for the brigade to 'stand to' in an emergency and face the enemy, it would have no doubt done so with distinction, displaying the same commitment and fighting spirit as the regular army.

Sadly, John Iscoed Williams passed away in February 2015.

Tanygrisiau Home Guard c.1942

Fourth row (top): Hywel Michael Jones, William Owen, Robin Jones, John Iscoed Williams, Aneurin Davies, Huw Jones, William Williams, Fred Ramskill, Iorweth Jones.

Third row: Jonny Jones, Evan G. Jones, Robin Ll. Jones, Emyr Jones, John Jones, Tom Harlech Jones, Alfred Humphries, Dan Roberts, Hugh Parry Thomas.

Second row: John Williams, John Thomas, Arthur Jones, Isaac Parry, William Henry Thomas, Lewys Moelwyn Jones, Robin Williams, Sam Jones, David Vaughan Griffith, George Washington Jones.

Front row: Glyn Jones Roberts, Owen Thomas Jones, John Edwards, John Arthur Jones, John Vaughan, William Jones, Arthur Davies, Dafydd Lloyd.

Blaenau Ffestiniog Home Guard

Fifth Row (Top): William Jones, Geufron; Robat Wynn Jones, 131 High Street; Chris Roberts, High Street; Dafydd Roberts, Park Square; Dafydd Seth Jones, Cloth Hall, High Street; David Griffith Roberts, Cae Clyd; Dafydd Roberts (Tŷ Cefn), Manod Road (Tad Gwilym); Not Identified; Owen Roberts, Cromwell Street; Robat J. Jones, Fuchas Wen; Not Identified; Not Identified; Fred Jones, Pen Bryn; William Hughes (Coed)

Fourth Row: Not Identified; Edward Jones (Ned Yank); Dafydd Griffith, Wynne Road; J. Ifor Edwards, High Street; Huw Idris Williams, Leeds Street; Emrys Williams, Fron Haul, Cae Clyd; Maldwyn Owen; Joe Evans, Tabernacle Terrace; Dafydd J. Roberts, Tanrallt; Not Identified; Owen Jones, Richmond Terrace; Martin Ll. Davies, Manod Road; Tom Hughes (Twm Bach), Pengelli Terrace; Ior Bach, Hafod Ryffydd; Not Identified

Third Row: Aneurin Jones, Bryn Teg, Cae Clyd; Edward Jones, 125, Manod Road; John Roberts, Eisteddfa, Tyddyn Gwyn; Ben Jones, Bodychain; Hugh Jones (Tad Agnes), Pen Coed; Dafydd Seimon Roberts, Cae Clyd; Dafydd Jones (Llandderfel), Congl y Wal; Lewis R. Lewis (Tad Eigra), Park Square; John Rodrick Williams, 142 Manod Road; Len Owen, Manod Road; William Jones, Pant yr Ynn; Joe (Fawr), High Street; William Jones (Capel Gwyn, Llan), Tyddyn Gwyn

Second Row: Alf Hughes, Manod Road; Jack Evans, Lord Street (?); Jack Jones (fish), 144 High Street; John Roberts (Fflacs), High Street; Bert Griffiths, Manod Road; Charlie Roberts (Sgt Major), Tanygrisiau; Captain Tom Williams, Maenofferen; Lt. William Osborn Thomas, High Street; Hugh Thomas, Cromwell Street; Ifor Thomas, 20 Manod Road; Ellis John Ellis, Glan Gors, Manod Road; Robat John Thomas, Britannic, High Street; Not Identified

First Row: Owen Jones, Pant yr Ynn; Eirwyn Lloyd Roberts, Manod Road; Ieuan Pugh (Congl y Wal), Manod Road; Jack Roberts (tyres), Wesley Street; R. H. Roberts, Cromwell Street; Caradog Roberts, Isfryn; Dafydd Griffith Owen, Picton Terrace; Dafydd Jones (diawch), (Fflacs), High Street; Aron Thomas, Manod Road; Gwilym Roberts (Tŷ Cefn), Manod Road; John Ifor Thomas, 2, Manod Road.

The Manod Slate Quarry and the National Gallery 1940–45

THE SPANISH CIVIL War created concern to all public bodies entrusted with the safekeeping of valuable national artefacts and works of art. In November 1936, assisted by Nazi Germany and Fascist Italy, the Franco regime bombed Madrid causing extensive damage. This demonstrated that the face of warfare had changed, and that indiscriminate aerial bombardment had the propensity not only to kill innocent civilians but also to cause irreparable damage to priceless national treasures as well.

The military had advised that London would be the first target if war was declared. The British authorities were already well aware of the dangers, and ministerial meetings to try and plan ahead had been held with directors of libraries, museums and art galleries in the capital as early as 1933. The discussions culminated in the creation of a list of country houses and other repositories, where material could be stored safely away from London.

During the Munich Crisis – which ultimately gave legitimacy to the German annexation of the Sudetenland in western Czechoslovakia – ten institutions, including the National Gallery, applied for space at the National Library of Wales,

Aberystwyth, and at the University of Wales, Bangor. To test the arrangements for moving the paintings from the National Gallery, two consignments of pictures were sent from London during the crisis, but, with the Munich Agreement newly signed and peace assured, the crates were returned to the capital unopened. This feasibility study had worked, and plans could now be prepared for removal of all artefacts, if and when it became necessary. Peace was only temporarily restored, and Germany eventually brought the world to war.

With the comparative quiet of the 'phoney war' period, 'All quiet on the Western Front' (an old WWI expression) became a familiar phrase. All this changed suddenly when the Germans started their blitzkrieg campaign on various European countries. With the collapse of France and the evacuation of our troops from Dunkirk, plans that had been made for safe storage of national treasures were now outdated, as the German forces had new airfields from which to operate in France. Country houses and similar locations which had been earmarked as safe storage for artefacts were now very much in the danger area.

In May 1940, plans were made to send the paintings out of the country, Canada being the preferred option. The prime minister, Winston Churchill, was consulted, and the idea was rejected out of hand, his response being: 'Hide them in caves and cellars, but not one picture shall leave the country.' The risk of sending them across the sea was too great, as, at that time, the U-boats were sinking Allied ships at an alarming rate. Churchill had further intimated that adequate protection for them, if necessary, be made underground.

Work continued to find suitable locations, and north Wales became the preferred area. Both the University of Wales, Bangor, and the National Library of Wales, Aberystwyth, had already being earmarked for use, but these were not sufficient on their own. The assistant keeper of the National Gallery visited numerous country houses, but they failed to meet requirements. The pictures would have to be carried, so a minimum number of steps was essential; doorways had to be high enough to facilitate moving large packing crates, and the question of humidity was vital. Suitable accommodation was needed for the accompanying gallery staff and guards. Eventually, Penrhyn Castle at Bangor appeared to fulfil all necessary criteria.

In August 1939, the majority of the paintings at the National Gallery were either moved to Bangor, Aberystwyth, or to Trawscoed (near Aberystwyth), whilst others were located at Caernarfon Castle and at Plas y Bryn, Bontnewydd. Trawscoed was problematic. Several of the paintings were stored in the library, but the house had an antiquated heating system operating below the library floor. This seriously affected the relative humidity of the room with the danger of disastrous consequences for paintings on panel and canvas. As the heating could not be turned off without affecting the whole property, blankets and pieces of felt had to be soaked in a nearby stream and hung up in the library until the humidity reached an acceptable level.

Problems were also encountered at Penrhyn Castle; the owner seemed to celebrate a little too often and was a danger to all as he and his dog stumbled about the various rooms which housed the paintings. The risk of having him fall on to paintings was too high, and this made the place unsuitable. Caernarfon Castle had many of the necessary attributes required, but the military also had plans for the place. The Eagle Tower, where many of the paintings were stored, was proposed as an observation post for the Air Ministry, and also the castle would be vital in the defence of the area if the Germans landed.

In the summer of 1940, the Blitz across Britain meant that the National Gallery collection had to find a more secure home. Aberystwyth, Caernarfon and Penrhyn Castle were major landmarks that were on the flight path of German bombers inbound to Liverpool and Birkenhead docks. The danger of them jettisoning their bombs on these places was a possibility that could not be ignored. With the threat of the military

Looking up Cwm Teigl towards the quarry

Looking down Cwm Teigl towards Llan Ffestiniog

requisitioning various buildings for their own use, the time had come to follow Churchill's advice 'to bury the treasures in caves and cellars'.

One of the features of north Wales was the abundance of slate quarries – to a large extent, the prosperity of the region was built on the slate trade. There was a distinct difference between the quarries in neighbouring counties. In Caernarfonshire, much of the slate was mined using an open-cast system, digging down the mountainside; in Merionethshire, by contrast, the slate was extracted by means of a system of underground, man-made caverns. The slate was carried out on small trucks on a narrow gauge railway track, and underground it was normal for horses to be used to haul the wagons to their destinations.

Many people have asked how Manod Slate Quarry (known locally as Bwlch y Slaters Quarry) was chosen for the storage of paintings. One rumour is that Lloyd George suggested the site. The quarry lay on the eastern side of Manod Mawr mountain and had one great advantage over other local quarries: its caverns were level as the slate seams ran on an almost horizontal plane. If it had been otherwise, great difficulty would have been encountered in moving paintings into the chambers. Another positive point in its favour was its isolation; Bwlch y Slaters was at least four miles from the nearest village and was literally in the middle of nowhere. The workings had a massive roof of at least 200 to 300 feet of solid rock which would defy any bomb.

Inside, it had six massive chambers which were ideal for the storage of pictures; the only snag was that the entrance tunnel was too small. With an opening of only six feet by six feet, it would be necessary to enlarge the tunnel to at least 13 feet 6 inches in height and ten feet in width, but this was not a serious problem, and one which could be resolved. A more difficult problem was the railway bridge on the unclassified quarry access road, the headroom of which was insufficient to allow large crates to pass underneath it.

In its heyday, the quarry was considered small in relation

to others in the area producing roofing slates and planed slate slabs. In recounting its story, many have stated that Bwlch y Slaters was disused, but this is not correct. Owing to the war, lack of orders, and labour scarcity, production was discontinued temporarily, but when it was eventually returned to its owners, slate production continued again.

Bwlch y Slaters Quarry

Pre-war, Bwlch y Slaters was owned by a Captain Mathews. The quarry manager was Wmffra Hughes, and Robert Baker (a keen Anglican and a lay preacher at St Martha's Church, Tyddyn Gwyn, Manod) was the administration and pay clerk. Richard H. Roberts, who later became a local councillor, county councillor, and then chairman of the North Wales Police Authority, was a young slate clerk in charge of all the newly produced slates and slabs for distribution.

The quarry maintenance staff comprised a fitter/electrician, Daniel Davies (a well-known dramatist with his own amateur dramatic company); Lloyd the blacksmith, who unfortunately suffered an accident at work and lost his thumb, which effectively meant that he could not carry on with his normal work; a stone mason called Hugh Pugh Roberts (who later became a local councillor); and a carpenter, who was my father, Eric Darbyshire.

The production side employed some sixty workers made up of rock men (working underground), slate dressers, and labourers. It was a close-knit workforce which, to a large extent, remained constant; meal breaks were taken in the *caban* (cabin), which provided a platform for discussions. It had strict rules of procedure, with an elected chairman and secretary who would convey the various resolutions passed to the appropriate authorities.

The workers travelled the seven-mile journey from Blaenau Ffestiniog crouched on the floor of an open truck, with a tarpaulin sheet over them if it was raining. They had to be at the quarry by 7 a.m. and finished work at 4 p.m. As in all works, they had their own unique characters, and John Q. was a noted miser. He bought stale bread to save money, and when asked why he was so miserly, as after his death his children would only waste their inheritance, he replied, 'If they get as much satisfaction in doing that, as I have in collecting it, so be it.' Such philosophy!

At the end of the working day, the homeward journey was by a different means altogether. Walking from Bwlch y Slaters over the summit of Manod Mawr, the workers met with the top incline of another quarry: Chwarel Graig Ddu (Black Rock Quarry). This was on the western slopes of the mountain some half a mile distant from their own works. They were allowed to use this incline and two others further down to make their way home to Blaenau.

The top incline was very steep, the middle moderate, whilst the bottom one had a gentle gradient. The preferred mode of transport for the workmen was unique to this quarry: a wood and steel contraption called a *car gwyllt* (a 'wild car', also referred to as a trolley) or *ceir gwyllt* in its plural form. The three inclines had a total length of approximately 1,800 yards with a fall of 1,040 feet, and normally this would be traversed in about eight minutes on a *car gwyllt*.

The body of the *car gwyllt* consisted of a two-foot long

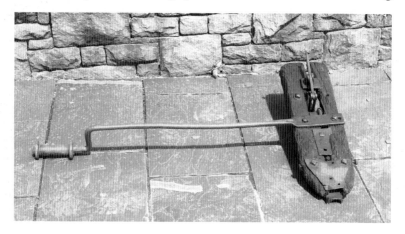

wooden plank some two inches thick and eight inches wide, on which the rider sat. A double-flanged wheel, mounted about a third to halfway along the underside of the board, rested and ran on one rail, whilst at the rear, a small, inverted V-shaped iron flange fitted over the same rail, acting as a skate on the downward journey. A brake lever was mounted between the legs of the rider, and when pulled backwards, rubbed on the front wheel to slow the *car gwyllt*. As the *car* reached speeds of over 40 mph on some parts of the inclines, the effectiveness of this lever must have been rather suspect.

Protruding from the centre of the board and above the wheel was a long iron rod with a double bend near its end terminating in a roller which rested on the left-hand track of the incline. The *car gwyllt* ran on the middle pair of the four rails of the double-track incline – a distance of three feet apart. On the main tracks, there were permanent iron rollers on which the steel cables to manipulate the trucks up and down rested which would have stopped the *car gwyllt* from being used on them.

The author remembers the thrilling sight of watching the *ceir gwyllt* coming down the incline, once at the bottom it was vital that the riders got off quickly as there was another *car gwyllt* following immediately behind.

Each working day morning the *ceir gwyllt* would be hauled up to the top incline ready for their next downward journey that evening. A charge of sixpence a month was levied on the users and this was distributed between the men responsible for hauling them back to the top.

The late Emrys Evans worked at the quarry from 1933 to 1939 when he joined the Royal Navy, the author is indebted to him for the history and anecdotes he recounted. His father, John Huw Evans, a slate clerk at the quarry, bought him a new *car gwyllt* at a cost of ten shillings when he started at the quarry. Uncannily, this very same *car gwyllt* is now on display at the National Slate Museum, Llanberis and is depicted in these photographs.

An old photograph currently on display at the Museum depicts Selwyn Evans (Emrys Evans's elder brother) descending an incline on a *car gwyllt*. It will be noted that he is wearing a trilby hat – a sort of 'badge of office' for a quarry steward.

Visible on both tracks are rollers and steel cables which hauled the full and empty slate wagons up and down the incline. This precluded the use of the normal track by the *car gwyllt* and clearly shows why the centre two rails were used.

In the same period the author remembers his father repairing a *car gwyllt* which included a new board for which he received half a crown. Each car was marked with the owner's initials or some other identification mark and it was the custom when one left the quarry for it to be sold.

Quarrying was a hard life; it was dangerous work with low pay. During the winter months, rock men would not see daylight at all during their working week. The author recollects the various characters who dominated the period, in particular, a Sunday morning conversation with a rock man named William Rowlands who was enjoying the winter sun. He was a very pious man, and he asked if it was a sin for him to sit and enjoy the sun on a Sunday.

To supplement their low wages, many of the quarrymen and their wives had small businesses. William Rowlands's wife, for instance, was involved in buying and selling – eggs and butter mainly. Another rock man, John Jones, and his wife were involved in lending money, especially to farmers. Mrs Jones also ran a type of agency business for farmers, finding suitable persons to work on their farms either as maids or housekeepers, or in some cases acted as a matrimonial agency.

The system of payments for the rock men and quarrymen was quite unique; they worked on a *bargen* (bargain) or subcontracting system. Teams were made up of rock men, slate dressers and labourers (who were paid daily). At the beginning of each month, a price would be agreed with the quarry's steward concerning their slate production for that month. At the end of the month, when production had been counted, i.e. the number of slates produced, the money would be paid out and was called the *tâl mawr* (the full payment). During the course of the month, they would receive a 'sub' from the owners, which would then be taken into account at the monthly settlement.

Some of these rock men were men of integrity and standing in the community – one being a farmer known as Yr Hen Gae ('The Old Field' – his name being derived from the name of his farm, Cae Canol or Middle Field). He was a very highly respected person and a pillar of the chapel – he was mainly responsible for the erection of Gwylfa Chapel at Manod. He hardly worked at the quarry but had a *bargen* there; every month he would argue his case for a good price for his output. He would then hire men to do the work at a daily rate, and at the end of the month show a good profit – whilst he had stayed at home farming! When he was contemplating leaving the area and had almost sold his farm, a public petition was instigated to try and persuade him to stay in the district, which as it happens, he did.

Wmffra Hughes, the Bwlch y Slaters manager, died in late 1938 and was succeeded by Mr Cadwaladr (Dwalad) Vaughan, who was in charge when the Ministry of Works signed a forty-year lease for the quarry. Mr Vaughan was responsible for enlarging the tunnel entrance to its current dimensions. A very competent and experienced rock man, all aspect of rock safety fell on his shoulders, and with his vast experience, he was able to guide and advise the authorities. When the entrance had been enlarged, Messrs John Mowlem became the main contractors to build the internal structures. At the time, it was Mowlem who were constructing the new airfield at Llanbedr, Merioneth. All the tradesmen (including the author) from the Ffestiniog area then working at Llanbedr were transferred to the quarry, including their foreman carpenter Mr J. I. Roberts of Tremadog.

Working underground was a unique experience, as the author can testify; the first reaction on entering the caverns was the feeling of warm humid air on one's face. Fortunately for us, there were electric lights to guide us through the tunnel until we reached the massive chambers where we were going to work. There was plenty of light there, a vast difference to the old quarry days when the rock men had to work by the light of a candle and, what is more, buy the candles from the owners. It was common knowledge that the chambers were being prepared to house the precious paintings etc. from the National Gallery.

Our work consisted in preparing and laying shuttering ready for the concrete bases of the buildings. The walls were of brick construction, and a crowd of London bricklayers did the job; they were a squad on their own, and they worked hard and erected the walls in quick time. This was the first time that the locals had seen bonus work; they seemed to throw the bricks into place, but their work satisfied the firm. Our other work was to erect roofs on the buildings and fix the necessary doors and frames.

During this time, the railway bridge on the access road was still causing a problem. Its headroom was insufficient to allow

the wagons carrying the large crates, containing the paintings, to pass underneath. The road had to be lowered by two and a half feet, but a new problem developed, as the new road was below the foundation of the bridge. This was resolved by inserting new concrete abutments under the old foundations, and to this day these can still be seen. When the crates started to be delivered to the site, it was only by deflating the tyres of the wagons that the largest crates were able to pass under the bridge.

Before the pictures could be housed at the quarry, each of the six chambers had its own air conditioning system fitted, which ensured four changes of air per hour and a constant temperature of 65°F at 42% humidity. During work in the caverns, huge droplets of water spasmodically came down from the roof of the chambers. It was said by the old rock men that it was the rain which had fallen twelve months previously on the mountain, and that it took that long for it to percolate through the mass of rock. Whether true or not is not known or proved, but very often such sayings had some element of truth in them.

After nine months of intensive work, the Ministry of Works announced that Manod Quarry was ready for occupation, and the paintings were conveyed from their six repositories in Wales to the quarry. The LMS Railway was responsible for bringing the pictures from Bangor – a distance of 40 miles – and the GWR Railway from the Aberystwyth district, 70 miles away. In both cases, the pictures were conveyed in container lorries. It took four weeks to transport the canvases, including the library, stores and equipment, and the paintings were stacked in rows for ease of inspection.

The library staff were able to constantly monitor the condition of all items stored in the quarry. They were assisted by hygrometers to maintain the relative humidity of each building, and conditions of light and temperature were kept at a consistent level (emergency generators were installed in case of breakdowns). In fact, the conditions for the paintings at the quarry were probably superior to those at London galleries.

As with all quarries, the potential for roof falls was always present, but Manod Quarry had a good reputation for safety, and the brick buildings were strong enough to withstand minor falls. In March 1943, some pictures were slightly damaged in a rockfall; about 300 paintings were removed from the affected area so that those damaged could be easily repaired. Mr Vaughan, the quarry manager, again examined and supervised the remedial work. No other falls occurred during the rest of the time the paintings were at Manod.

Parts of the following collections were held at the quarry: the National Gallery, the Courtauld Institute, the National Portrait Gallery, the Soane Museum, the Victoria and Albert Museum, London, the Walker Art Gallery, Liverpool, and the Fitzwilliam Museum, Cambridge, as well as collections from a number of other galleries. A part of the Royal Collection was also housed at Manod. These priceless works were guarded by a staff of fourteen, under the leadership of the head attendant Mr E. B. Harrison. Their storage at Manod Quarry was deemed to be a success, and not one of the pictures suffered during their stay in Wales.

The paintings were returned to London in 1945, but the Ministry of Works retained the caverns at Manod for quite a few years after the expiry of their lease, and it was only after a high court action in 1983 that the owner was able to reclaim ownership of the quarry.

An interesting cartoon appeared in *Punch* at the time of the return of the paintings to London. It depicted an old lady telling the gallery attendant: 'My sister tells me that most of the stuff now in the gallery came from a cave in Wales!' Manod Quarry deserves a mention for the vital role it played in ensuring that a good part of our treasure and heritage was not destroyed in WWII. The National Gallery was hit at least nine times during the Blitz, which caused much damage to the building. When plans were prepared for renovation of the gallery, they included the installation of air conditioning for the conservation of the paintings. The importance of constant temperature and humidity could no longer be ignored. The lessons learnt at Manod Quarry during the war ensured that all major galleries adopted the same methods for the conservation of their art works.

Recollections of Trawsfynydd

TRAWSFYNYDD ARTILLERY CAMP was one of the oldest military establishments in the Merioneth area. The army came to Traws at the beginning of the last century and established a small camp at Bryn Goleu. In 1906, the establishment bought land around the area we know as Bronaber and also the historic farm Rhiw Goch, reputed birthplace of St John Roberts the Catholic martyr.

The camp and surrounding ranges, comprising around 8,000 acres, were to be used by the regular and Territorial armies for artillery training; Rhiw Goch farmhouse, though a listed building, was adapted to become the officers' mess. The land was extensively used during WWI, as the ranges were reputed to be the best in the country, and at a later period in that war, it accommodated German prisoners of war. The small hamlet of Bronaber (the name taken from a nearby farm) grew alongside the camp and was mainly a line of tin shacks along the main road. Known locally as 'Tin Town', it consisted mostly of cafes and shops, together with a petrol station. The hamlet did a thriving trade and proved a boon to the troops.

During the interwar years, the camp kept its doors open, continuing to train the regular and Territorial armies in the art of artillery. It was divided into three sections: North Camp, Depot, and South Camp. The Garrison Maintenance Section (all civilians) had their compound near the camp centre, and this included an electrical generator to produce power. The camp gave employment to numerous locals, but Trawsfynydd was very parochial and did not like outsiders coming to work there. This created a bit of discord but provided spin-off work for Trawsfynydd village itself, with the Tudor family taking advantage of the opportunity to supply shire horses to transport equipment from the railway station to the camp. The late David Tudor related to the author that, as the camp closed during the winter months, the horses were redeployed extracting timber from the forest, which was the beginning of their successful timber business.

I was part of the maintenance team for a period in 1941. There were six of us, all teenagers, who had been taken on as improver apprentices. Of the six, I was the only one not local to Traws. Without exaggeration, we were taught by the finest and most capable tradesmen, and memories of the characters working there still remain in one's memory today – Ellis Jones, general foreman, Dick O'Neil, plumber, Jack Menyn and Ifan Barbwr, stonemasons. Ifan had a small brass 'Put & Take' spinning top which showed on different faces what you had won or had to put in the kitty. Ifan had an uncanny knack of getting his spin to land on 'Take all' far more often than the rest of us. Other characters included Moss Jones, a joiner who was also the licensee of a public house in Trawsfynydd; Harold Rees, a handyman and caretaker of the sewage works; Bert Jones, a painter from Llan Ffestiniog; Dafis, a brush hand; Ned Morris, salt of the earth, who was respected and esteemed by all (he later became a county councillor); Elsyn Lewis, plumber's mate; Oliver Meredith, general labourer; his brother Dick,

in administration; and Ypres,[2] a joiner from Gellilydan. An old photograph taken in 1938/9 shows that the maintenance staff comprised some fifty local men, which helped the local economy.

The work was mainly general maintenance of the camp, as well as the building and erecting of observation sheds on the ranges, so that the officers could observe the accuracy of the shelling. As the camp increased in capacity, huts had to be erected in North Camp. Nissen huts were the standard accommodation for troops throughout the UK and were a quick way of erecting living quarters. Once the concrete foundation was laid, bricklayers would build a three-foot high perimeter wall with pillars; semi-circular steel ribs were then bolted to the pillars, and corrugated iron sheets laid lengthwise between them and held in place with tensioned galvanised steel wire. Wooden purlins were fitted on the ribs and preformed corrugated sheets then nailed to them. Care had to be taken with the corrugated sheets; they were not galvanised but had been immersed in some oily substance to protect them from rust, and the edges were razor sharp. Some huts had dormer windows inserted; the ends were made up of wooden boarding and heating was by coal-burning stoves with cast-iron chimney pipes.

The squad also had to work outside the camp area. We were taken to Rhug Hall near Corwen by army lorries, where we were responsible for converting part of the hall to accommodate the Western Command. Rhug Hall was owned by Lieutenant Colonel R. V. Wynn of the 6th Corwen Sector, Home Guard, who later became Lord Newborough.

During the same period, an additional camp was opened on Morfa Harlech, and part of the squad was employed there. A contingent of Indian soldiers came to Tŷ Llwyd, camping by the station, and preparatory work had to be done to

---

[2]   Ypres Neave Hughes, colloquially knows as Ipri. There seemed to be a national tradition during WWI to name a son after where his father had fallen in battle.

accommodate them. Trawsfynydd Camp had all the facilities, a large NAAFI, a superb cinema, and a dance hall with transport laid on to bring visitors to the venue. Our work was finishing by 1941–2, and I was directed to work with Costains Ltd on the new extension runway at Llanbedr.

***

The late John Norman Davies, a native of Trawsfynydd who retired to Llangefni, wrote numerous articles in Welsh about his childhood memories of Trawsfynydd during the WWII period. These were published in the Ffestiniog district community paper, *Llafar Bro*. He kindly allowed excerpts of his work to be published in this book:

Camp Traws

About two and a half miles from the village of Trawsfynydd, on the road to Dolgellau, is the small hamlet of Bronaber – the old church on one side, the school and the tin shacks on the other. Today it's a different village, with numerous wooden log chalets built on the road leading to the Rhiw Goch Hotel. This was the site of Camp Traws, the military camp which became part of Traws's history in the last century. Memories from my boyhood are full of events of that strange place. Before I drown in reminiscences of my childhood, it would be better to have a few facts about the place. It was started as a small temporary camp on land belonging to Bryn Goleu at the beginning of the last century, but in 1906 a permanent camp was established by Rhiw Goch, which was split up into two sections, North Camp and South Camp.

At the same time, a new platform and a military yard were added to the existing GWR station at Traws, with a new bypass road leading from it; this would take all the goods, wagons and heavy guns to the camp, and they would not have to manoeuvre through the village. The road can be seen today;

the top half of it started by the gates of Pen Cefn Cemetery and terminated near the river bridge. As children, we watched the procession of heavy guns drawn by shire horses trundling down the road, while nearby, soldiers could be seen drilling in a field. Normally, a contingent of troops would come and stay for a fortnight's training during the spring and summer, but around September the camp closed until the following February, giving maintenance staff the opportunity to renew and repair, whilst a few soldiers remained for security.

In the 1930s and at the beginning of WWII, the demand increased for extra personnel and machines at the camp, and the hamlet grew in size to include eating places, cafes, shops and a petrol station; these became very popular with the troops and locals alike. One of my best friends, Derek Davies, lived in Waverley Cafe, where I spent hours devouring egg and chips cooked in the small kitchen – no wonder the place was full of soldiers! We would be invited to the camp cinema because of our connection with the Waverley Cafe, and we were able to see and hear very well-known artists taking part in the ENSA concerts – all for nothing as we were the 'Waverley kids'.

By now, the old Rhiw Goch farmhouse had been converted into the officers' mess, with the soldiers living in permanent huts on the camp. During the war, it was home to soldiers from all over the world, and I remember the lads coming back from Dunkirk with all their hopes and aspirations shattered. Later it became an Italian prisoner of war camp, and I can still remember the prisoners: Mimi, Mario and Marionni. During this period, goods from the military yard at the railway station were still being carried on Ned Fôn Pugh's lorries, and we always managed to get a ride to the camp.

There was also a military range for gunnery and bombing practice; red flags would be flown at the summit of the peaks when firing was in progress, and it always seemed to rain when the big guns were firing – the drizzle did annoy us.

The camp maintenance squad travelled there daily from Traws on one of Ned Fôn Pugh's open lorries and were supervised by William David Evans, who was employed as a 'civil servant' in the role of 'barrack warden'; he wore a special uniform to denote his position. In WW1 he had been awarded the Military Medal for his heroism, and I remember him as an upright, ramrod of a man with distinguished eyes.

After 1945, the camp became quieter and its purpose changed; the need now was to get rid of surplus shells, high explosives, and ammunitions. By 1950, the camp was nearing its end as a military establishment, and it was closed in 1958.

For a period afterwards, it reopened until 1963 as accommodation for workers who were building the new atomic power station at Trawsfynydd. When the station was completed, the old buildings were demolished, the site landscaped and sold, and log cabins were built on the site and sold as holiday homes.

The camp played an important part in the history of Traws. Over the years, many came from afar to find work, to build the railway, and to construct the lake, the dams and the atomic station, but they did not change us. I believe more than anything it showed our strength, our environment, and the creed of Dafydd Iwan's ballad: 'Ry'n ni yma o hyd' ('We are here still').

***

Megan Falconer lived in Tŷ Llwyd Terrace by the GWR station. Her father worked at the camp, and she remembers him leaving for work to catch Ned Fôn Pugh's truck in the early morning. Megan stated that this was the happiest period of his life, as his specific job was to shepherd the sheep. When firing took place, his duties entailed moving the sheep from the designated firing area and taking them to a safe pasture. Megan was allowed to go with him to Pen y Stryd and enjoy herself at the farm.

[The author had occasion to visit the camp whilst working for the Deudraeth Rural District Council in the early 1960s. It looked desolate and unkempt. There was one solitary timber shed to be seen, and, on investigating, he met Lewis Griffiths or 'Lewis Jeru' as he was known. He lived in a house adjoining Jerusalem Chapel, about a mile to the south of the camp, and was the War Office's representative and caretaker for the camp. I still remember seeing Lewis whistling outside his shed; the sheep pricked their ears and would all trot towards him for some titbits. This, I gathered, was a daily occurrence. A few months later, an official from the War Department visited and was amazed that a caretaker was still there. Needless to say, Lewis became unemployed soon afterwards.]

The Red Flag

Today, how many residents of Trawsfynydd remember the Royal Artillery heavy guns firing over the ranges behind the village hills? Not many, I think. Live rounds were fired from the direction of Yr Ysgwrn and other farms in the Cwm Prysor area towards Abergeirw. On impact, the explosive detonation could be heard all over the mountains and vales. This was the place to practise, even though it was part of our heritage; we lived with the firing every spring and summer.

Very large red flags were hoisted on the mountaintop to show firing was in progress. As children, we were well aware what this meant and of the firing that followed, which sometimes lasted a whole week. We soon became acclimatised to it and accepted it as part of everyday life. Despite the flags, we were not afraid and did not consider the dangers involved. We would crawl to the red flags and watch the shells exploding, the puffs of smoke, the flashes where live rounds were landing on the ranges.

The camp had a vast influence on the village for over fifty years. Special trains arrived on Sundays to the new station, transporting soldiers, horses and guns, marring the Sabbath but adding colour to it. The horses were deployed to tow massive wagons and armed vehicles; it was a sight to see them being harnessed to the guns. On the command of the band, they marched down the military bypass road with barely enough room to pass over the bridge and onwards to the camp. We always knew what was happening at Bronaber: in the camp, the cinema, the ENSA concerts, the shows, and, of course, the football matches. We also saw prisoners of war from Italy and Germany behind barbed wire, also commandos and SAS billeting in the Coed y Brenin area.

Apart from the guns, for a period special Anson planes used the ranges for bombing practice. Gathering over the Rhinogs, they flew over Trawsfynydd Lake and village towards the ranges. During the Anson bombing runs, we were fearless; lying underneath the flags, we could see the faces of the pilots and crews clearly.

In the fifties, a squad of soldiers lived in the camp. Their work was to clear the ranges of unexploded ordinance, which was partially buried; it was very dangerous work. Permanent notices in large bold letters had now taken over from the red flags, warning of the danger. Trawsfynydd is noted for its rain – heavy rain and high winds in winter, and light showers in the spring and summer. Some used to say that you could forecast the weather by studying the flags. It was true that after a lull in the firing it often rained, but we knew the firing had not caused this.

Traws Railway Station

My home was close to the station, and all I had to do was climb over the fence to get the morning train to school. The engine gave a short sharp whistle and it served as a clock. The 6 a.m. workers train, the 7 a.m. school train, the 10 a.m. for shopping, the 4 p.m. school train, the 5 p.m. workers train, the 7 p.m. evening train, and the last train at 8 p.m. before closing the gates. On Saturday nights, there would be a late train, the 10 p.m., for the convenience of cinemagoers and drinkers after enjoying themselves in Blaenau or Bala.

Sunday was the day for military use and inspection trains. The troop trains changed the atmosphere of the village completely from the normal tranquillity of a Welsh Sunday to a bustling, noisy day. Before the advent of the modern vehicle, the troops brought colour and excitement to our world: the engines hissing by the platform near the military yard, troops descending the trucks and carriages, heavy guns being offloaded from special low-level railway wagons. With horses disembarking from their horse boxes, the yard was a kaleidoscope of colour and movement, and the sound of different voices and intonations was wonderful to one's young imaginative and receptive mind.

We were given the odd copper or two if we went to the Co-op for fags for the soldiers, and sometimes a drink of sweet tea from the big urn. There was the thrill and joy of being allowed to hold the horse's head whilst the officer rearranged his Sam Browne belt over his shoulder, and, more than that, to see the shine of his sword and his revolver, which was always on his belt.

At last, the horses and guns were ready to move, the soldiers in their formation waiting for the command to proceed, and, when it came, the drum and the band took over and started their journey of two miles to Bronaber Camp. We participated in the wonder of being able to see and hear such scenes and movements, pondering perhaps what else the train could bring to us.

Later, we saw Bren carriers taking over from the horses, light tanks instead of the heavy guns, and soldiers from foreign countries such as India, Poland, France, Canada and the United States. We wondered at and felt the pain and anguish of the troops who had had to suffer and endure in the evacuation from Dunkirk, and there was always a reception when a contingent of special trains arrived in Traws to take refuge and shelter under our quiet hills.

More than anything, I remember the little dog which had been abandoned by a soldier in the station when he was leaving.

The dog adopted us and came to live at Tŷ Llwyd Terrace – we named him Spot. One day, he left us to follow the trail of another lonely soldier on to the train – a case of once a soldier's dog, always a soldier's dog.

Bombs over Traws

Liverpool suffered tremendously from the bombing between October 1940 and May 1941. Over 4,000 people were killed during the Liverpool Blitz, as it was called. Between October and Christmas 1940, 300 attacks were made on the city, with 365 people dying between 20 and 22 December. On one night, 165 perished when an air raid shelter was bombed.

Because of its strategic importance on the River Mersey, Liverpool received as much attention by German bombers as London did. Planes flew across our county to bomb Liverpool on a nightly basis. On moonlit nights, the Glaslyn and Dwyryd rivers were marker paths for the Dornier and the Heinkel planes, which followed them towards our north coast and onwards to Liverpool. During the Blitz, we could hear the hum of the German planes above our heads, creating trepidation. Sometimes because of fierce opposition by our planes and the ack-ack guns, they would turn around and head back to their bases in France or Germany, jettisoning their bombs as they did so – and that's what happened in Trawsfynydd one night in October 1940.

On this particular night, we heard the usual drone of the planes before going to bed and trying to sleep. In the early hours of the morning, we were awakened by the loud noise of a plane flying lower than usual. Suddenly, we heard a scream and a whistling noise overhead, and then explosions – one after another – either side of the station. The house shook to its foundations. It all happened in less than a second and was followed by a dreadful silence. We rushed downstairs, and my father went out into the street. He saw there was nothing he could do except remain and give succour to his family.

The next morning, we saw how close the bombs had been to our house and how lucky we had been. Eleven bombs had been dropped in a pattern: seven on Tŷ'r Felin land by the boundary wall with Craig Dân, less than half a mile away, and four on Y Pandy land near Tŷ'n Griafolen, again within half a mile of our village.

The official report was that the planes had been forced back from Liverpool and lost their bearings over the Welsh mountains, offloading their bombs willy-nilly as they tried to make their way back to base. Perhaps that was the truth, but on clear moonlit nights the station, railway and houses would have been clear from the air – targets which would have proved useful to the enemy instead of jettisoning their bombs haphazardly elsewhere.

According to the experts, pinpoint accuracy in bombing was impossible; to bomb a target, many bombs were dropped to cover an area like a blanket. I believe that is what happened in Traws that night, and it was not an accident that the bombs fell so near to the station. The station was an important part of the military set-up, and the Germans had strategic maps which would have shown the importance of the station to the military camp at Bronaber. What would have happened had they bombed a far more important target, the Cwm Prysor Viaduct, thereby cutting the Bala–Blaenau railway link?

William Joyce (Lord Haw-Haw), the German spy, stayed in Maentwrog before the war, and he would have had knowledge of the camp and railway station. By the time he was broadcasting from Germany with his call sign 'Germany Calling, Germany Calling', all he had gleaned from his trips to this area would have been passed on to his masters. We all listened to him, but we would have taken up arms had they come to Traws.

Note: In the editorial notes to the article in *Llafar Bro*, the editor states that William Joyce is believed to have visited a friend, John Philby (a leading British fascist of the time), who rented a house named Coed y Bleiddiau, situated between Dduallt and Tan y Bwlch, close to the narrow gauge Ffestiniog Railway. His son, Kim Philby, was a member of the Cambridge Five in the 1950s and was later unmasked as a KGB agent.

Cae Bomer (Bomber Field)

It was a fine day in September and I was at the back of the house with my father, who had just come home after his duties with the Royal Observer Corps, which had its base not far from our house at Pen Cefn. Their job was to watch the skies continuously, day and night, and register any plane movements and their directions, as well as to determine their origins and identify them. Suddenly, the silence was broken by the noise and sound of planes firing above us. We saw a large black plane turning and twisting around Cwm Prysor way, trying to avoid a small, fast RAF plane. My father said the big plane was a German Dornier. Smoke could be seen coming from its tail, and it was losing height and heading towards the village bridge. We lost sight of it as it flew towards Bronaber Camp. An RAF Spitfire was following and firing at it, and later we saw the Spitfire doing a 'victory roll'.

My father rushed back to the observation post, whilst I borrowed a bike and with other village lads cycled towards the camp. As we rode over a hump in the road, we could see the massive tail end of the plane in a field; it had a large bold swastika on its side that seemed to overwhelm and scare us. The Dornier had landed on a hump between the main road and a small farm road. The pilot had miraculously managed to land the plane, but it had broken into two parts. The main body was on the hump, with the wings and cockpit resting on top of the two walls adjacent to the farm road.

We could smell the fumes and saw that telephone poles and wires had been damaged and thrown everywhere across the road. I remember two airmen jumping from the cockpit and a dead airman lying by the tail. A lorry with armed soldiers arrived from the military camp. Their presence did not stop us collecting pieces of Perspex, which we could make into rings by inserting a hot poker through them.

Rumours were rife. We heard that a woman, who was gathering blackberries close by, had offered her handkerchief to one of the German airmen; some said that she was a German who lived in Traws and was able to speak the language. We also heard that it was the pilot who had been killed. It was said that the gun had been fired by one of the crew, who was supposed to be a Gestapo member, and afterwards that another crew member had taken over the controls.

Our school train was used to transport a crew member, under military escort, into custody in England. One of the crew was kept apart from the other two, and to our minds he had to be 'the Gestapo'. We were listening to the warring speeches of Churchill on the radio and willing to believe any story, and we were also more than willing to 'up it' and fight the Germans on our mountain terrain if the need ever arose!

But the facts are more real than that of a teenager's memory. The plane was shot down on Saturday, 21 September 1940; the Spitfire pilot was Flying Officer Dennis Adams and he had been ordered to stop the Dornier from taking photographs of Liverpool. The planes met around Denbigh, and the Spitfire followed the Dornier for fourteen minutes before shooting it down over Trawsfynydd. One of the crew was killed, and he was interred with military honours at Pwllheli.

In a different article, Megan Morris, a fifth-former at the Ffestiniog County School who lived near Bronaber, recounted her recollection of the events in the 1940 Christmas edition of the school magazine *Blodau'r Grug*. She wrote:

> On the Saturday afternoon, I was out in the garden when suddenly I heard a plane overhead and then a heavy thud as if something heavy had been dropped. Looking up, I could see a British plane making trails in the sky and heading towards the military camp nearby. After leaving the trail it disappeared out of sight.

I was keen to know what had happened, and before long somebody came by to say that a German plane had been shot down less than a mile from my home. I ran to the house to get my coat and hurried to be an eyewitness of the scene. Quite a few cars passed by, and in one I could see a British officer with three airmen with him. I could see that one of them had been injured as blood was oozing down his face; he was, as I was later told, the German pilot.

As I neared the scene, I could see many people had gathered in the field before me, and there was a long line of cars parked along the main road. Then this great massive plane came to sight lying across the road leading to Tyddyn Sais Farm. As the plane came down to earth, it had hit a telegraph pole and had pulled all the wires, and they were dangling all over the road and field. By now, the soldiers had arrived and kept the public away; they roped the area as it was believed that bombs were on board the plane and could ignite at any time, but nothing happened, and the public pushed their way towards the plane ignoring the danger.

The plane had a crew of four, and the mechanic had been killed and the pilot injured. I was told the plane was a Dornier 125 (model 1939) and that it was a Spitfire that had shot it down.

By the evening, there was much activity, and cars were slowing down to have a look. Some high-ranking officers came to inspect the plane, and this was sufficient for the crowd to think that there were no bombs on board. When I went home at 9 p.m., there were many people still there.

Next day and throughout the week, more people came in their hundreds, all hoping to get hold of souvenirs. Then, on the following Sunday, a squad of RAF men came to clear the plane and debris, and soon there was nothing left.

This was the most frightful incident of the war for me, and I treasure a souvenir which I had, a small metal plate indicating that the plane had been made in the Ruhr, Germany.

John continues:

The Dornier pilot was Leutnant Rolf Book, and the crew were Feldwebel Jensen, Feldwebel Kuhl, and Unteroffizer Pelzer – the engineer who had been killed. The Spitfire pilot, Pilot Officer Dennis Adams, was from B Flight of 611 Squadron detached from Tern Hill to Manchester Ringway. After the war, Rolf Book rejoined the Luftwaffe and lived in Berlin. This is how he described the incident:

> We had finished taking photographs over Liverpool and were on our way back to France at a height of 28,000 feet when we were attacked by a Spitfire; with two engines damaged, we were lucky to be able to land at all. Officer Pelzer was killed in the first encounter, and he was buried in a place called Pwllheli to the west of Trawsfynydd.[3]
>
> I well remember the girl who gave me her handkerchief; she was pretty. The fact that she married a German from Berlin gives me great pleasure. I stayed in the military camp before being transferred to the military hospital in Chester. I remember Dorothy Fox, a nurse who looked after me. From there I was taken to Stratford-upon-Avon, the only place that I did not like in England and Canada. At the end of January 1941, I was taken to Canada, and in 1946 I spent some time in England before being sent home to Germany in December 1946.

Mr R. E. Williams of Tyddyn Sais recounts his experience:

> I shall never forget that Saturday. It was around 5 p.m. and I was in the kitchen when I heard the sound of a plane. I looked out through the window and I saw an aeroplane coming straight for the house. I ran out and saw it miss the house and fly low over the fence. A Spitfire was hovering above it. I saw them throwing things from the plane; I realised afterwards that they were parts of maps.
>
> It was easy to see the German markings on the plane. The plane got caught on a telephone pole and wires, and I saw that the pole had split in two and that half of the plane had then fallen in the field and another part on the access road to the farm.
>
> My father and brother came quickly to the house; they had seen the plane flying low through Cwm Prysor and the Spitfire firing at it. I was a member of the Home Guard and my father in the Royal Observer Corps. We went to the plane – we were

---

[3] Pelzer was reinterred after the end of the war in a German War Cemetery in Cannock Chase, Staffordshire.

the first there – and we took one body out. A soldier from the nearby camp then sent us away from the plane. The seven-year-old daughter of the farm was gathering blackberries by the hedge near where the plane landed; another girl on the main road waiting for a bus was trapped by the telephone wires. The local bobby PC Thomas arrived, and I had to make an official statement to him.

The captain in charge of the soldiers was Captain Roe; he lived in the village. The field came to be known as Cae Bomer (Bomber Field).

Below is part of a letter written by Kit 'Bryn Re', a young woman who lived close to Tyddyn Sais. She was the person waiting for the bus when the bomber landed.

I have little to say about the incident on an afternoon so long ago, and I was only around twenty years old. I don't remember much about the war, the shortage of food and so on, especially living on a farm in the country. To be truthful, there was no change in my mode of living, as I made the best of things, and we enjoyed ourselves dancing etc. That afternoon, I was waiting for the bus around 5 p.m. when I saw the Spitfire flying quickly towards Cwm Prysor and Bala. I heard the firing, then I saw this big black thing coming towards me like a beast from space and I saw the telephone pole being hit. I ran across the road and squatted by the gate, the telephone wires falling around me. I saw that the plane had landed in the nearby field and that there were pieces of metal everywhere. It turned and moved and then rested between the two stone walls either side of the farm road which I had just walked on. I jumped on top of the wall and saw a Spitfire flying low and the pilot waved to me. I shouted to a man who was passing on his bike 'Look', and he came back. I jumped down from the wall and made my way to the plane. After the smoke had cleared, I saw it was a German plane. I saw two men jumping out and they asked me if there was a doctor available; I had to say 'No'. By now, people and soldiers had arrived; I couldn't believe that so many could come in such a short time. I am afraid that my meeting was very short. I remember giving him a handkerchief to wipe his face, I remember seeing his bloodied knees, his clothes were wet and stained. I was afraid that he was severely wounded and worried that I could not reach him to help him because of the height of the plane. I saw them once again when they were taken away by car by the military officers; when he was crossing the wall, he smiled at me and I smiled back. I can't believe whilst writing this today that this person is still alive and asking questions about the incident. I can't get to grips with the fact that we are talking about 'The Boy with the Blonde Hair from Germany'. That's how I remember – so long ago.

Kit goes on to say that she visited Berlin often and was one of the first persons from north Wales allowed to visit East Berlin after the war, where she met and married a German citizen.

Indians in Traws

When I was a youngster, Craig Dân (Fire Rock) behind the station was quite a romantic place. Today, there isn't much left of its past glory; it is now a quarry and workplace. Standing on Tŷ Llwyd land, it was situated on the far side of the railway bridge and military yard. Nearby was Pwll Corddi, a small pool from which a leat or culvert ran to take water to a nearby waterwheel; by opening or closing a sluice valve, water coursed out and turned the wheel so that the farmer could churn butter – hence the name Pwll Corddi (Churning Pool).

Craig Dân was our playground, where we would play 'Cowboys and Indians' and become the film star cowboy 'Tom Mix' and fight the Sioux. To us, the wonder was that genuine Indians came to camp at the bottom of the rock.

It was April 1942 when a contingent of Indian soldiers with their mules arrived from France to camp in the Llanfrothen and Nantmor area. Their expertise was to fight in mountainous regions and to transport equipment on the back of their mules. After Dunkirk, they trained on the Moelwyn and Cnicht mountains whilst the establishment decided on their future. About fifty of them came to camp at Tŷ Llwyd; these were the soldiers of the Royal Indian Service Corps. We were surprised to see them and their tents below Craig Dân; not only was their skin different to ours, but also their speech, dress and habits. The tents were placed in a line between the rock and Pwll Corddi. There were about six men to each tent with a fireplace and a big black cauldron outside. They squatted to eat curry, which they cooked on their fireplaces. They ate using their left hand, as was their usual practice, putting pieces of meat on a round piece of bread which they had baked. We were able to watch them and they gave us a taste of chapatti and meat.

They kept sheep at the back of Tŷ Llwyd and Rhiw Cefn hilltop, where the Royal Observer Corps had their special observation post. Four soldiers were kept permanently there as shepherds, two to each flock; nearby, a large tent had been erected close to the stream. Being Muslims, the sheep had to be slaughtered according to their religious rites and faith. They wore turbans on their heads, were unable to speak English, and were from the lower caste of their community. Their dress was a pair of strong boots up to their knees; around their legs they wore a sort of stocking, whilst over their trousers and military jacket they wore a long light coat, which looked like a frock and reached down to their knees. Two officers were in charge of them; they came from the upper caste and had had a good education and were conversant in English. They wore highly polished brown leather boots which nearly reached their knees, had a Sam Browne belt over their shoulders, and a hard turban on their heads.

As my father was a member of the Observer Corps, his post was near to their camp, and he became acquainted with one of the shepherds, Aladitah. He came to our house with his friends on a Sunday morning to listen to a Hindustani programme on our crystal set; others went to various houses for the same purpose. The two Indian officers used to go to Tŷ Llwyd, where Bob and Gwenno Griffiths lived; matters that concerned them all were discussed there.

Their daughter, Mair, recalls a local teenager who liked to

play tricks on them; he had a liking to sneak into the house and change the times on the clocks, open the sluice valve, or release the animals from their pens. One day, the pigs were discovered to be roaming free and the sluice valve had been opened. Being Muslims, the Indians could not abide pigs or their meat. On seeing what had happened, the two officers ran to Tŷ Llwyd shouting 'Hurry, hurry, the water is coming and the pigs are running, our men will kill them.' Our teenager had been up to his tricks again!

Addendum to the Indians

The Indian soldiers or, more correctly, the Indian Muslim muleteers, came from what was then the Rawalpindi area of India, now in Pakistan. At the beginning of the war, the British military realised they would need animal transport and, at short notice, requested that the Indian government procure four companies of muleteers to be deployed in France. Company 22 was captured by the Germans and companies 25, 29, and 30 were evacuated from Dunkirk but had to leave their animals behind. They were taken to Cornwall and then to Abergavenny, and for three and a half months they stayed at Llanfrothen and Nantmor training in mountain warfare on the Cnicht and Moelwyn mountains. Company 30 was camped at Llanfrothen, whilst 25 and 29 were at Nantmor. Since the mules had been left in France, replacement mules were imported from America, and horses for the officers were acquired from the region. They came to Porthmadog Railway Station by means of cattle trucks in the first week of April 1942, three trains in all, bringing about a thousand men with a few British and Indian officers.

They had an Indian doctor and a vet. The mules and horses were exercised every day, three abreast, and it took an hour for them to pass by, the vet at the head of the troop on a white horse. It was estimated that about a thousand animals were involved.

It is said that there is still a spot on the Croesor–Nantmor road called Pont Troed y Mul (Mule's Foot Bridge). Legend has it that one of the mules got its leg into a gap between two large slate slabs over a culvert, and they could not release the animal, which had to be destroyed, leaving the foot stuck between the slate slabs! The mules were taken to the Dwyryd river to practise swimming, which later stood them in good stead in Burma. The muleteers were not originally armed, but they did go to the firing range at Trawsfynydd for firing practice.

They camped in rows in round white tents, their animals tethered in rows on 'standings'. A bugle would sound when it was feeding time. Afterwards, the animals were taken to the river for watering. At the end of their stay, the Indians moved on to Scotland, returning to India in 1944 to fight the Japanese in Burma. Their presence in Traws left a lasting impression on the locals, many of whom still remember the lovely smell of chapattis cooking.

Yanks in Traws

By watching the television and seeing soldiers doing their duties in Afghanistan, I notice the children always gathering around them; this also happens in Syria, despite the atrocities. Perhaps it is in the nature of children to want to see, know and touch. I remember in my early days how we gathered around the soldiers at the camp and station, fascinated by the British, French, Polish and Indian soldiers. It was with grief that we saw our troops returning from Dunkirk, and we gazed in fear at the Italians and Germans behind barbed wire at Bronaber Camp.

The American soldiers came to the outskirts of our village in May 1944, resting here before going on to fight on the beaches of Normandy in June 1944. They had nothing to do with Bronaber Camp; they were two independent regiments waiting for embarkation at one of the major ports prior to D-

Day. They came to Traws unexpectedly during the night. Some pitched their tents on Tyddyn Sais land near Bronaber Road, whilst others were by the dam near the lake. The small tents (bivouacs) were sufficient for two men. Their camp comprised a fenced-off compound within which lorries and jeeps were parked in a circle with tents at the centre – reminiscent of the method used by cowboys to safeguard themselves from attacking Indians.

An armed sentry granted permission to enter the compound. The troops were not free to roam outside, but soon they came to greet us by the fence. In time, we were able to crawl towards their tents; they loved to see children and thrilled to hear Welsh being spoken. To us, their accent was also strange and reminded us of the language of the motion pictures we saw at Blaenau cinema. It is thought that they came from Brooklyn, New York, but they did not look in good physical condition, and it was said that these were the type of men who would be thrown in to fight at the initial landings. There were about five hundred of them with a small squad of black soldiers serving in both regiments. There was no obvious mixing between the white and black soldiers; to us, at the time, to see a black soldier was a sight to behold.

Very soon, the troops realised that we could shop for them. They gave us half a crown or more to run errands for them. Surprisingly, most of them would ask for bread; our bread still retained its taste, despite the rationing and hard times. They also enjoyed our cakes, if available, and our cigarettes were a treat for them. They did not understand our money, and we often kept the change. Often we had chewing gum and chocolate for carrying fresh milk to them; we also loved their cigarettes. In particular, I remember the 'Lucky Strikes' – they were priceless bargaining items at school. Jini's little shop by the bridge did good business as we supported her, though PC Thomas kept a very sharp eye on us.

The troops played baseball – a new kind of game for us.

The ball was much smaller than our rugby ball, and it was a game with a lot of noise and shouting under strange rules. They also sang a lot with small banjos, ukuleles and mouth organs. Songs from Brooklyn were heard mostly – songs which really were not suitable for children to take home. I remember one soldier telling off his mates for being indecent in front of us and bringing shame on their country. It was not easy to know who the officers were; a small badge on the shoulder showed the rank, and discipline was not that strict. Their clothes were of good material and their boots were of the best. When I spoke to one of the officers about our football and the trouble acquiring football boots, he gave me a special present: a new pair of their military boots. My father converted them for use in football, and I used them at school and college.

A frightening experience I had in their camp was when I made friends with Jessi, who was in charge of the bazooka which belonged to his group. He took me near some tents and strapped a rocket gun on me. It looked like a pipe on my back. He ordered me to aim at Tŷ'n Twll but not to pull the trigger. I had both a sense of power and fear in those few minutes.

These lads left Traws as quietly as they came, and by the morning of 6 June 1944 most of them had been killed on the beaches of Utah and Omaha in Normandy. Out of the 6,603 American soldiers that landed that morning, 2,499 were lost in the early hours. I hope that they carried a little of the peace of our hills with them on that fateful day. Their families probably never knew about the rest they had at Traws, and very few of us remember anything about them now, after all this time. We should remember the thousands who perished on 6 June and also remember their sacrifice.

Home Guard

In his concluding article, John Norman recounts his memories of the home services. Like all other places, Trawsfynydd had a local defence force made up of two platoons: Mr Hayes the bank manager (à la Mr Mainwaring in the TV series *Dad's Army*) was its commander, with his second in command being William David Evans, who had been awarded the Military Medal in WWI. He was a fine man, the silent type, tall with a strong character; at the time, he was working at Bronaber Camp. The Home Guard consisted of men over military age, farm labourers (a reserved occupation) who were exempt from military service, and men who were not fit for active service.

There were about twenty in each platoon; they trained twice a week in an outbuilding behind the Cross Foxes Hotel. In winter, they had lectures and drill practice etc., but in dry weather they trained outside with hand weapons. Once there was quite a consternation amongst them, when a mortar was accidently fired and the missile went through the roof; fortunately, nobody was hurt. Manoeuvres were carried out, and the Home Guard had to defend Traws in a mock battle with the officer cadets from Barmouth, who were trying to capture the village. These would start on Saturday evening and go on through Sunday to the consternation of the worried local residents.

Some local men joined the Fire Service, with its HQ at Llwyn Celyn; others joined the Special Constabulary to assist the police. During this period, there were two or three air raid wardens, who made sure that all blackout regulations were observed.

Near Cae Pandy, a building had been built for the use of the Royal Observer Corps, whose job it was to watch and record all aircraft movements and relay the information to their HQ at Capel Curig. Part of the building was made up of an underground office with a telephone, and there were also sleeping quarters and a strong periscope. Outside, there was a platform and a powerful telescope allowing the observers to plot aircraft courses, and displayed on a nearby wall were the silhouettes of all aircraft for instant recognition. Ten local men worked in pairs on day and night shifts at the post.[4]

***

Trawsfynydd Artillery Camp was dependant for most of its communications and supply needs on the Bala to Blaenau Ffestiniog branch line where it joined the main GWR line at Bala Junction. The military had its own station and sidings at Trawsfynydd, with a private road to skirt the village, and it is a miracle that these facilities were not targeted by enemy aircraft. Opinion today suggests that the bombs which were dropped were not simply jettisoned by the German bombers as initially thought, but were in fact dropped to a pattern and in line, just as one would expect on a bombing run on a railway line. Fortunately, they missed their target.

The twenty-five mile branch line climbed steadily from Bala to Cwm Prysor Station at a height of 1,278 feet, then crossed the nine-arched Cwm Prysor Viaduct and skirted along a ledge cut into the mountainside towards Trawsfynydd. The line boasted the most spectacular breathtaking views and ran through wild and desolate country. In winter, ferocious weather, high winds, hail, and heavy snow were always a possibility.

Special trains arrived at Trawsfynydd from all parts of the country, full of troops, tanks, ammunition, and all sorts of equipment as was required. These loads could not be hauled by the normal Pannier engines, and were quite often double-headed with engines such as 'Moguls' or 'Manor', and even then needed banking assistance to reach Arenig or Cwm Prysor.

---

[4]   The author gratefully acknowledges the assistance and valuable insight provided by the late John Norman Davies in relation to his childhood days in Trawsfynydd and his recollection of wartime events.

In a local newspaper, driver Gwilym Aled Jones, a native of Trawsfynydd, recounts his own experience of bringing a special train to Trawsfynydd during the war. He had a twelve-coach troop train with 400 soldiers on board, destined for the camp and gun ranges of Trawsfynydd. The weather on this particular day was ferocious, with high winds and freezing conditions. Climbing a steep gradient through the small hamlet of Capel Celyn, his train came to a halt, the wheels spinning even though he was driving a GWR 2251 class 0-6-0 engine. It was a day to remember. His sand had run out, but he was able to inch his way to Arenig Station. There he uncoupled the engine from the coaches and proceeded 'light-engine' to Trawsfynydd, where he was able to replenish his sand. He returned to Arenig to rescue the stranded troops, who were by now nearly frozen in the unheated coaches. Eventually, three hours late, the troop train with its shivering passengers reached their destination.

After the war, several trainloads of unused ammunition were taken to Trawsfynydd and disposed of on the ranges. The noise, echoes and vibrations of the explosions could be clearly heard as far away as Blaenau Ffestiniog. It was the end of a chapter.

Barmouth – the Home Front

THE TOWNS, VILLAGES and hamlets did not take long to acclimatise to the new conditions which would show them the grim reality of war. Young people had had to leave their homes either to go and work in industry or to join the armed forces; older people and those who had retired had to come back and fill the various posts which still had to be maintained. Civilians had to cope with identity cards and ration books – virtually every type of food, clothing and fuel was rationed.

Statistics from the *Barmouth Advertiser* show that within the first six months, ninety-seven locals had joined the various services: Royal Navy (13), Royal Marines (1), Merchant Navy (7), Royal Air Force (16), and 60 to the army. These included all the reservists, militia men and the territorials, but, worst of all, the statistics showed that one had died whilst on home defence service while another had been killed in action. The reality of war had come home.

The local authorities had various problems, which included the upheaval caused by evacuees coming to their area, with all the troubles that that entailed. Another interesting piece in the *Advertiser* dates from August 1940 – a Councillor enquired if everything had been settled with regards to a Cleaning Station to temporarily treat evacuees not in a fit condition to enter private billets. The Evacuation Officer replied that a property had been taken over for the purpose and that this had been agreed by the Ministry of Health. The Council resolved to communicate with the W.V.S. to obtain a Caretaker for the Cleaning Station.The problems of the evacuees also affected the Barmouth County School. Their minutes for the period show that in late 1939 they had 266 pupils, including fifty new pupils and eleven refugees (fee paying). Parents had been critical of the school's decision to admit the eleven refugees, although no local children had been denied a place as a result. In late 1940, the school's minutes show that there were now 273 pupils, including thirty evacuated children, and that there were a further forty to fifty evacuated scholars who had taken up residence in the school district but who were unable to gain admission to the school.

In July 1943, it was resolved that fifty-five special places be offered, subject to the existing rules, to scholars who were not evacuees, in order of merit. It was also resolved that ten special places be offered to evacuees in order of merit subject to the home authority accepting financial responsibility. A motion that no evacuees be admitted was defeated.

Another interesting item, which does seem consistent with the time, appears in the school minutes of September 1942. It records a decision by the governors to ask the clerk to make the following appeal, namely that: 'Mr M. G. Evans, a member of the teaching staff [later to become the headmaster], be not directed to join the local Home Guard and that the headmaster and clerk do attend to the matter if necessity arise.'

All the local papers had articles instructing the public on how to deal with various air raid precaution (ARP) matters, especially in relation to incendiary bombs. Whether the instructions were of any use is debateable, but it kept up public vigilance with regard to the threat of bombing and its effects. Gas masks had become part of everyday life – even children going to school had to carry them – and instructions were given on their use.

Another problem which the ARP wardens had to contend with was the enforcing of the blackout regulations. All windows and doors had to be lightproof and breaking the regulations meant a court fine. Numerous cases came before the magistrates and about ten people appeared at Barmouth Court on blackout-related charges. Various excuses were given for violating the regulations – one being that the window had been covered with blackout material but that, because it was partially open, the wind had blown the material inwards, showing the light. However, in all cases, the defendants were found guilty and fines of two pounds were imposed.

During this period, the *Barmouth Advertiser* had a column under the heading 'Barmouthians in the Colours', in which they reported who was home on leave, who had been injured, and who had been unfortunately killed in action. It gave the locals news about their friends and relatives, especially when fellow Barmouthians met in foreign lands as often happened. In the 19 July 1945 edition, it was reported that Leading Seaman Glyn Jones was on leave in Barmouth and staying with Mr & Mrs David Griffith, Tŷ Clyd. His father, Captain John Jones, was serving with the United States Merchant Navy, and the 1 July 1943 edition reported that he had been promoted to the rank of lieutenant commander in the United States Naval Reserves. Sometime before, Captain Jones had had grim experience serving with convoys in some of the North Atlantic's most dangerous waters. Another titbit reported that R. J. Thomas of the RAF had been featured in a broadcast on Indian wavelengths with his noted RAF Welsh voice choir. He had been presented with a watch by the members in appreciation of his service as a conductor.

However, the pattern of life still clung to its old traditions. The Barmouth Mixed Choir managed to survive, and the various local societies also kept their heads above water, albeit with a diminished membership. As expected, the goodwill of their members prevailed throughout the period and was of great assistance to the general wellbeing of the town.

As in all wars, casualties were incurred, and the locality suffered like so many other places. Barmouth lost ten men, Dyffryn lost four men, Dolgellau lost twenty-six men and one woman, Harlech lost eleven men, Tywyn lost fifteen men and one woman, Aberdyfi lost thirteen men, and Trawsfynydd four men. These were all young people who had no choice but to join up, and in certain cases one might ask was it necessary for them to die.

Some of the incidents in which these men died have been recorded. Rowland Rowlands's ship, HMS *Rawlpindi*, went down after a battle with the battleship *Tirpitz*, an encounter in which there was no hope of victory. Rowland had served in WWI and had taken part in the Zebrugge raid. Another interesting case is the death of Hywel Jones Griffith, a Royal Navy reservist, who was recalled at the beginning of the war and served on the armed merchant cruiser *Patroclus*, which was sunk by a German U-boat on 3 November 1940 off the coast of Northern Ireland. *Patroclus* had been shadowing SS *Casanare*, acting as an escort to protect the vessel from German surface raiders, when the *Casanare* was torpedoed. *Patroclus*'s captain decided to speed towards her to pick up survivors; his staff disagreed with this decision, as the U-boat was still in the area, and advised the captain that, if they stopped to pick up survivors, they would be sunk within half an hour. The captain refused to listen to their arguments and is reputed to have said, 'If I don't stop, I will never be able to show my face in Liverpool again.' He was again reminded of Admiralty orders forbidding the exposure of ships to U-boat attacks and is again reputed to have said, 'The Admiralty is not in command of the ship.' *Patroclus* dropped depth charges near the scene with the intention of scaring off the U-boat, but *U-99* fired two torpedoes, one of which struck the ship near its stern. The ship's crew, plus survivors from the *Casanare*, had to abandon their respective vessels and take to their boats.

The 365 survivors from the *Patroclus* were picked up by HMS *Beagle* and landed in Greenock; *Patroclus* broke in two, the stern capsized, and the bow sank slowly. HMS *Hesparus* commanded by Captain MacIntyre attacked *U-99* but had to pick up survivors from HMS *Laurentic*.

U-99 was commanded by one of Germany's most famous U-boat commanders, Kapitanleutnant Otto Kretschmer, who gained notoriety by sinking more Allied tonnage than any other U-boat commander. Just four months later, in March 1941, Captain MacIntyre, in command of the destroyer HMS *Walker*, finally cornered and damaged *U-99* south-east of Iceland. Otto Kretschmer had to scuttle his U-boat but made sure his crew were saved and taken on board the destroyer. Of the forty-three members of crew, only three lost their lives.

Another interesting event was the return of a prisoner of war, Flight Officer Jackie Ellis, who had been a prisoner in Germany for about four months. He had been part of a bombing mission to Berlin and had been attacked by enemy aircraft close to the German capital. After his plane was hit and they had to bale out, Jackie descended in his parachute but hit a tree on landing which knocked him unconscious. When he came to, it was dawn and the Germans arrested him. He was taken to Gestapo headquarters and later removed to a basement which was pitch-black. He was moved along the basement, and suddenly the Gestapo switched on a flash lamp. On the floor, he saw the bodies of three British airmen whom the Germans wanted to identify. They adopted such tactics to see how Jackie would react and to ascertain whether he was a member of an air crew or not. He was taken to the centre of Berlin, which was still burning after the raid, and later removed to a prison camp in Poland. As the Russians advanced, they were forced to move, and for twenty-five days they marched aimlessly across country before being liberated by British forces.

Two other prisoners, Leading Seaman Evan David Jones of HMS *Repulse* and David Elio Roberts, a supply assistant on HMS *Mata Hari*, came home after enduring captivity under the Japanese. Another Barmouth man, Chief Wireless Officer Robert Hughes, served on the Arctic convoys. He was taken captive and spent considerable time in a prison camp in Germany. Their stories have been published in *Barmouth Sea Heroes*.

Many Barmouth lads received military honours in various theatres of war; the names of some have already been mentioned. There are others, but it is also possible that some recipients of honours will never have their names recorded as their deeds have been lost over time. The *Advertiser* again has some names:

> Bombadier J. Shone of Royal Regiment of Artillery of 4, Goronwy Terrace, Barmouth was awarded the Military Medal for outstanding bravery in the fighting in Malaya.
>
> Ellis Mawddach Evans also awarded the MM.
>
> Sergeant Neville G. Jessop of West End, Marine Parade also awarded the MM for great courage and devotion to duty at Anzio, Italy.

In the end came peace, and what a joyous relief: normality returned, the lads coming home, and parties everywhere. The editorial in the *Advertiser* summed up feelings at the time:

> There will be no fruits of our labour in the material sense. Our rewards will lie in the satisfaction of knowing that we have helped to save civilisation and of seeing the free and happy faces of nations that, through our efforts, have been born again.
>
> In difficulty and disaster we acquitted ourselves well. Let us show that in victory, we can act with the same steadfastness, the same restraint and the same dignity we displayed to the world in the hard days that are past.
>
> First, therefore, let us give thanks that we can dedicate ourselves, in all humility to the task which we took up in 1939, the task of ensuring that the Rule of Law shall prevail in every corner of the globe. The last five years have changed our lives, our thinking, our values. We have been awakened from dreams of easy living; we have learned to put the country before our private interests, we have fought alongside men of many nationalities and learned to respect them.
>
> This is Britain's great hour, we meet it with courage and hope. With deep-felt thankfulness we say 'This Time We Won't Let Them Down'.

Captain John Parry and the Barmouth Home Guard.

Captain John Parry's Military ID Card as a serving Home Guard Officer.

Captain John Parry's Certificate of Transfer to the Reserve on Demobilisation on 2 July 1914.

Mr Joe Finnegan

'Old soldiers never die, they simply fade away'[5]

I HAVE TO admit, I suppose, that 'Finnegan the Fruiterer' seemed a bit of a mouthful to say, but there was little doubt that to a small boy such as I was at the time, the man himself appeared like a character straight from a storybook – almost larger than life, in fact! (That was saying something when you consider that the town in which we lived was about as chock-full of 'characters' as a melon is of pips.)

In Barmouth, Mr Finnegan hawked around a selection of fruit and vegetables on his coaster barrow. The bodywork of this vehicle was painted a glistening green, except for the end of the handles, where the wood had been left bare and become polished to a shine by the constant grip of the owner's sinewed hands. The wooden-spoked wheels of this glorious contraption were attired in a coat of bright pillar-box red paint that caused them to tinkle as they spun around when the equipage was under way.

The wares, whose merits were shouted abroad by Mr Finnegan, were set out in a colourful display that struck the eye with the reds and light greens of glossy apples, the yellow of bananas and lemons, the soft bloom of green and purple grapes,

---

[5] This article was written some time ago by Roy Speight, who gave Peter Crabtree permission to put it forward for publication. Something not mentioned in Roy's article is that, during the summer months, Mr Finnegan wore his white tropical uniform, medals and hat.

the red of tomatoes, the frothy whiteness of cauliflowers, and all the multiple hues imparted by a mixture of the bounties of the earth. If you did actually buy a couple of pounds of new potatoes or four oranges or a punnet of mustard and cress, Mr Finnegan would moisten a convenient thumb across his tongue and, with a flourish, tear off a brown paper bag that bore the device 'Fyffe's Bananas' in blue capital letters on its side from a bunch pierced through one corner and tied to a strut on the barrow.

This man may have been a humble purveyor of fruit and veg, as I knew his everyday self, but when I pictured him as a young man, my mind's eye transformed him into some kind of legendary folk hero, for Joe Finnegan had been a soldier in South Africa about thirty years before. Ordinarily, I suppose, this fact might have escaped my notice, but Mr Finnegan was not only proud of his past exploits, but was a patriot into the bargain, and, as a result, continued to sport a replica of the uniform he had worn in South Africa about thirty years before.

His thinning grey hair was cut short in military style and was topped by a genuine bush hat. The brim turned up at one side bore a meticulously clean and shining regimental badge that reflected the sun's rays with dazzling brilliance.

The dark brown jacket was neat and carefully brushed to remove every stray hair and every speck of dust. The buttonhole sported the most perfect red or yellow rosebud, depending on what was best from Joe's garden plot at the time. Set in a colourful row at the level of his top pocket were the brave ribbons that he had won at Ladysmith and Mafeking, whose attached medals tinkled musically as he walked along.

The well-cut cavalry breeches curved gracefully about the thighs, whilst below his knees a pair of khaki puttees was wound with mathematical precision from his ankles up round the calves of his leg. Then there came a further shining delight: the prospect of Mr Finnegan's boots. These were of black leather, to which a vigorous application of spit and polish had imparted a surface rarely seen outside the confines of a mirror frame, and their sparkling allure vied with the glowing badge on his hat above.

All this glory was enough to turn the head of a small boy in admiration, but the effect so far almost paled into insignificance when one took into account Joe Finnegan's expressive face. It still seemed to retain the deep tan acquired in South Africa all those years ago and was sufficiently unusual to draw attention to itself, its weathered lines and crevices creating an effect like that of crinkled leather.

Then there were the eyes: dark and direct and piercing, so that if one happened to be caught in a glance, it was as if the man saw right into you and laid your soul bare. With eagle eyes like that, how could you possibly hope to hide anything from this man of steel and whipcord?

That left just one more item to complete the ensemble: the crowning glory, the wonder of wonders that almost bordered on the realm of the supernatural. The old warrior carried the most wonderful moustache! It wasn't one of those full and bushy ones; it wasn't one of those thin and droopy ones; and it wasn't one of those clipped toothbrush styles. But, from one end to the other, it must have measured at least three inches in length. This was a monument set in wax, as if arrested in time. It seemed as if it might bid fair to claim the title of the eighth wonder of the world – immutable, unchangeable. The fibres of hair were twisted like finely drawn strands of silky cotton and tapered to a point at both ends. It was impossible not to be full of admiration for the architecture of that wonderful moustache. Surely, a man who looked as glorious as this must have won medals for heroic deeds and the utmost bravery? Perhaps even been decorated by Queen Victoria herself. Who could tell?

But then, suddenly somehow, Joe Finnegan's age began to show and he began to look like an old man. The autumn winds caused him to change from the dandy's white silk scarf that he had earlier worn, to the comfort of a woollen one that now crossed the front of his meagre chest. His voice, always a bit raucous and grating, was muted to a rather ineffectual scratchy whisper. He developed a bronchitic cough, and those same winds brought tears to his old eyes – eyes that all those years before must have gazed like those of a hawk across veldt and kopje; across grassland and river and beyond scrubland and rocky slope.

That moustache lasted for as long as I can remember the old man, but one day his mortality was proved when he caught a cold standing by his barrow with its multi-hued cargo of edibles and calling his wares in a bitter wind. The glory that had been Joe Finnegan began to diminish and fade. My memories of him prove that old soldiers never die, but the truth of the matter was found in the second half of that adage when the old fellow quietly faded away.

***

Joe Finnegan, one of Barmouth's characters, lived during the 1930s in Llyn Du at a house called Ladysmith, just opposite the Royal Antediluvian Order of Buffaloes (RAOB) HQ – the old New White Cinema.

Joe Finnegan volunteered for duties in the Home Guard at the age of 68, three years above the age limit. His duties were confined to the armoury, and he was excused drill duties according to Robert Ifor Roberts, who served alongside Joe for a period. Joe Finnegan served in three wars, the Boer War, WWI and WWII, and served as a regular soldier for over twenty-three years, a record he could be proud of.

GVI   RI

This scroll commemorates

W. Jones, O.B.E. Master
Merchant Navy

held in honour as one who
served King and Country in
the world war of 1939-1945
and gave his life to save
mankind from tyranny. May
his sacrifice help to bring
the peace and freedom for
which he died.

Scroll to commemorate Captain William Jones (affectionately known as 'Captain 'Wil Bermo') and Master of the *SS Logician*, who was in Convoy OB218 (20 ships) bound for Montreal, leaving Liverpool on 24 September 1940. Three days out of Liverpool the convoy was attacked by U-boats; the *Manchester Brigade* was torpedoed by *U137* and all crew including the convoy Commodore and his staff were killed. Captain William Jones took over the duties of the convoy Commodore. Under his command the convoy arrived at its destination with only the loss of five merchant ships.

Recollections of Barmouth 1939–40

by the late Nia Cooke (née Williams), Cardiff

DURING THE WAR years, I lived with my parents and two brothers Iolo and Iwan at Twyni, North Avenue, a street about three hundred yards from Marine Road and the promenade, beach and sea. [Nia's father was the late W. D. Williams, the local schoolmaster and a native of the Corwen area.] At the end of the street stood Marine Mansions, a very tall building where the officer cadets from the training unit were staying. Twyni ('sand dunes') was a good name for the house, as the terrace had been built on sand, and behind the houses there were still plenty of sand dunes stretching as far as the Min-y-Môr Hotel (this was before the council houses were built in Princess Avenue).

The soldiers carried out their manoeuvres and training on the flat area of ground behind our house. They erected a row of wooden frames with sandbags hanging on them and these were used for bayonet practice. Sometimes my brothers and I would watch the men practising their skill on the dummies whilst we were safe in our own backyard. The soldiers, in batches of four or five with their fixed bayonets, would run towards their targets shouting and making an unearthly noise to the command of their officers. Such fun for us! I was only about five at the time, and little did I know what was happening, only that the war was behind our house.

One day, my mother was hanging out the washing on the line in the back garden when an officer came past very fast in a jeep or truck, which threw sand all over the clothes. My mother gave him a piece of her tongue and inferred that he had no idea how to drive a vehicle around sand dunes without creating a mess. In his best military tone, the officer retaliated by saying, 'Madam, I've just come back from the war in the desert in North Africa; I think I know what I'm jolly well doing!'

Some of the officers came to our house for a cup of tea or a snack supper, generally on a Sunday evening. They were glad to have the welcome of local Barmouth residents. It was nice to have a conversation and hear about their families and the places they came from. I don't remember their names, but I do remember two of them in particular, one from Glasgow and the other from Yorkshire. The English lad was very nice and quiet, whilst the Scotsman was exceptionally jovial. He also had a moustache, and he would insist on kissing me as he was leaving after his visit. *Ych a fi!* ('yuck!').

Occasionally, I would see the ceremony of the passing-out parade, which would be held on the Black Patch, the tarred area in front of the Marine Hotel. To the beat of drums and band, the soldiers marched in their best uniforms, displaying all the glamour of their medals and colours. As children, we enjoyed the occasion; we could march behind them whilst trying to copy them with our arms and feet. However, we couldn't match their timing, even as we shouted 'left, left, left, right, right'. The sergeant major used to go mad and threaten us, while we fled from there in case he caught us – such fun!

The Barmouth Primary School at that time was in the middle of the town and with the main street adjoining it. During our playtime or dinner break, we could look at the world passing by from the yard: people shopping in the lovely shops in the Arches, all the transportation of the town passing by, lorries carrying soldiers from places higher up the coast. As children, we used to gather by the school boundary wall and shout at the Americans, who were camped at Llanbedr: 'Any gum chums?'

Usually they would throw small packets of gum across to us, and we all scattered and fought to try and recover them.

One night, coming home on the bus from Harlech with my mother, where we had been to see Nain (grandmother), I was taken ill. The bus was full of Americans going for their 'night out' in Barmouth. I distinctively remember some of them giving me packets of gum to try and comfort me, a five-year-old child. I kept the precious gum for the following day! I still remember those few precious memories of Barmouth when I was a very young girl during WWII.

Cartoon: Don James

The author is grateful to Nia for her recollections of the period. Although these were originally written in Welsh, it is hoped that the translation has not lost the feeling, tone and quality of her letter. Sadly, Nia passed away in early August 2014.

Barmouth
Home Guard

By Robert Ifor Roberts, Singen, Germany
June 2009

BRITAIN WAS IN turmoil in June, 1940 with our land forces having been over-run by the German army on the Continent, and the consequent evacuation of our decimated troops at Dunkirk and the French channel ports.

Churchill's call for the formation of a volunteer citizens' army was met in Barmouth, as indeed in every town and village in Britain, with an enthusiastic response. It was feared that an invasion of mainland Britain was imminent, the Channel Islands having been already occupied, and an invasion via Southern Ireland being a distinct possibility.

These events have, of course, been adequately documented in official records of the times together with the accepted view that the timely formation of a widespread volunteer army, and Churchill's stirring rally-call to 'fight in the fields and on the beaches', together with other factors such as the supremacy of the Royal Navy and the determined resistance of our RAF Fighter Command, did indeed make the German High Command think again and fail to press home their undoubted advantage.

The reality was very different. Our gallant forces were severely overstretched and under-equipped and a determined attack upon our shores would surely have been successful.

No such defeatist thoughts entered our minds as we rushed to enrol with the Local Defence Force (LDV) to be known later as the Home Guard, in response to Churchill's call to arms.

I was sixteen at the time and sitting my matriculation exams at school but I had already volunteered for the Navy and been told to wait. Among my contemporaries joining the LDV were my two best friends, Albert Milliner and Trevor Griffith Davies, also other friends such as Albert Whitehouse, Robert Crabbe and Evan John. Like myself these lads would soon be serving in the regular armed forces.

Among the older members there were several veterans of the First World War, and indeed one, namely Finnegan the Greengrocer, who had seen service in the Boer War. He was to become our armourer and was excused patrols and drill. Other names that come to mind are Gwylfa Wynne (Butcher) with the rank of Sergeant, Bob Crabbe, Iorweth Richards (Crosville, Bus Driver), and John Evans. There were also several others whose call-up had been deferred but who would eventually be conscripted into the various armed services. Among these were Robin Pugh (Joiner), and Glyn Roberts (otherwise known as Kelly) and Meirion Rowlands.

Our Commanding Officer was the much respected Mr. Parry (Gardener) of Bryn Mynach who carried the rank of Captain.

Our HQ was at premises in Jubilee Rd., part of the Lion Garage where our armoury was located. Drill and basic training in unarmed combat, bayonet drill and the likes took place in the Arrowe Hall across the road. We had no weapons at first, and drilled with dummy wooden rifles. We were however soon to be given some vintage Canadian Ross rifles. Later we would be issued with proper Army battledress, and the Armoury provided with standard Lee Enfield rifles, plus a few hand grenades. Up to then our weapons against tanks would have been home-made petrol bombs known as Molotov cocktails.

From this it might well be gleaned that we were, at first, more of a danger to ourselves than to any potential enemy, which can be illustrated by a couple of incidents which could well have been taken out of the *Dad's Army* script. Our main duty in the early days was standing night guard on Barmouth Bridge. We were to challenge anyone approaching with the customary commands.

Among our ranks we had an older comrade who had an unfortunate stammer. A pedestrian crossing the viaduct late at night in the blackout was a rare event so that the opportunity to utter the challenge was welcomed as a relief from the boredom. We usually took it in turns, but not when we had (let's call him G!) with us. We always let him make the challenge arguing that it was his right as the senior member. Yes, it was not very praiseworthy, but quite funny when the words came out (partially at least) *'Halt who gggggggggggg-goes there?'* The approaching individual was often too confused to reply, especially if it was some local walking home after a night in the pub. Not conduct conducive to good order.

On another occasion, after our Company had been issued with (joy oh joy) a coveted Lewis machine gun, we were on the beach at Dyffryn engaged in target practice, it came to our friend's turn (G with the stutter!). As he was lying prone firing away the CO approached and stood over him issuing an order. With due respect and military discipline our friend sprang to his feet with both he and the Lewis gun stuttering away and spraying bullets all around and everyone diving for cover in the sand dunes. You would be surprised to hear that G was in the course of time called up into the regular Army, underlining just how short of manpower Britain was.

Another incident which could well have resulted in a fatality, but has also a funny side to it, occurred when four of us were preparing to stand down at first light after a night on guard duty on Barmouth Bridge. We were in a little shack which had been allocated to us for shelter when off watch on stand-by, it had a tin roof, with an oil lamp suspended from it inside, and two bunks for the two off watch. The four of us, Trevor Davies, Jack Parry, myself and an older comrade, whom I shall refer to as 'M', were unloading our rifles as was customary in going off duty. As it was not yet daylight we needed the light of the lamp. We were all half asleep as I watched 'M' go through the routine of unloading. I was dimly aware that he had miscounted the rounds that he had removed from his gun, but did not react fast enough when he raised his rifle in the approved manner to squint up the 'spout'. There was an almighty bang as his gun went off in the confined space and the light went out. When we had recovered to some extent from the shock, one of us lit a match. The shot had blown a huge hole in the tin roof. But not only that, Jack who had been standing in front of 'M' was in a right state. Fortunately the bullet had missed his head, but his hair was standing straight up from the blast and his face was all black with the soot from the lamp. He looked for all the world like the stereotype golliwog of comic movies. It was perhaps this subliminal association of ideas, together with a certain reaction to shock, coupled with huge relief that our friend Jack was still in one piece, that caused Trevor and me to burst out in a spontaneous bout of uncontrollable laughter. So infectious was this that the others soon joined in, eventually to subside with the realisation of what might have been. Not only that, but Jack was the son of our Commanding Officer. Naturally we all had to answer questions why the rifle had been discharged, but we quite truthfully said that the proper drill had been carried out, omitting to state, of course, that no one should point a gun to any person's direction. No action was taken, and if anyone should think that this sort of incident happened only in the Home Guard then they have not had much experience of the armed services. Friendly Fire? It's still happening!

I must relate a really comical situation that I witnessed on one of our many exercises. These war games were often held in conjunction with other military units in training in our area, which our local HG company would often outwit through our better knowledge of the local terrain. On this particular occasion our unit was defending the hills above Panorama and I was stationed as a lookout above the old road to Bontddu, to report likely advancing 'enemy' movements. I had a clear view from my position at the head of a small valley which had a dry-stone wall extending up the middle. I soon became aware of two opposing patrols advancing simultaneously, one each side of the wall which both were using as cover. Being close to the wall they were concealed from each other but not from me. It was with great amusement that I observed the leader of each small group periodically raise his head to observe the land on the other side, but as it happened, never at the same moment. I waited gleefully for this as it was like an episode from a Laurel and Hardy film I had seen. In such manner they progressed along the wall each unaware of the other's presence, until eventually they arrived at a large gap in the wall. Then of course there was utter confusion. No one could say who had captured whom!

Of such stuff, of course, was *Dad's Army* made; but the real Home Guard that I saw was very different from the fictitious Captain Mainwaring's delightful bungling company. During my two years with them, until I was old enough to be called up into the Royal Navy in early June 1942, I saw our unit develop into a disciplined, well trained and well equipped body.

With the ever diminishing threat of invasion the HG was able to take over from the army, many of its more mundane duties, such as guarding bridges and railways and vital installations, thus releasing its troops for front line service overseas, e.g. North Africa, or preparing alongside our American allies, for the Second Front on the mainland continent. Was the formation of the HG the beginning of 'the long fight back?'

There is no doubt that the Home Guard gave us youngsters a good grounding in basic military discipline and skills, thus easing considerably our subsequent entry into the Armed Forces proper, and greatly facilitating the otherwise arduous basic training.

I look back with no little pride on my days with the LDV and the Home Guard nevertheless, sixty-nine years on; I still enjoy watching *Dad's Army*.

Footnote

Robert Ifor the son of the late blind harpist of Barmouth 'Telynor Mawddwy', volunteered for duties in the Royal Navy as a youngster, and had been accepted by the selection board for training as an observer (navigator), but was turned down after failing a rigorous eyesight test. He later joined the Navy and was trained as an Asdic operator and in 1943 with a group of naval personnel went to America to advice the Americans of the potential of Asdic Operations and to show how sonar beams could plumb the depths of the ocean searching for submarines. He later served on frigates and minesweepers. His brother also served in the Royal Navy and was taken prisoner by the Japanese. (See 'Barmouth Sea Heroes')

The Battle of
Barmouth

AN INCIDENT HAPPENED in February 1944 which has been dubbed 'The Battle of Barmouth'. In that period, the risk of a German invasion was still a possibility. The thinking was that the Germans would make a quick assault on southern Ireland and then use it as a springboard to invade the UK. North Wales was considered particularly vulnerable as the coast here would be suitable for the landing of assault craft. Security was still very much to the fore in the area, although, for now, all remained peaceful.

However, Barmouth's peace was rudely shattered on 18 February 1944 by the sound of rifle fire from the vicinity of Dinas Oleu, a hill overlooking the town. This created a bit of a panic as the military knew no exercises were taking place in that area, and there was always the possibility that the gunfire was a diversion created by enemy agents. Troops were sent up to investigate but could not find anything.

Sitting on a bench on the promenade were three young boys thoroughly enjoying the sight of troops combing the land around Dinas Oleu. The boys also knew full well that the unseen enemy the troops were looking for was in fact them. They were the ones who had been firing the rifles earlier that day. Great fun! They had managed to steal rifles and ammunition from the Royal Marines armoury by watching the guards and entering the armoury through a window. They stole three rifles and 400 rounds of ammunition, and then went up the hill to shoot rabbits and tin cans. It was the noise they made which had attracted attention and caused consternation and panic.

Much has been written about the incident, and fact and fiction have become mingled so much that it is impossible to have a clear picture of what really did happen. The three lads have always stayed silent about the events, and sadly today only one survives and his recollection is poor owing to advanced years. At one time, rumour had it that the lads had taken 5,000 rounds of ammunition, but, according to old sweats, the weight would have been too much for them to handle and the figure given above is more realistic.

Eventually, the lads decided to go back to the hill, probably to retrieve the guns and ammunition. It was then that the marines found them and they admitted what they had done. The marines took them through the streets and up to Porkington Terrace, where they were treated to a meal of meat pies and rolls. Having played truant from school that day, they were by then extremely hungry.

Obviously, there was consternation within the Royal Marines; security was of prime importance, and the fact that their armoury had been broken into by young children did not bode well – what would have happened if it had been the enemy? It is not known what repercussions there were in the unit, but their slackness damaged the reputation of the marines badly in the area. Naturally, other units took advantage and made rude and derogatory remarks about them, which added insult to injury.

The three lads were arrested by the police and charged, and on 28 February 1944 they duly appeared in Barmouth Juvenile Court. The register of the court of summary jurisdiction sitting at Barmouth states:

Juvenile Court 28th February 1944.
Name of Informant or Complainant: Inspector D. Lewis Davies, Barmouth
Names of Defendant:
> Glyn Jones, 13 yrs 11 months, Victoria Buildings, Barmouth, *Mrs Elizabeth Jones, Parent.*

John David Lloyd, 11 yrs 7 months, Sunny Side, Barmouth,
Mr William Lloyd, Parent.
Robert Glyn Evans, 13 yrs 9 months, Doctor's Building,
Barmouth,
Mr Ernest Evans, Parent.

Nature of Offence:
Stealing 3 Service rifles, value of £6 each & 400 rounds of 22
ammunition value 12/- on Friday 18th February 1944 from a
Miniature Range, the property of the Admiralty.
   A plea of Guilty was recorded.

Minutes of Adjudication:
   Glyn Jones: Ordered that he be sent to an approved school on
1st March 1944 viz – Stockport, Cheshire. Court fee waived in this
case.
   John David Lloyd: Ordered that he be sent to an approved
school on 1st March 1944 viz – Crewe, Cheshire. Court fee payable.
   Robert Glyn Evans: Fined £1, his father bound over in the sum
of £5 that the boy would be of good behaviour for twelve months,
boy to be indoors no earlier [*sic*] than 8 p.m. each day and to
report once weekly to Probation Officer.

Magistrates:
   Miss C. Somers OBE, DL, JP; J. Llew Davies JP;
   Dr J Pugh Jones JP.

The sentences seem harsh. It is not known whether the boys
had legal representation, nor whether anyone had provided
them with a character reference. Why should the youngest
of the group be penalised more than the others? One would
assume that the youngest would have been a follower rather
than a leader and, as such, should have had a more lenient
sentence or even just a court warning. Also, why was he the
only one who had to pay court fees?

It could perhaps be argued that events outside of Barmouth
influenced the sentencing. The *News Chronicle*, one of the
national daily papers, had published a report about the
incident and brought the question of security to light. How did
the paper get hold of the story? Was there a breach of security?

A prominent journalist and editor at the *Barmouth Advertiser* was taken to Dolgellau Police Station for questioning, as it was believed that he was the one who had breached the security code. It later emerged that an OCTU cadet, who had worked for the *News Chronicle* prior to joining the army, had been the one to inform the paper.

Owing to the publicity, it was said that Winston Churchill became aware of the incident and demanded action from his Home Secretary, Herbert Morrison. He is reported to have said that if the boys had been shooting at the marines, they should be charged accordingly. At the end of the day, the truth was that the Royal Marines had lost face and somebody had to pay. As far as we know, only the lads paid the price for what was at the most a boyish prank, but it did show a severe lack of security on the part of the marines, and the question does arise, had there been a genuine enemy infiltration, what would have been the outcome? In a way, the boys did the marines a great favour.

Anthony J. Perrett's book *The Royal Marines in Wales* (1992), published by the Royal Marines Historical Society, provides the following account of the incident:

It is not so much the men of Crete Camp[6] who made a name for themselves so much as three local boys Glyn Evans, Glyn Jones and Dai Lloyd who caused a stir that was reported in the Sunday Express of February 1944:

'With three rifles and 400 rounds of 0.22 ammunition, three boys aged 12 to 14 defied a platoon of marines 36 strong, led by two subalterns, in the Welsh mountains around Cader Idris. For two days and nights they carried out their own guerrilla warfare, only surrendering under the protection of a white flag and reduced to two rounds of ammunition.

On Thursday the boys broke into the armoury of a camp at Barmouth. Three rifles and all the ammunition were taken.

---

[6]   Crete Camp, Barmouth.

Soon [after] the theft was discovered a hue and cry started.
The Lieutenant Quartermaster was recalled from leave and the
Brigadier's batman sent after the young desperadoes.'

When bullets started whizzing round his head, he decided
that reinforcements were needed and went back for the
Regimental Police. They in turn retired in the face of superior
enemy fire and the National Fire Service were called out. They
also gave up. The boys were out all night on the mountain and
shot two fowls belonging to a local poultry keeper. They then
went to a disused mine in the mountains and dug themselves
in.

'On Friday a platoon of marines, 36 strong with two subalterns
set out on the chase. They tracked the boys down and the bullets
began flying again. The platoon got under cover and prepared to
attack. Firing blank cartridges they made a frontal assault on the
boys' position, but had to retreat. Reinforcements were sent for
and a Captain came to supervise.

Ammunition was running low and the boys flew a white flag.
Out they came with just two rounds, but without the rifles which
have not been found yet. The three boys were marched back to
their home town under an escort of eight marines. The boys were
placed 'under restriction' at their homes but last night went to the
local cinema, fêted by all the boys in the neighbourhood.'

Prime Minister Winston Churchill was furious and
demanded to know if the boys had fired on the Marines, and
if they had, should be charged with attempted murder, but
Herbert Morrison, the Home Secretary placated him and the
matter was hushed up. That was until reporter David Jack got
wind of it and produced a lengthy article in the Sunday People
of 27 April 1975 when the War Cabinet papers of the period
were released and the correspondence between the Prime
Minister and the Home Secretary appeared.

He contacted the Corps but was told all the records of this
incident had been destroyed, so he pieced his evidence together

from the reports of the court case and local men of the town who were then boys.

What came out of the enquiry was interesting from the point of view of the resentment of the local populace to their 'invasion', compared to all the friendly reports in coverage of South Wales. One wonders whether this had anything to do with the high concentration of Welsh language speakers in the area, a different breed of Royal Marines or locals, or perhaps a higher concentration of troops. This is pure speculation because it is clear that not all the civilians in the north were anti-troops, no more than everyone in the south welcomed them with open arms. Certainly a Nationalistic mood prevailed in the north.

However the report did uncover this resentment as one person explained:

> 'Barmouth had been a peaceful little town before the war, then we had two 'invasions'; firstly the evacuees from Liverpool, then an invasion of English soldiers, making us talk English instead of our own language.'

There was even a case of a 'rotten tomato throwing' shopkeeper, as the Marines marched the boys through the town! I would hasten to add that these three lads have since led law-abiding lives and are respected members of the community; they were, at the time of my research, all still alive, and incidentally are friends of Jock Steele, our former MT Sergeant.

I have heard Barmouth referred to as 'The Gibraltar of Wales', and it certainly bears a resemblance, being virtually a one-street town at the base of a massive rocky mountain side, and during the war was heavily garrisoned, with Navy, Army and RAF as well as the Corps.

From the very lengthy report I highlight some relative facts. Because civilians were not evacuated from the area, and in fact were, in two cases at least (Iceland and Crete), actually inside the camps, security was said to be very lax and they were able to watch everything that moved in or out, such as ammunition trains, etc. The young boys, often bored watching the Marines play their war games, saw their means of playing 'Cowboys and Indians' for real. They claimed to have first taken a Bren gun from the rifle range when some officer cadets went off to brew up in their billy cans, but seeing the cadet concerned getting told off by the sergeant, they produced the gun and said it was just a prank.

> 'They knew where the rifles were, having watched the armoury at Crete Camp for ages. It was in one of the houses that was normally well guarded, but with the weather being hot, a window was left open and in an opportune moment they slipped through it and got the rifles and ammo. The official statement said it was 400 rounds, but the boys claimed they had taken 5,000.
>
> We fired and fired for hours on end, but we never hurt anybody ... they fired blank cartridges to try and scare us out in the open ... When they caught us they gave us a whole Swiss Roll to eat ... They marched us through Barmouth with fixed bayonets and we were locked up ... From the hill we had a view right over the town and we could see them coming for miles.'

The lads paid for their foolish prank with an appearance at Barmouth Juvenile Court and the incident which became known locally as 'The Battle of Barmouth' lasting about 36 hours and at one point said to have involved 1,800 troops in the hunt, was understandably hushed up by the authorities. It is not clear if the rifles were ever found, or are still hidden in some cave on the mountain.[7]

Certainly the 'Battle of Barmouth' was a well-kept national secret but in the midst of government many questions were asked about what had happened in a sleepy Welsh seaside town. Churchill was certainly not amused.

Under the thirty year rule, documents and reports about the 'battle' were released to the Public Records Office and on 27

---

[7] This account of 'The Battle of Barmouth' has been reproduced with the permission of the Royal Marines Historical Society.

April 1975 the *Sunday People* newspaper carried an account by their investigative reporter, David Jack:

> It was the day the Russians smashed through German defences in Estonia; 600 Lancasters and Halifaxes bombed Stuttgart; Hitler launched radio-controlled mini-tanks as his 'secret weapon' on the Anzio beach-head: and fighter ace 'Cat's Eyes' Cunningham got a bar to his D.S.O.
>
> And what was absorbing Winston Churchill, overlord of our war machine on that March day of 1944?
>
> He was angrily writing orders for an immediate investigation... into an escapade of three naughty boys.
>
> Those three boys, now middle-aged men, met in a reunion at a Welsh pub last week to talk again of the Battle of Barmouth.
>
> With rueful grins Dai Lloyd, Glyn Evans and Glyn Jones admitted to me that they were the teenage desperadoes who so angered Churchill 31 years ago.
>
> It was they who caused the Great Man to break off his round-the-clock D-Day preparations to demand to know what caused such a rumpus in the sleepy Welsh town.
>
> It was they who had taken rifles and ammunition from a Royal Marines camp, climbed into the hills above the town and 'dug-in.'
>
> They fired off hundreds of bullets and kept the military brass-hats in confusion for 36 hours until the Marines winkled them out.
>
> 'The Marines marched us three boys through Barmouth with fixed bayonets,' recalled fishmonger Glyn Jones, now known as Jones the Fish.
>
> The truth about the incident was never made public.
>
> But now, among secret War Cabinet documents just released to the Public Records Office, it can be seen that the Prime Minister demanded from Home Secretary Herbert Morrison a detailed official account of what he called 'this extraordinary affair.'

Reports at the time told of Marines held at bay by boys directing a withering fire from their hill hide-out.

In a dramatic note to Morrison, Churchill wrote:

> The point is: did the boys fire with bullets on the Marines? If they

did the case is grave and they should be charged with attempted murder.

We really cannot have young hooligans setting out upon Royal Marines with bullets.

The sound of gunfire had caused a scare in Barmouth where citizens thought German paratroops had landed.

But few people today know the identity or the three pranksters who made Churchill so angry. Indeed, it required some espionage of my own to track them down.

I found Dai Lloyd at the ambulance station at Dolgellau.

After a brief interrogation he gave in with a grin and admitted: 'Yes, I was one of them.'

I found Jones the Fish in his shop at Towyn, 25 miles away. And eventually I traced Glyn Evans, who is also in the ambulance service.

So we arranged the reunion in a pub on the banks of the River Dovey, where they talked of those 36 hours when they kept the Royal Marines in confusion.

Dai Lloyd, 14 at that time, said:

They reckoned we took 400 rounds of ammunition, but it was 5,000 rounds. The authorities were trying to play it down because they were embarrassed about their lack of security I suppose.

We fired and fired for hours on end, but we never hurt anybody From the hills we had a view right over the town and we could see them coming for miles.

We even strolled back to the beach and watched them combing the hills for us. What a laugh!

Glyn Evans, who was 13, recalled:

The Marines didn't know who they were looking for because our cover was so good. They fired off blank cartridges to try to scare us into the open. And when they caught us, they gave us a whole Swiss-roll each to eat.

It was all a silly childish escapade. But boys will be boys.

Indeed, after extensive investigations, Home Secretary Morrison reported to Churchill: 'There is no evidence that the boys shot intentionally at Marines or anyone else.'

The only living things among the various targets selected by the high-spirited youngsters were some chickens, 'It was the poultry-keeper who started off the alarm,' said Glyn Evans.

The lads paid for their prank with an appearance at Barmouth Juvenile Court.

And 900 Fortresses bombed Berlin; London's air raid roof-spotters were reorganised; Phyllis Dixey carried on stripping at the Whitehall Theatre.

And Churchill went back to winning the war.[8]

---

[8]   The above was reproduced with the kind permission of the Trinity Mirror Group © Mirrorpix.

Wartime Barmouth: Memories of a Teenager

by Robert Wyn Jones

THE TOWN WAS inundated with military personnel, and swollen even further with the influx of troops from various adjoining military establishments. The army was secure in the town; the OCTU and the Royal Marines were in control.

The Royal Artillery was based at Tonfannau, the RAF at Llanbedr, and a few Polish soldiers were camped at Llwyngwril.

The OCTU at Barmouth had a motor transport unit attached to it, instructing in the driving and maintenance of lorries, cars and motorcycles. The military took over the top floors of hotels and large boarding houses for billeting purposes. The Black Patch (the area between Marine Parade and the Promenade) was used for drills, marching and parades. If the windows at the primary school were open, the pupils could hear the instructors shouting out marching orders. This intrusion was not popular with the headmaster.

The military had an office in Plas Mynach, with an assault course in the woods. There were also ATS personnel stationed here. (ATS – the Auxiliary Territorial Service – was the women's branch of the British army during WWII.)

During this period, an army cadet force was formed for young teenagers of the town. Under its supervision, we were taught the skills of drill, weaponry and map reading, utilising the assembly rooms in the high street for these activities. The instructional lectures we attended proved invaluable when the time came for national service at the age of 18.

There was a .22 rifle-shooting range in Park Road, situated underneath what is now Lewis's Furniture Store (where the present Elim Church is based). The OCTU very kindly provided the youngsters with a football kit and we formed a team called the Barmouth Eagles.

The troops were entertained in the old concert hall, opposite the railway station where the fairground is now located. Well-known artistes from the world of show business attended; it was run by the Entertainments National Service Association (ENSA).

Most of the Royal Marines were based near Arthog; they had taken over the upper floors of the terrace known as 'The Crescent', and several Nissen huts were erected there. Similar structures were built in Barmouth, and their concrete bases are still there. Two concrete sentry boxes were positioned on the road leading from 'The Crescent' to what was then the Barmouth Junction Railway Station. They survive to the present day in a good state of repair.

In Barmouth, a Navy, Army, and Air Force Institutes (NAAFI) cookhouse existed close to Porkington Gardens.

There were two Nissen huts in Barmouth: one below Abermaw Terrace, and one within the grounds of the Min-y-Môr Hotel. The latter hut stored army physical training equipment. The Royal Marines had a couple of DUKW (D – designed in 1942, U – utility, K – all wheel drive, W – dual rear axles) amphibious vehicles, which were launched off the beach. These were found to be rather unstable.

Every Sunday evening there was a community singing event at the Pavilion Cinema, together with solos from local singers. The compère was the Royal Marines padre.

The Royal Marines had an assault course on the Fegla Hill near 'The Crescent'. They had various names for their camps: 'Gibraltar' (Llanegryn), 'Iceland' (Arthog), and Barmouth, I believe, was 'Crete'.

They constructed a football pitch behind the sand dunes at Fairbourne (where the small golf course is at present) and had a very good team. One particular cup competition was held in Barmouth, the final being between the Royal Marines and a Royal Navy team from HMS *Glendower*, the naval training camp at Afonwen, Pwllheli (which became a Butlin's holiday camp after the war). The Royal Navy won 4–3.

There was a Spitfire squadron at Llanbedr with a firing range set up in the sand dunes. A target was erected, and the planes practised firing their wing-tip machine guns. When the range was dismantled, we youngsters used to collect the empty cannon shells which were strewn everywhere – they were solid brass.

Sometimes if we were on the beach at Barmouth, a Spitfire would suddenly appear from the Llanbedr end, flying extremely low – so low in fact, the pilot would wave to us.

I still remember the squadron lettering on the side of the planes: 'ZPB' followed by a number. The pilots seemed to be mostly Poles and Czechs and must have been connected in some way with the Battle of Britain. One Spitfire actually flew under the widest span of Barmouth Bridge at very low water.

The occasional sea mine would be washed up, and hastily made signs would be erected on the promenade: 'Danger – Unexploded Mine – Keep Off Beach'. The mine disposal squad would then be sent for. There was a nasty incident when a mine came in with the incoming tide and was bobbing around in the harbour, very close to the bridge. Luckily it beached itself at Traeth y Borth Wen where it was dismantled.

There were several wooden poles dug into the beach at various places. I never discovered what the reason was, but they were no doubt connected to the war effort.

Barmouth also had a branch of the LDV, better known as

Barmouth Army Cadets 1942

the Home Guard. In addition, there was a Royal Observer Corps section, a few land girls (who worked on local farms), and a couple of special constables. We had gas mask training at school and, of course, the usual clothing and food ration coupons.

There was a military tailors establishment in Church Street (where Barclays Bank now stands), which provided uniforms and repairs for the military. It was run by a Jewish family from London. The WVS was also ongoing at that time.

Many aircraft flew around the area, and there were a few tragic crashes; an Avro Anson, for instance, crashed behind Cell-fawr, at Bwlch y Llan. Another crash occurred in the sand dunes between the Round House (Tŷ Crwn) and the present-day leisure centre. The plane was, I believe, a Miles Master aircraft, and the accident happened during what was then called 'War Weapons Week'.

We had a few evacuees from various places. There were also Italian prisoners of war housed at Lawrenny Lodge in Porkington. They seemed to spend most of their time carving models from pieces of wood whilst sitting in the park opposite. We had a few French sailors in the town, although I must confess, I don't know where they came from or what they were doing here.

The radio kept everyone in touch with the latest war news, and various light entertainment programmes were broadcast for the factory workers – for example, *Workers Playtime*.

Our two cinemas also kept going. The *Barmouth Advertiser* reported the whereabouts of local servicemen and servicewomen wherever they were serving. It also reported on casualties and prisoners of war.

Compared with the bombing of larger towns and cities in the UK, Barmouth itself remained unscathed. However, our war memorial tells its own story of tragedies connected to the families and friends of many of the town's residents. This little town of ours certainly played its part in the war and had its fair share of all the sadness it left behind.

To the Barmouth Boys

All Barmouth boys in khaki, air force and navy blue,
Your relatives and friends at home convey their love to you.
You left the dear old home town to serve your noble king,
Some on the raging battlefield and others on the wing.
Some on the rolling billows and some along the bed
To hunt the lurking menace, for Britain must be fed.
We know your thoughts will wonder to happy days you knew
So far away in Bermo with others of the crew.

The Institute at Pen-y-cei is still going good and strong,
Where in the winter evenings you'd sing a good old song.
And there's of course the library you know just by the green
Where many a stirring game was played by players young and keen.
We'll keep the tables warm, lads, until the happy day,
When you return to Bermo, your handicap to play.

The old town's very quiet now to what it used to be
But happy in its ownership of sons across the sea.
The war can't last forever, lads, with all its blood and sweat,
And by the grace of Him above we'll beat the Nazis yet.
The blackout will be banished, the lamps will all be lit,
And Bermo will be glad to say her sons have done their bit.
So 'Hwyl fawr, hogia'r Bermo', wherever you may be,
May God protect you always by land, by air, by sea.

Walter J. Pugh
2, St George's, Barmouth

160

164 Officer Cadet Training Unit (OCTU)

by Peter Crabtree

THE OFFICER CADET training unit (OCTU) arrived in Barmouth on Thursday, 12 September 1940 at about 2 p.m. and virtually took over the town. The unit orderly room (admin) was at the rear, in the part of the old assembly rooms above Davies's Chemist. The unit guardroom was the old building up the steps by the Buffs (the New White Cinema that was).

A Company took over Cors-y-Gedol
B Company – the Min-y-Môr
C Company – the Marine Mansions, now known as the 'Arbour'
D Company – the Marine Hotel, recently converted into luxury flats

Nissen huts were erected in various building spaces in the town for lectures. Also used by the unit were Arrowe Hall at the end of Jubilee Road (burnt down in 1947, I think), the church hall, and, of course, the old assembly rooms (unit dances etc.).

Our parade ground was the tarmac area opposite the Balmoral Café, known as the Black Patch. Regimental Sergeant Major (RSM) Charlie Copp was the terror of the unit, who used to put the cadets through it on the drill parades. A 6 ft 2 in.

Coldstream guardsman, Copp was the second senior RSM in the British Army at the time! RSM Britten was the senior – a man who, it was said, could project his voice for up to a mile.

Copp even marched a squad into the sea for being 'idle' and put a cadet on a charge for freewheeling past the guardhouse – because he should have been pedalling! He was idle on a bike!

The first commanding officer, until about 1943, was Lieutenant Colonel Cadogan. He was succeeded by Lieutenant Colonel Paul Bryan DSO, MC, and Bryan was succeeded by Lieutenant Colonel Darling in October 1945. (Bryan was demobbed before the unit left Barmouth and therefore did not command 164 unit at Eaton Hall near Chester.)

The last 'passing out' held on the Black Patch was on Thursday, 15 November 1945 (I know this because I was on that parade myself). Lieutenant Colonel Darling, who was later promoted to the rank of general, commanded 164 at the time.

The OCTU had 'occupied' Barmouth for a total of five years, two months, and three weeks. In late November 1945, the unit at Barmouth disbanded and reformed at a Nissen hut camp in the grounds of Trentham Park, near Stoke-on-Trent. Here it remained until late 1946/1947, when it moved to Eaton Park near Chester. The unit finally ceased to exist sometime later, and by then it had trained hundreds of officers, many of whom made the supreme sacrifice. A memorial lamp hangs above the choir stalls in St John's Church, Barmouth in their memory.

Whilst I was doing my OCTU training at Barmouth, I was put on a charge for losing a small wooden handle which was part of an entrenching tool carried by each soldier. I was marched into the CO's office (Lietenant Colonel Bryan of all people) and given a dressing down for my carelessness, but when I agreed to pay eleven pence (old money) to replace the tool, the charge was dropped! The eleven pence was deducted from my pay and appeared on my paybook in red ink!

***

Peter left the army (Welch Regiment) with the rank of lieutenant and went on to Loughborough College to attend a three-year course on physical education. He then entered the teaching profession and taught for six years at Segontium Secondary School, Caernarfon, and then at Ysgol Ardudwy, Harlech, where he stayed until he retired.

There is no official history of the 164 OCTU at Barmouth, which was based in the town for just over five years. Some insight has been gained into the unit from those who held command as well as those who trained there.

In July 1940, 164 OCTU was located in Colchester, moving to Barmouth on 12 September of that year. Barmouth virtually became a garrison town; hotels, boarding houses, and private homes were all commandeered. The upheaval in the town must have been enormous. The local people would have been shocked by the sudden influx of servicemen and servicewomen with all the equipment and the transportation they had brought with them. The locals had to contend not only with losing their houses, but also the assembly rooms, the Arrowe Hall, and the new White Cinema building as well. The takeover was complete, and Barmouth people had to learn to adjust to the new conditions. Little did they know that the occupation would last for over five years.

The authorities had looked for a quiet place with suitable terrain for training 'would-be officers' in field work and allied subjects. The sixteen-week course was intensive and designed to train infantry officers, who were granted a week's leave on completion. Before being accepted as cadets, they would have attended a War Office selection board (WOSB), and the majority would have served in the ranks initially.

The 164 Officer Cadet Training Unit comprised of four companies – A, B, C and D – plus headquarters staff. Each company comprised around one hundred men. Initially, all cadets would join D Company before being allocated a training company; Peter Crabtree was in B Company. Each company was again divided into platoons. The total strength of the unit was not far short of a thousand once administrative, training and medical staff were taken into account.

The unit was commanded by very well-known officers who had proved their worth in various theatres of war.

Lieutenant Colonel Cadogan was the first commanding officer, and he commanded until 1943, when Lieutenant Colonel T. W. G. Stansfield DSO became commandant. Later in the same year, Lieutenant Colonel Paul Bryan DSC, MC was appointed commandant; he had come direct from active service in Italy. His career in the army had blossomed from being a private in a pre-war territorial regiment to a sergeant and then a commissioned officer. He had served in France until the country's fall, and his battalion had been evacuated from Cherbourg.

In 1942, Bryan saw action in Algiers and was part of the advance into Tunisia. He distinguished himself and, early in 1943, he was promoted to second in command and awarded the Military Cross. The battalion reached Tunis in May 1943. Bryan was given the command and had to prepare his men for the Sicily campaign. In September 1943, they crossed into Italy. At the end of that year he was awarded the DSO for his outstanding leadership. The battalion also had to take part in the fighting at Casino and saw the monastery being bombed by the Germans. Later in the spring, Bryan was rested and returned to Britain.

He was appointed to command the 164 Officers Cadet Training Unit at Barmouth. In accepting the post, he also brought with him two of his senior aides from his time in Italy to support and run the unit.

Paul Bryan had been born in Karuizawa, Japan; his father, the Reverend Dr Ingram Bryan, was a lecturer at a university there. Bryan attended a convent school in Tokyo until the age of eight, when he was sent to St John's School, Leatherhead. He studied modern languages at Gonville and Caius College, Cambridge. He took up a position with a clothing manufacturer in London but found the work rather dull. As the talk of impending war increased in 1938, he joined the Territorial Army as a private and was eventually selected for a commission.

In 1939, he married Betty Hoyle. Their first child, Elizabeth, was born in 1942, and stayed with her parents in Barmouth. Their second child, Felicity, was born in 1945, and their third, Bernadette, in 1948. Whilst at Barmouth, Betty took an active part in the life of the town. A programme has survived of a dramatic evening's entertainment held at the concert hall, the proceeds in aid of the Barmouth Welcome Fund and Dolgellau and Barmouth District Hospital. The evening's president was Mrs Betty Bryan, and amongst the cast were family members of Peter Crabtree.

Betty Bryan died in a swimming accident in Marbella in 1968, and in 1971 Paul Bryan married Cynthia Duncan. Bryan was very proud of his daughters. The eldest, Elizabeth, became a distinguished paediatrician, and Felicity became a literary agent and writer. The youngest, Bernadette, became an Anglican priest and was one of the first women to be ordained. Sadly, she died of cancer in 1995.

Paul Bryan became an MP in 1955 and held various offices in the Conservative Party. He was knighted in 1972 and retired in 1987, but he continued to live at the Yorkshire farm which he had bought in the early 1950s. He died at Sawdon, North Yorkshire, in October 2004 at the age of 91. His occupations were listed as politician, farmer and company director.

In his reminiscences, Roy Hobbs mentions several properties which he remembered as being used by the 164 unit, but there were other buildings which had been commandeered by other services such as the Royal Marines. He does not mention the Richmond Hotel, which seemed to be the focal point for the cadets' amusement, the assembly rooms, or the café by the railway bridge known as 'Phyllis's Café', where cups of tea and buns were always available. Phyllis Hartley, the proprietor, was awarded the BEM (Military) for her services.

The marines had their own camp called Crete – a series

of Nissan huts located near the Panorama Hotel. Huts were erected near the Min-y-Môr Hotel and opposite the Birmingham Garage. There was also a NAAFI canteen near Lawrenny Lodge and a miniature rifle range located in the old quarry area. An assault course was erected near the Round House (Tŷ Crwn). This was a delight for the local children, who happily played on it when it was not under supervision and being used by the troops.

Details of the training at the OCTU are not available, but the cadets would have had to attend lectures on tactics and do practical field work. This necessitated travelling to the Trawsfynydd ranges, which meant that the unit had to have efficient transport facilities with all the necessary staff. The Black Patch, as it was called (opposite the Marine Parade houses), served as the drill square, with the regimental sergeant major in charge. The area to the north, where the council estate is now located, was also used as a practice ground. Penrallt, at the top of the hill, which housed the hospital, was at one time the home of Harold Lowe of RMS *Titanic*. The corner shop by the National Westminster Bank had been taken over by a firm of Jewish tailors – Messrs Alkit from London. Austin Reed rented the first floor of Mona Cafe, and the O'Briens had the Compton Stores – the first shop in the old assembly rooms just past Christ Church. They employed local labour to make uniforms in a property across the road to their shop known today as Goodies Café. The vestry at the Ebenezer Methodist Church was also used by the WVS as a canteen for the troops. Plas Mynach was commandeered for the use of the ATS, and it housed approximately sixty girls.

Paul Bryan's tenure of command came to an end in October 1945, when he was demobilised. The command was taken over by Lieutenant Colonel D. L. Darling, who took the unit to Trentham Park. In July 1946, both he and the unit moved to Eaton Hall, Cheshire, where it was eventually disbanded.

In later life, many of the cadets who attended the OCTU in Barmouth became well-known personalities. There was the cartoonist Roy Ullyett, the composer Roy Parker (who co-wrote the song 'There'll always be an England'), Hugh Wheldon, and Sir David Willcocks (conductor, organist, composer, and conductor of the Kings College Choir, Cambridge), to name but a few. Sir David served in the army for five years and was awarded the Military Cross.

Also Alan Whicker, who was mentioned in dispatches, and became a well-known broadcaster and author; in his book *Whicker's War*, the author mentions his early training with the 164 O.C.T.U at Barmouth. It was only post war, on his return to the area, that he realised what scenic magnificence the county offered. His training was so intense that he had had no spare time to appreciate it during the war years.

164 OCTU was a unit which trained hundreds of officers who still have nostalgic memories of the period. These will never be forgotten, but nor will those days ever return. A lamp, presented by 164 OCTU, hangs above the choir stalls at St John's Church, Barmouth, as a memorial of their time in the town.

Major Bob Smith

(the author of *Khaki Shorts*)

BOB SMITH WAS a fellow cadet with Peter Crabtree at the 164 Officer Cadet Training Unit, Barmouth, until late 1945 when the unit was transferred to Trentham Park, Stoke-on-Trent, where they completed their training. The regimental sergeant major of 164 OCTU was Charlie Copp, and Bob Smith's description of him is typical of a British Army RSM at that time: 'Shine and Bullshit'. Bob described him thus:

> The pinnacle of excellence, or the one who terrified me most, was Warrant Officer Class One Charlie Copp of the Coldstream Guards. He was the regimental sergeant major of 164 Officer Cadet Training Unit (OCTU). He stood out from all others like a lighthouse on a barren shore, towering over most of his flock by at least six inches and wearing a uniform into which he seemed to have been poured. He was the epitome of military perfection, from tip of his nose-flattening peaked cap to the brass ferrules on his highly polished pace stick.

His way of treating recruits was typical of the period. To us today, the shouting and bawling may seem unnecessary, but, as both Peter Crabtree and Bob state, ultimately they had to admit that the endless drills and verbal haranguing made them look, feel and act like soldiers – and perhaps help them to get to know themselves as well.

Many stories exist about RSM Copp's time at Barmouth. On one particular day he was giving the cadets a rough time when an old lady appeared on the parade ground waving an umbrella in a threatening way and hurling abuse at him. Quite unperturbed, he roared, 'Get out of my square, madam. Sergeant Major, take this lady away.' Once he roared at a cadet: 'You there, yes, that little fellow, you are marching like a ruptured duck.' The parade ground in Barmouth was only about 100 yards from the sea, and RSM Copp took great delight in parading the cadets at the double in the soft sand, rifles held aloft. There is a rumour that on one occasion he even marched the cadets into the sea.[9]

9   Permission to make use of Major Bob Smith's recollections has been given by his daughter Gilly.

Major Roy Rees

In his book, *Age Shall Not Weary Them*, Major Roy Rees recollects his wartime period at Barmouth. The author relates how Major Rees remembers his times there in March 1941:

ORIGINALLY FROM SWANSEA and stationed at Scarborough, Roy had been selected as a candidate for commission and travelled to do his training at Barmouth in March 1941. In those days, the journey entailed changing trains at Leeds, Manchester, Chester, and Ruabon, where there was a three-hour wait for the Barmouth connection.

On reaching his destination, he found that his quarters were in the Barmouth Hotel, that still had civilians staying there. He shared a small but adequate bedroom with two other cadets. The training consisted of drill exercises on the seafront and lectures, with provision for sport. As a cadet, his uniform was distinguished by a white band around the cap, a red stripe on the right shoulder indicating that they were infantry, and a white one on the left indicating that they were from the officer cadet training unit.

Field exercises were very much to the fore; some were night exercises involving Barmouth Railway Station. Towards the end of the course, the cadets took part in an extended exercise which entailed climbing to the top of Cadair Idris, supposedly in a hostile situation, but it was all very exhilarating. At the end of the twelve weeks, the cadets had to fill preference forms for regiments they hoped to join, but things did not always turn out as they wished.

In his book, Roy recalls his experience of an assault landing on Barmouth beach – a 'combined operation' with the Royal Marines from across the river. Having had to wade through chest-high water to reach the assault boats, they were soaking wet before embarking. The boatswain, having little knowledge of the beach, arrived at what he thought was the drop-off point and ordered the troops to disembark some distance from shore – a point that they quite rightly thought was not the intended drop-off place. One keen cadet threw caution to the wind and jumped overboard; he disappeared completely and had to be rescued at the end of a boathook.

The boatswain agreed to bring the craft nearer the shore, where the troops were able to jump into water that was about four feet deep. They then carried out their assault on the town. On completion, a short rest was called for!

Lo and behold, RSM Copp arrived from somewhere and decided to give them a half-hour drill in their soaking wet uniforms with water sloshing about inside their boots and packs as they marched up and down the promenade.

Three Miles of
Memories [10]

During the Second World War Roy Hobbs from Christchurch in Dorset spent four years in Barmouth. This week at the age of 90 he returns to the seaside town for a trip down memory lane...

IN AUGUST I visited Barmouth, which in 1940 became the base of the 164th Officer Cadet Training Unit whose task it was to turn private soldiers into officers.

Somewhere quiet and free from military action had to be found and Barmouth was chosen. I spent four years there and on my recent visit I called at every building that had been commandeered from 1940 to 1945. Almost every step stirred my memory.

Standing at the train station revived many because in wartime the one train in on Saturday in summer arrived at 5.30pm choc-a-bloc with holidaymakers, many of them young girls who worked in the munitions factories of Birmingham, Wolverhampton, Crewe, Liverpool, Birkenhead, and many of us were young men of 20 or so. Each Saturday, a crowd of us would wait for the train, sort out the best-looking girls, offer to show them to their digs and carry their cases. This usually assured us one or two weeks pleasant female company and occasionally led to romance.

The only train out on Saturday was the 12.30pm so having carried our girls' cases to the station, we would see them off

---

[10]   Roy Hobbs, 'Three Miles of Memories', *Cambrian News*, 9 September 2010.
       Permission to use and print this article was kindly given by the *Cambrian News*.

with fond farewells, a kiss, tears and promises to keep in touch. At 5.30pm we met the train in and repeated the process.

From the station I walked to the south of the town and went into the foyer of three flats which had been a commandeered hotel housing most of the HQ personnel and where I lived for four years. The name Orielton Hall is still on the wall outside. Across the road is Penrallt Guest House which had been the unit hospital in which I once spent several days after falling oﬀ my bike on a mountain path and rolling for 30 yards before hitting a stone wall.

I stopped at Lawrenny Lodge where the MT staff (drivers and motor cyclists) lived.

Close by was Porkington Terrace where the upper crust of the ATS, i.e. the typists and secretaries, lived.

I turned right and walked toward the beautiful Panorama Walk, then right to Mount Argus where half the ATS girls had lived. My first wife was billeted there and we married in December 1942.

The name of the building has changed so I went to the front door and asked the receptionist if it had previously been Mount Argus. She told me it had and when I explained the reason for my enquiry, the lady, far too young to remember the war said: "*Sit down and tell me about it*". A cup of tea and half-an-hour later I went on my way toward the town centre until I came to some steps on my right.

There were probably 50 going very steeply from the road to a white house where my commanding officer Colonel Bryan had lived with his wife Betty and daughter Elizabeth. Those steps tested me in my 20s. Now at 90, I had to struggle a bit.

The colonel was remarkable. In May 1939 at 22 he joined the Territorial Army in Kent as a private and by October he was a sergeant. He was then selected for a commission and became an officer. He fought in France, North Africa and Italy and was awarded the Military Cross, the Distinguished Service Order and Bar and in 1944 he became the youngest colonel ever in the British Army, aged 28.

I admired the colonel and when in 1945 he went to London to get demobbed I went with his belongings to his home near Huddersfield. I stayed with the family for a few days, then he rang the OCTU and arranged a week's leave so I could visit some relatives in Manchester I had not seen since before the war. After the war, the colonel became Sir Paul Bryan and an MP.

I walked toward the town centre past the quarry where, in wartime, youths had broken into an ammunition store and stolen rifles. They took pot shots at people, hitting one man in his rear end. A team of marines was called to deal with the matter and the youths were arrested.

I stopped to have a drink at the Last Inn and from there I could see Barmouth Bridge. I remembered a spitfire pilot had flown under it during the war although the beach at low tide was only about 40 feet below.

Passing the next hotel, which had been the Sergeants' Mess, I reached the centre and took a look at a bucket and spade shop that had been the NAAFI canteen. I walked to the north of the town and looked at Plas Mynach, a hotel which housed other ATS girls. Turning back I went into the grounds of what I remembered as The Cliffs Hotel but is now called something else, and The Ferns guest house next door. The Cliffs had been the main Officers' Mess and The Ferns housed ATS officers and a few girls who worked in the main mess.

I spoke to a lady in The Ferns and spent half-an-hour giving her and her husband a history lesson and said if she looked under the first floor window sill of The Cliffs under the lead flashing she would see all my details scratched in the lead.

From there and over the railway bridge until I reached Heol-y-Meirion, I knocked on the door where my old army pal Benny Woolven lives. He married Dora, a local girl, and remained in Barmouth after the war.

Benny was pleased to see me and we were soon talking our way through the war years. When I said *"You're 95 this year aren't you?"* he said *"Yes, tomorrow."*

Before I left I wished him happy birthday and he cheered me saying that by calling and spending three hours I had given him the best present he could have wished for.

I walked along the sea front and in my mind's eye I could see soldiers and their girlfriends sitting on the promenade steps admiring the sunsets as they had all those years ago. After one last look at the sea and the mountains, I made my way to the station.

I was met at Minffordd by my family and taken for a lovely meal at the end of a very interesting day, where almost every step of my three-mile walk through Barmouth held a memory of a very happy period of my life.

Live Ammo

An interesting letter has been discovered by Hugh Roberts, Henddol, Barmouth, appertaining to the field firing exercise of the 164 OCTU, Barmouth. It seems that the inhabitants of various farms and small holdings in a specific area were warned that their land would be used for live ammunition practice by the unit and the precise times given. In this particular instance, the area is given as Llyn Cwm Mynach, which is situated up a mountainous road about three and a half miles north of Bontddu. The area is now managed by the Woodland Trust and is being restored to broadleaf forest.

Tel. Barmouth 162.   CI/R/D74

Subject:- Field Firing.

To:-, The Addressee.

    The firing of live ammunition will take place as follows during w/c 28 January 45.

Date   28 January 45.

Time.   0900 - 1700 hrs.

Area   Ground north, south, east and west of Llyn Cwm Mynach.

Weap   3" Mortar
               2" Mortar
               S.A.A.

Warning   DO-NOT, AT ANY TIME, touch or pick up any strange object which may be found lying about, but report the matter to this H.Q. immediately.

                                           D.J Duffy
                                     Major. Capt.
                             Chief Instructor.
           164th (Infantry) Officer Cadet Training Unit.

Barmouth
22 Jan 45

OCTU – White Tape

The B Company magazine *White Tape* was written before the OCTU left Barmouth, although the company was stationed at Trentham Park by the time it was published. One of its editors, A. B. Niven, was presented with the Belt of Honour at Trentham. Peter Crabtree was one of the platoons' representatives on the board of *White Tape*. In his 'Au Revoir', the editor states:

> Though we have moved to Trentham Park, we still hold dear many happy recollections. Such familiar scenes, easily recalled, are still fresh in our memories: the Assembly Rooms, the Richmond Club, the Royal Hotel – and Phyllis.

There are numerous articles in the magazine. Some are reproduced below to illustrate the humour of the period and the cadets' ability to have fun under dire conditions.

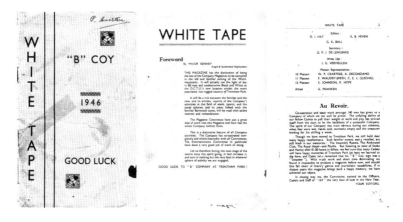

Learning to Drive an Army Truck

Let it be known that no military force in human history has had in its power such a potentially lethal weapon as did the British Army when it entrusted a 15 cwt truck to my tender supervision.

The event is still talked of in whispers in the area – Wrotham-Meophan-Tonbridge. In fact, I have it on very reliable authority that the local yokels will probably pass the story on for generations to come.

To return to the story, my first introduction to the joys of driving was under the somewhat harassed tuition of a driving instructor (D.I.) at Wrotham (I think he was the first Scotsman I've met who knelt down and prayed to every conceivable saint in the driving-cab of any vehicle). Within two hours of the happy coincidence of our meeting he'd already christened me 'The D.I.'s Despair'.

Now to you who know perhaps a little more than me of the 'innards' of a truck (this probably includes 99.9% of the population above the age of 12 years) will know that inside on the floorboards are a certain number of gadgets. Going from port to starboard these include the clutch, the steering-column and wheel, the footbrake and accelerator. Aft of these comes the handbrake and a thingumajig called the gear-lever. On a panel above are a number of dials, the only one of which a driver of my calibre needs to use is the clock, if fitted, to remind one that it is time for tea.

There's nothing easier than starting a truck. One merely has to release the handbrake and away she goes, of course, it all depends on the ground, as Capt. Wood would say. If one was parked uphill one went backwards. If by some miracle of chance one was facing downhill one went forward. However, by manoeuvring with little plugs and levers it is possible to start the engine going. My first attempt at so doing is memorable, never before has any internal combustion engine so nearly mimicked the antics of a kangaroo. Anyway as soon as the D.I.

had finished whispering sweet nothings into my ear, I really managed to get the thing going.

Next I was taught the workings of the gear-lever. The gear-lever is a rod with a knob on the end, introduced into army trucks to produce weird grating and rattling noises to warn cyclists to get on to the pavement. In fact, it is the modern equivalent of the medieval cry 'Bring out your dead!'

My next lesson was in stopping of the vehicle. This isn't so easy. There are three main ways of accomplishing this; first, by running into something; secondly, by backing into something, and lastly, the right way. If you are anything like myself as a driver (which heaven forbid) you probably also own the sort of foot which covers both the foot-brake and the accelerator at one and the same time with dire results to both. I am sure my D.I. must have been a very religious man from the way he kept both hands in an attitude of blessing, hovering over the hand-brake, also from the fact that he often muttered words which sounded like Latin to me; still I am probably mistaken.

Such then are the most enthralling moments of my army career as a driver and the most worrying of other people's. I have, however, had several offers of an agent's job with one or two insurance firms whose number of life-policies has rapidly increased since I was let loose on the surrounding countryside – so I still have hopes!

E. C. Mundy

Poisonalities

NEXT COMES

Cadet Woolnough, Supreme Commander of the Men-y-Môr partisans. He distinguished himself in a recent sharp skirmish with the Tal-y-Bont Maquis, when, with one of the NAAFI's rock cakes, he single handed knocked out a self-propelled pea shooter mounted on a hot-chestnut barrow disguised as Stevenson's 'Rocket'.

Incorrect Method of Whisky Appreciation

I had twelve bottles of whisky in my cellar, my wife told me to empty the contents of each and every bottle down the sink, or else! I said I would, and proceeded with the unpleasant task.

I withdrew the cork from the first bottle and poured the contents down the sink, with the exception of one glass, which I drank; I extracted the cork from the second bottle and did likewise, with the exception of one glass which I drank. I then withdrew the cork from the third bottle and emptied the whisky down the sink with the exception of one glass which I drank.

I pulled the cork from the fourth bottle and poured the bottle down the glass which I drank.

I pulled the bottle from the cork of the next and drank one sink out of it and threw the rest down the glass. I pulled the sink out of the next glass and poured the sink down the bottle. Then I corked the sink with the glass, bottled the drink and drank the pour.

When I had everything emptied, I steadied the house with one hand and counted the bottles, corks and glasses and sinks with the other, which were twenty-nine. To be sure, I counted them again and when they came by I had seventy-four and as the house came by, I counted them again and finally had all the houses and bottles and corks and glasses and sinks counted, except one house which I drank.

AEA Licudi

'Advt. Poser by an Honest Artist'

Do you get up in the morning with a headache and a nasty taste in your mouth? Do you have pains in the back and joints? Does your stomach ache after eating a good meal and do you see spots before your eyes?

If you do, then you are in a HELL of a MESS!

Ysfradonian

'The Phantom Few'

I stood on a lofty hilltop and watched the clouds scud by
While high above there soared the lark, up in a wind-swept sky,
I looked towards the eastward and saw like streamers pale
Against the perfect sun-lit blue a phantom vapour trail.
The roar of ghostly engines came, the drone of harnessed might;
The sound we only knew too well, we heard both day and night,
And In my mind I saw the glint, the flash of sun on steel;
There forty German bombers flew, so distant yet so real,
Those phantom planes were overhead, just as they used to be,
And in their bellies hung the bomb that fell on folk like me,
I felt the ground begin to shake, and all that sapphire blue
Seemed fading swiftly into night, the sun could not shine through,
The sky was dark with outspread wings, and hope sank in my breast,
When suddenly I saw a glow which came from out the east,
Just like a symbol of the dawn a phantom squadron came;
Twelve British Spitfires roaring up, their wings all tipped with flame;
Up, up and up to awful odds, 'through hardship to the stars'.
I saw their ghostly tracers shoot like meteors to Mars.
The German bombers scattered then, and turning tail they fled,
But two came whining to'ward the earth in plumes of black and red;
The phantom planes had disappeared, my heart was light again,
And there across the span of world the rainbow after rain;
The lark, the fleecy clouds returned, the sky was brightest blue;
I knew I'd seen their ghosts in death – the Spirits of 'the Few'.

G. Woolnough

In Convoy

This is not so much an article on troopship convoys, on which some of you may have travelled, but of the great food-carrying armadas.

Little recognition was given to these ships and their crews until the latter part of the war. It was they who carried the supplies which were necessary for our very existence, and therefore they should have our heartfelt thanks.

I shall now write about a typical convoy which left the Americas in the summer of 1943. You may wonder why I said 'the Americas'. The reason is that the ships came from widely separated places – Hudson Bay, Buenos Aires and Peru. The convoy consists of a polyglot collection of ships ranging from the type with only one main hold to the larger passenger ship converted for food for supply carrying purposes.

The ships first assemble in ports up and down the coastline. Here they take on board their cargoes consisting mainly of square airtight tins. It was these tins that were so important in saving shipping space. Some of them are oddly shaped to fit in awkward parts of the ship, but the majority of them are square. The cargo being loaded, the ships then wait for their sailing orders. In this case they come from New York, since there the convoy commodore, usually a retired rear-admiral, resided. The main assembly was also to take place at New York.

Our orders came and we steamed up to the assembly point, hugging the coastline to minimise the submarine danger. Arriving in New York we spent a whole day picking up convoy stations. The sea there is a mass of coloured bell-buoys and each ship goes to its allotted buoy. At dawn the next day we set sail in nine lines of close on ten ships each. The ships sail half a mile astern of each other and the distance between each line is a mile.

Our only escorts for the next two days were two converted passenger ships armed as convoy raiders; later, the escort was strengthened by two more similar ships and a destroyer escort of 21 vessels. The latter joined us on the third night out, and by that time forty other ships, mainly tankers, had joined the convoy.

The crossing took exactly four weeks. The extra week was caused by the attention of two German Karrier planes which forced the convoy to deploy about four hundred miles off Iceland. The main crossing was uneventful except for a submarine attack which was beaten off by the escort before it inflicted any damage.

There are some interesting facts about convoys. One is that they must sail either with or against the current to prevent the rolling of the ship from loosening the deck cargo. Once we sailed four hundred miles in the wrong direction as a result of this. Another is the tankers, which all carried deck cargoes of aircraft. In a rough sea, the only indication of the tankers' presence was the aircraft bouncing, apparently, from wave to wave. Four tankers broke their backs but still managed to stay in the convoy.

Over here the ships were 'sorted' according to their freights and sent to various ports. The escort went back with the next returning convoy and so the great work, with all its hardships and perils, goes on over again.

Equipment

A newly initiated member of the PBI [poor bloody infantry?] on arrival at his unit is generally issued with certain set pieces of 'Equipment, soldiers for the use of'. With a cool, collected and analytical eye, let us now examine these as they appear to, and arc used by, the private soldier.

Of major importance of course is the rifle. This is a concoction of wood and metal provided to give the private something to keep clean and keep his mind off more important matters. Its uses are various, besides being something to carry on drill parades and providing a prop whilst on sentry-go. It is said that it makes a useful toasting fork when 'avec-la-bayonette'. Judging from appearances, it is also possible to dig trenches in very wet and muddy ground.

Following the rifle in priority – comes the bayonet. Besides the use previously referred to, it can be made to open a can of milk, and makes a good coat-hanger when stuck into a tent pole. This is facilitated by its shape, which is that of an eleven inch nail, plus attachments.

After having mastered the intricacies of the fore-mentioned articles, the recruit should next turn his attention to the webbing kit supplied.

When first given him, this consists of one huge Gordian Knot; the first two days of Army life are usually spent in unravelling this mystery. Having more or less successfully sorted out the various straps included, attention is next diverted to the separate portions.

Firstly, comes the small pack, this supposedly containing a water-bottle and cork, mess-tins and ground sheet. Mess tins are found on 'Admin Inspections' to be in one of three conditions – rusty, split or greasy. Although originally intended to convey 'grub' from cookhouse to mouth, they are usually convenient for the purpose of blancoing (the soldier's joy), shaving or pressing trousers. Water-bottles, strangely enough, are used almost exclusively for carrying water.

Ground sheets, intended to provide shelter from all forms of unwelcome moisture, are usually quite futile for this or any other purpose. Devious other objects have a knack of finding their way into small packs – such as bundles of love-letters, 'snaffled thunder-flashes', even mouse-nests by no means being the exceptions.

The rest of the webbing consists of straps of varying lengths and sizes, of which two are generally kept to provide support for one's denim trousers, and two are lost. Thrown in with these are a pair of pouches, basic, which in 'chic' condition are usually crumpled, slightly oily and permanently undone; as is usual with all army kit, in two ways, too loose or too tight, generally the former.

The whole of the webbing can be worn in three ways, known colloquially in fashion circles as 'Brassiere', 'A-la-Parachute' and 'Loincloth'. Let us examine next some of the personal clothing of the infantry-man. Socks, for example – when issued, these were grey and have a hole one end in which to put one's foot. After a few weeks' wear, having somewhat of the characteristics of the chameleon, they are to be found black, and one can put one's foot in either end.

Well, having now a rough insight into the 'wherefores' of army kit, let us now regard the 'whys'.

Everything in this army is for a reason, and this is no exception. We have it from Very High Authority that the whole constitutes Britain's latest secret weapon, the very sight of it on the battlefield having a devastating effect on the enemy's morale.

E. C. M.

Punctures

Lesson 9
Instructors' Notes – a parody on how the army does it!

Instructors will impress upon their men the need for care and knowledge in handling the puncture and will emphasise that a drill is of urgent importance in its quick and thorough mending.

Reference to Appendix 2, part 11. Cycle accessories; Contents of a Puncture Repair Outfit

Stores. One bicycle, one puncture repair outfit; a small quantity of drawing pins; one pump; practice inner tube.

(i) Explain
The bicycle has two wheels around whose circumference is a treaded tyre; in peace-time said to be made from rubber; an illusion not worthy of continued existence in time of war.

Within the outer tube is a second tube which is normally unseen and somewhat resembles a German sausage. This is connected to the outer air by a simple structure known as a valve.

The valve is merely an aperture in a manner similar to a guard room – allows entrance but no exit!

(ii) *Description*. Explain and Demonstrate
(a) A regulation length of tubing having been attached at one end to the valve and at the other end to the pump (see lesson 8 for details); controlled pressures upon the pump handle; followed by sudden withdrawals, will produce swelling in the tyre of the bicycle (if the swelling is unevenly distributed what is known as a 'Service Burst' may occur, and the demonstration will cease forthwith). This procedure is termed 'pumping up'.

The Squad should not be practised on any instructors' machines.

(b) Pointed materials may infiltrate through the outer tube of the tyre group and cause deflation of the inner tube.

This is known as a puncture and may be recognized by a hissing noise similar to that heard in lecture rooms; and occasionally laid down to sleep.

The Squad should not be practised on any Instructors' machines.

(iii) Carry out 1A of Dismounting (as taught in lesson 111)

(iv) *Examination* – Outer Tube. Explain and Demonstrate.

(1) Safety precaution. Remove valve and examine small segments of rubber therein to ensure that it is in no way broken. It is the duty of all ranks at all times to ensure that rubbers are not perished or holed.

(11)Examine outer tube for positive signs of infiltration.

(v) *Stripping.* Explain and Demonstrate

(a) Remove all valve accessories. Place these with care in left hand tunic pocket. Do not leave on the ground, since elaborate formulae will be required to pin point their position, i.e. third brick, wall 3 p.m. position small daisy, 2 yards left crack in ground. Range cards will not be provided for this drill.

(b) Outer Tube, tyre levers may be available. Explain that spanners, spoons, bayonets, bars etc. may be improvised (a demonstration for trained soldier, instruction may be laid on later; in which the bicycle sustains a puncture near the cookhouse; and the cyclist improvises his mending with spoons, suet puddings, porridge and any other locally found substitutes).

The laid down drill is that one lever shall always be inserted under the outer tube and that there shall be a continued endeavour to insert the remainder. Emphasise that there must be a danger area of 3 feet in all directions, since levers are liable to be catapulted into the air without due warning.

Instructor's Note.

Up to the moment there has been no issue of protective clothing for safeguarding personnel against this catapulting. Respirators may be worn, but the units own standing orders. When two or three levers have been successfully inserted, one edge of the outer tube should be levered out, and the inner tube pulled gently from underneath.

It may be found simpler to upturn the bicycle (after dismounting) as per 1(a) for examination and stripping. Wheels may ONLY be removed at the direction of an officer of field rank.

(vi) *Examination* – Inner Tube, Explain and Demonstrate, Squad imitating

(a) Find valve accessories and replace. Fix pump. Take first pressure and continue as necessary. Remove pump. Listen for hissing and search arc of tube from right to left in the laid down rule to locate the point of incidence.

It should be impressed upon squad that in the excitement of locating punctures, it is extremely simple to lose their position. They should hold the tube in the left hand at its punctured point, and open repair outfit with right hand, take out indelible pencil (See Appendix-Cycle Accessories) and neatly draw a small ring about the aperture.

(b) Punctures will not always be located by the sound of hissing; in this event further apparatus in the form of water within a suitable receptacle (steel helmets forbidden) is available. Water need not be pure, but canal water is not advised since its density will prevent free passage. (For Trained Soldier demonstration; cookhouse soup may be used with the exception of that which resembles canal water.)

Place inner tube by tactical bounds in the water, observing discharge of air. This will be the location of puncture. Ring round as above.

(vii) *Mending, Explain and Demonstrate. Squad Imitating.*

(a) From repair outfit take instrument resembling a vesta match, lick end and apply vigorously to clean region of puncture. Officer Cadets will be issued with damp service flannelette in lieu of licking. They will ensure that the flannelette is damp at all times.

(b) Take tubular container marked 'rubber solution'. Remove cap, apply by squeezing over vicinity of hole. Ensure that container has been used before, otherwise unseal by pricking.

Inexpert squeezing of an unused container will cause
fluid to emerge over fingers and trousers. It is difficult to
explain stained trousers. Apply solution over puncture with
forefinger of the right hand.

(c) Allowing solution to congeal and grow tacky, take rubber
patch and remove linen backing. All ranks are advised to
allow one finger nail to grow longer than the others for
this purpose.

Officer-Cadets are advised to cut all the finger nails
shorter. Press patch firmly over the hole.

(d) Take small hollow metal square, in which is contained a
set portion of French Chalk. (Explain: that it has never
been discovered why this was so named. It is apparently
no different from English Chalk. Many things, however,
are attributed to the French which the country has in
common.) Grate chalk over patch. Ample allowance should
be made for the wind in judging the grating aim. Rub
chalk well in around the patch.

(viii) *Assembling.* Explain and Demonstrate.

(a) Replace inner tube. It is invariably too large for the
circumference of the wheel. Since there is no way of
overcoming this defect, no drills are laid down; and men
are expected to use imagination. Poke valve stem through
hole provided; screw on valve accessories. Fix pump and
inject between three or four cubic inches of air. Remove
pump.

(b) Attempt to replace outer tube. It is invariably too small for
the circumference of the wheel. Employ levers according
to applied principles of attack; one lever keeping the
tyre edge down while another is put through a flanking
movement of a few inches. If further levers may be
brought into use as reinforcement a pincer movement
should be attempted; otherwise the outer tube may burst
forth again where it was levered into position. Squad will
offer small prayer before the replacement of the outer tube
(it is unlikely that it will be answered).

(c) Fix pump and pump up.

NOTE – If as is probable, punctures prove unmended,
instructors should not apologise to squad, since this lowers
vital prestige and thereby affects the morale of the British

Army as a whole. He will blame pump.
    (d) Upturn bicycle again if necessary.
  (ix) Question Squad.
    Ensure safe collection and return of drawing pins.
    Emphasise all points.

K. M. D.

10th Battalion Royal Welch Fusiliers (Territorials). Taken at Barmouth, September 1939.

Rear: George Jones, Tommy Williams, Cyril Buckley, Frank Ingram, Will Lloyd, John Llewelyn Griffiths, Raymond Morris, D. Ffoulkes, Tom Murray, Will Jones.

Centre: Stanley Jones, Robert Griffiths, William Jones, Meirion Owen, C. J. Jones.

Front: Evan Lloyd Williams, Bob Crabbe, Gwilym Jones, Howell Griffith, Robert Roberts, Ernest Evans, William Charles Roberts.

Seated: Richard Griffiths, Eirlys Morris, Morris G. Roberts.

Barmouth Lifeboats and Coastguards

THERE WAS ONLY one lifeboat and coastguard station along the Merioneth coast, and this was in the port of Barmouth. Aberdyfi had lost its lifeboat station in 1931, but did have an Outward Bound school, established there in 1941.

The activities of the town's lifeboat crew could not be disclosed during the war itself for security reasons, and it wasn't until 24 January 1946 that the *Barmouth Advertiser* was finally able to print and recount some of the wartime tasks undertaken by members of the crew. The *Advertiser* devotes some of its space to giving a vivid account of what they achieved and praises the crews for their devotion and heroism:

Rescues by Lifeboat
Barmouth Men Honoured
Heroic Work in War-Time

Four members of Barmouth lifeboat crew have received official notification from the Royal National Lifeboat Institute that it had been decided to award them the 1939–1945 Star for outstanding lifeboat service during the war years. They are Mr John Ellis Morris (Coxswain) and his son Mr William Morris and Mr John Jones and his brother Mr Edward Jones.

Between 1939 and 1945 they were the regular members of the Barmouth Lifeboat crew on twenty-five occasions when the boat was launched for service to rescue airmen and merchant seamen from Cardigan Bay. The official recognition of their bravery discloses the nature of the rescues, which could not be given previously owing to security reasons.

On one occasion the Barmouth Coastguards reported that a ship called the *Amy* had got into difficulties during the night on the St Patrick's Causeway while coming from New York to Liverpool. Owing to a terrific gale the vessel, which was loaded with ammunition, crashed into the causeway and was aground and liable to blow up at any moment. The Barmouth lifeboat reached the helpless vessel in record time despite the darkness and an eighty miles an hour wind. They rescued eight members of the crew and brought them to Barmouth. They returned to the ship and stood by for fifty-one hours until assistance arrived and it was removed.

On another occasion SOS signals were observed in the same vicinity from a vessel known as the *Vick 111*, which had lost its propeller in Cardigan Bay while proceeding from Liverpool to Portsmouth. There was a crew of six on board who suffered from exposure and want of food after being adrift for several hours in the cold. The Lifeboat stood by until a naval ship arrived and took over.

This rescue was followed a little later by the launching of the lifeboat to assist a minelayer which was in difficulty between Barmouth and Aberystwyth.

Great anxiety about the Lifeboat's safety was felt in Barmouth on a subsequent occasion, when it was called out to the assistance of a Dutch ship loaded with ammunition. While proceeding from Newport, South Wales, to Belfast, this ship had got into difficulty during the height of a terrific gale and in the pitch darkness. The lifeboat, assisted by flares from the vessel, reached it after battling for a long time in the heavy seas and gave assistance until daylight, when the crew succeeded in repairing the damaged engines.

On several occasions during the war the lifeboat was launched to search for aircraft which had been reported by coastguards to have crashed into the sea.

The Barmouth Lifeboat Station was established in 1828 and is one of the oldest in the kingdom.

In reality, this recognition of their work did not reflect the dangers and risks they had undertaken or the fact that their support had been given on a voluntary basis.

In the UK, the coastguard is primarily concerned with search and rescue and is still to a large extent a voluntary service. It plays no role in the day to day maintenance of sea markers and buoys, which is the responsibility of Trinity House, nor has it anything to do with customs and excise enforcement, which is the responsibility of HM Revenue and Customs. The service does not have any lifeboats of its own but does on occasion have the use of an MCA Falconer, a type of lifeboat used in areas where there may not be a lifeboat provided by the Royal National Lifeboat Institution (RNLI). The service can lease commercial helicopters and tugs to provide search and rescue cover in certain areas. It also maintains a number of search teams specialising in rescue from cliffs and mud and is the coordinating body for the maritime rescue service. The coastguard plays a vital part in the saving of lives, be it on land or sea. It does not get the publicity or adoration of its associate organisation, the RNLI, probably owing to two factors. Firstly, that the coastguard was originally created to combat smuggling (it was called the preventative service) and came under the jurisdiction of customs and excise; secondly, that it is a state-funded service that unlike the RNLI is not dependent on voluntary contributions. Basically, however, their work and aims are similar, and to a large extent both organisations work well together without any discord, jealousy or animosity.

The history of the coastguard goes back about 200 years, and during that time it has operated under different names. Its first duty was to curb the smuggling which was rampant during that period. As smuggling diminished, the service was taken over by the Admiralty, which saw it as a reserve force for the Royal Navy, and the main role of the service became that of saving lives. From its earliest days, signalling was the coastguard's forte, and this was the greatest value of the service to the navy. Exercises were conducted twice daily, using semaphore flags and telegraphy as well as flashing lights at night. However, with the coming of the telegraphic system, communications between stations containing life-saving apparatus, or between sites where lifeboats stations were located, became much easier.

In 1911, an Admiralty instruction stated that they did not accept responsibility for life-saving duties, but that coastguards were to render every possible assistance to the local life-saving service as far as it was compatible with their proper duties. The Board of Trade took over the supervision of a number of private life-saving bodies which had been formed as well as responsibility for maintaining 'Rocket' life-saving apparatus and breeches buoys, but they remained dependent on the assistance of the coastguard for their effectiveness. These were the forerunners of the modern auxiliary service. A rocket company consisted of twenty-five men known as volunteers; they could not be members of the lifeboat service as both units could be called out at the same time. The volunteers assisted the coastguards, and they held regular sessions to practise firing rockets and setting up breeches buoys. Next to the lifeboat, the rocket is now the most important means of saving lives from shipwrecks.

During WWII, the coastguard provided telegraphy training for the Admiralty as well as coast-watching duties. After WWI, the coastguard had taken over responsibility for all rocket equipment and become the unit we know today; at the same time, they had ceased to be part of the armed services. Subsequently, full-time coastguards were assisted by auxiliaries drawn from local communities.

Today, HM Coastguard is responsible for the initiation and coordination of civil maritime search and rescue within the UK maritime search and rescue region. This includes the mobilisation, organisation, and tasking of adequate resources to respond to persons either in distress at sea or at risk of injury or death on the cliffs and shorelines of the UK. The Coastguard Act of 1925 had conferred on the coastguard the above responsibilities, which also included all life-saving activities (including the RNLI) and the training and inspection of all life-saving companies.

Barmouth Coastguard Station is part of the Holyhead district, which covers an area extending from the Dee estuary in the north-east of Wales to Friog in Cardigan Bay. It has five substations located within it: Aberdaron, Abersoch, Criccieth, Harlech, and Barmouth.

An interesting 'WRECK SERVICES' document has come to light; it records an incident on 22 November 1944 when a ship ran aground near Dyffryn. The report, by a member of the life-saving apparatus crew (LSA) (unfortunately none of the volunteers' names are given), describes their work in saving lives and the conditions under which they had to manipulate the heavy gear and ropes to the scene of the shipwreck.

Wreck Report
22 Nov. 1944

A message was received by telephone at the Barmouth lookout from the District Officer, Caernarfon at 13.52 on 22/11/44 to assemble the LSA crew and proceed to an unknown vessel reported aground, half mile off shore near Dyffryn Lookout.

Mr J. A. Davies was contacted by telephone and requested to proceed at once in his motor lorry to the LSA House on the Quay. Most of the LSA crew were out of town, only five members could be mustered, the help of five volunteers was accepted to make the crew a workable number. The crew were assembled by 14.20, owing to the delay of the motor lorry the company did not leave Barmouth until 14.45. The fringe of the sand dunes at Dyffryn was reached at 15.29, from this point a half a mile of sand dunes had to be traversed to reach the beach, which necessitated the hand transportation of the gear to the beach, which took some considerable time. The rocket machine was in position and ready to be fired at 16.05 when the District Officer arrived, he then took charge of the proceedings. At this time the visibility was 200 yards the wind SW5 with continuous rain and the tide about 3 hours ebb.

The District Officer decided to use the rocket pistol in preference to the Rocket. The pistol was fired by the District Officer and was the means of getting the line aboard with the first shot fired.

The whips were soon hauled abroad and the breeches buoy made fast using the 'B method'.

The crew of six men were hauled ashore without mishaps by 16.45. The LSA Company then stood by awaiting further instructions.

The District Officer instructed the company to cast off and stow the gear, this took a considerable time, due to the state of the gear and the continuous rain, the half mile of sand dunes had to be traversed again, with the gear half as heavy again due to being wet, had to be hand transported back to the lorry. At 18.30 the gear was stowed, the LSA Company together with the six survivors were transported to Barmouth arriving at 19.15. All the company were wet through but well satisfied with the results obtained.

The vessel was the Motor Vessel Green Finch, an Admiralty Mine Layer.

HMS *Green Finch* was the former French tug *Lama*. This was seized in 1940 and renamed *Green Finch* and was used as an observation minelayer during WWII; she was returned to her owners in 1945.

Any person conversant with the sand dunes at Dyffryn will know how precarious these are, and having to carry heavy equipment through the loose, shifting sand in atrocious weather deserves some recognition. Normally, the equipment and ropes would have been on a handcart, and one can only assume that, owing to the terrain, it would have been impossible to manipulate a cart over the undulating sand dunes and that they therefore had to be manhandled.

The auxiliary officer in charge at Barmouth Station during and after this period was Mr Robert Henry Williams, better known as Bob Henri. He received the British Empire Medal (BEM) in the King's honours list in 1946. The *Barmouth Advertiser* stated that he had been complimented for his efficiency and had been the recipient of many messages of tribute for his bravery. An amusing story appears in the *Coastguard's Cutter*:

Some rescue operations do not receive the gratitude from the victims which they deserve. Mr R. Williams of Barmouth rushed into the sea to rescue a woman who was drowning. He pulled her out on to the beach, where she lay unconscious. Attempts to revive her were unsuccessful, so he gave her the 'kiss of life'. She quickly recovered, but instead of thanking him for rescuing her, she smartly slapped his face!

Phyllis's Café, Barmouth

Plas Mynach – The ATS of 164 OCTU

Red Duster

It isn't just a flag to us but part of who we are,
It flew astern from every ship we sailed.
From Liverpool to Singapore and through the Panama
It filled us with a pride which never failed.
Sometimes tattered, sometimes torn, raised each day at morning's dawn,
It told the world of who we are and where.
And across the seven oceans it weathered every storm
To keep our country strong, and firm, and fair.
It flew not just in peacetime but bravely went to war
Where the conflict raged across a flaming sea,
And it shrouds our fallen shipmates upon the ocean floor
Who gave their lives to keep our nation free.
No politician's pen stroke can take away the pride
That wells within to see that flag unfurled
And they'll not besmirch the memory of all those who have died
In every ocean on our fragile world.
Our flag must stay until the day we have no ships to sail
And the piper sadly wails the last lament,
And we'll leave it then to history to tell the famous tale
Of a flag which flew so proud where ere it went.
So join the battle, show no fear, let our banner fly,
Let it sail through stormy waters and grace the morning sky.
And when we all must heed the call to make the final muster,
One last request, please let us rest, beneath the old Red Duster.

David Partridge, NSW/ACT Branch (Vindi Boy, 1956)

Penrhyndeudraeth Gwaith Powdwr / Cooke's Explosives

FOR GOOD OR bad, the explosives factory at Penrhyn was established nearly 150 years ago, the little hill overlooking the Dwyryd estuary being deemed to be the ideal place to produce explosives. The first account we have is that it was established in 1865 and was called the Patent Safety Guncotton Company. It was duly licensed in 1876 and became part of New Explosive Company Ltd. In 1908, the factory became the Steelite Explosive Company manufacturing patent 'Steelite' explosives.

In 1845, a German chemist had discovered that by mixing cotton with various acids he could produce guncotton, which could be used for military purposes and as a propellant for cannons. It could also be used for blasting but was a dangerous substance.

In 1872, an explosion at a guncotton factory in Stowmarket killed two of its principals and thirty other workmen and injured about ninety others. It had been assumed that guncotton was dormant and safe until it was fired, but it seemed that the heat in the atmosphere had ignited it. Guncotton was later superseded as an explosive, but it is said that the Syrian rebels of today have gone back to basics and are making and using guncotton for use in their fight against the authorities. It is very likely that guncotton made at Penrhyn was used in campaigns during both the first and second Boer Wars (1880–1 and 1899–1902).

During WWI, the Penrhyn factory suffered a massive explosion. It was subsequently taken over by the Ministry of Munitions and became known as His Majesty's Factory, Penrhyndeudraeth. In 1926, a Mr R. T. Cooke purchased the factory; he was already the owner of the Miner's Safety Explosive Co. and had been associated with the explosives industry since 1902. He combined the work of both companies but did not officially amalgamate them. They produced explosives for the coal-mining and slate-quarrying industries under the new name of Cooke's Explosives Company Ltd.

The factory covered twenty-eight hectares of land and, when in operation, a no building zone was created around the perimeter of the factory area.

To transport the explosives, a small ship – the SS *Florence Cooke* – was built to the company's specifications at South Shields. She was based at Porthmadog and registered in Sunderland, the company's address being given as Maiden Law, County Durham. She carried raw materials and general cargo to Porthmadog and took the firm's finished products from Penrhyn to the Tyne; she was also able to carry a few passengers on board. At the beginning of the war, the Admiralty commandeered her and she served as an ammunition ship in Milford Haven and Scapa Flow and also took part in the Normandy landings. She was released by the Admiralty in 1945 and returned to port, where in 1959 she was sold as surplus to requirements. By then, road transport was more convenient and quicker. A fleet of trucks built to order was obtained, and these were painted a distinguished chocolate-brown colour so they could be easily recognised and avoided.

The natural topography of the three parallel valleys was deemed an ideal site for the factory buildings, with the natural slope of one of the valleys allowing the nitroglycerine mixture to be moved by gravity – a safer method than pumping and one which minimised the risk of ignition. The factory manufactured a variety of explosives including guncotton, nitroglycerine, picric acid and trinitrotoluene, as well as detonators and numerous patented mining explosives.

An ARP report from the mid 1940s states that just over 500 personnel were employed at Cooke's Explosives: 150 men and 100 women and, in the Miner's Safety Explosives, 121 men and 116 women with 18 staff members. At that time, the factory worked two shifts, but later it was said that there were three shifts worked in a full day, the shifts being based on the locality one came from: Porthmadog, Blaenau Ffestiniog, Barmouth etc. Locals from the Penrhyn area worked their own shifts. The ARP report makes interesting reading, covering the staff safety requirements which had to be attended to. For the shelter, it was stipulated that there should be seating, lights, a lavatory, accommodation, gas-proof curtains, drinking water, picks and shovels, and emergency exits. It was a requirement that all workers knew which shelter to go to on hearing an air raid warning – which was considered very likely – and preparations were made to safeguard everybody.

Instructions were given that all personnel had to carry a gas mask at all times. The risk of bombing was very high. A train driver (Edwin Lloyd) has recounted his experience of being on a goods train transporting explosive material from Cooke's at Penrhyn. They had stopped at Drws y Nant Signal Box, Dolgellau, for a break and a cup of tea when a German plane came over and dropped bombs ahead of them – had they not stopped, the train would have been in their path. In a way, it's surprising that targets such as the explosives factory at Penrhyn, Barmouth Bridge, the Britannia Bridge, the Menai Suspension Bridge, the Conwy Bridge, and the Cwm Prysor Viaduct near Trawsfynydd were not targeted. The destruction of such structures would have caused chaos to both the civilian population and the military. It is said that Cooke's during WWII produced 5,000 tons of military explosives per year as well as filling 17 million grenades.

After the war, Cooke's returned to normal peacetime business and continued to develop new, safe industrial explosives with the National Coal Board, which required 'permitted explosives' suitable for use in gas-filled coal mines. Other factories had failed to produce this type of explosive, and the success of the Penrhyn Works was commemorated in the explosives named Penobel 1 and Penobel 2, which acquired their name from a combination of the words 'Penrhyn' and 'Nobel'. A later feature of the site was a ballistic pendulum, which was erected in 1980 to gauge the strength of these permitted explosives.

Production of explosives peaked in 1970, when some 9,000 tons of explosives were produced annually. Penrhyn was considered the most sophisticated operation of its kind in the world, but work finally ceased in 1995 following a decline in demand for nitroglycerine-based explosives. After it had been decontaminated and decommissioned, the area was given to the North Wales Wildlife Trust by Imperial Chemical Industries (ICI). Today, the factory site has been transformed, and it is well worth a visit to explore its heritage and the wildlife of the area.

After the war, Cooke's used the underground caverns at the disused Croesor Slate Quarry as a storage facility for their explosives, and later ICI bought the quarry. After the Central Electricity Generating Board (CEGB) had finalised their plans for the pumped storage scheme at Tanygrisiau, it was realised that the Croesor Slate Quarry would be in close proximity to the Stwlan Dam and that a vast amount of explosives were still stored there! If some event was to ignite the explosives, that would be the end of the Stwlan Dam and other ancillary buildings in the scheme, so the explosives had to be moved from the quarry. It was said that they were taken out to sea and dumped, this being deemed the best way to dispose of them.

With the increase of production in various ordnance factories, the authorities had a problem of storage. Explosives by their very nature had to be kept in a safe and secured environment and be generally stored at a constant temperature. It was also necessary to keep them safe from human and animal intervention.

201

Old and disused mines/caverns were adopted throughout the country. In Merioneth, two such facilities were utilised, the first of these being Hendre Ddu Quarry in Aberangell near Machynlleth. This was owned by a Mr T. O. Williams when it was taken over. Its isolated position made it an ideal site for the safekeeping of ordnance. The access to the quarry was modified in 1941. Previously, there had been a tramway running most of the way from the quarry to the local Aberangell Railway Station, but this was scrapped, and a new road, capable of taking vehicles, was put in place. It is not known what ordnance was stored at the quarry nor how they were stored. According to Mr Edwin Williams, the grandson of the then owner, two local nightwatchmen with Alsatian dogs patrolled the area. He remembers the names of the dogs as Letan and Diane.

It is not known what surveillance there was during the day or whether the army had any presence on the site, but one has to assume that, given the dangerous nature of the substances being stored, security would have been tight. It is understood that the munitions continued to be stored at the quarry for quite a period after the war.

The other mine taken over was the Llanfair Slate Quarry near Harlech, which is situated on land belonging to Cae Gethin farm. This quarry had ceased production in 1906, but the chambers were still intact and its tramway to the various chambers still in place. Five chambers were used, and platforms or stages were built in them to accommodate the ordnance; it was said that 2,000 tons of TNT explosives were stored there. They came in wooden boxes, the TNT wrapped in an oily type of paper. A goods train offloaded these cases at the nearby railway station at Pensarn, and then they were conveyed in trucks, by road, to the quarry. A similar process, in reverse, took place when explosives were sent from there. Security was similar to the Hendre Ddu Quarry, with watchmen and Alsatian guard dogs being used. The present owners of the quarry – Mr & Mrs R. Owen – have created a tourist attraction out of the old mine and farm.

By a strange coincidence, T. O. Williams of Hendre Ddu was the father of Mr G. O. Williams of Blaenau Ffestiniog, who took the Ministry of Defence (MOD) to court in order to regain possession of the Manod Slate Quarry. Another son, Mr W. O. Williams of Harlech, cleared the Llanfair quarry of all the tramway and ancillary objects after the war.

It is not known if the Penrhyn 'Gwaith Powdwr' supplied any of these caverns with its material, but we have a report of a train driver taking explosive materials on a train to England. It has to be asked how safe these caverns were with their lethal ordnance stored in them. Were the public even aware of the risk of them exploding?

An incident in November 1944, when an underground munitions storage depot exploded at RAF Fauld near Burton-upon-Trent, provides an indication of how dangerous such sites could be. The explosion, which killed around seventy people and 200 head of cattle, obliterated 450,000 cubic metres of water in a storage reservoir and left a crater some 100 feet deep and 250 yards across. A subsequent inquiry blamed lack of supervision and safety rules, and it was thought that the explosion occurred when a person used the incorrect implements to remove a detonator, causing a spark which ignited the dump.

No wonder the Central Electricity Generating Board panicked when informed that the Croesor Caverns, adjoining their pump storage scheme, were full of explosives!

Harlech Anti-Tank Artillery Camp & The Harlech Military Railway

OF ALL THE military camps and installations in the area, Harlech Camp is the one with the least information available about it. Moreover, what is available is mostly hearsay. Local people seem to have had very little contact with the camp or knowledge of its existence. During the war, a spur ran from the GWR main line just north of Harlech Station and proceeded towards the Morfa crossing over the A496 road. Today there is absolutely no trace left of the line or route, and to the younger generation it may seem incredible that such a line existed at all.

The camp was built in 1941 by Messrs John Mowlem and Co., civil engineering contractors from London who also built the Llanbedr Air Force Camp and adapted the caverns at Bwlch y Slaters Quarry, Blaenau Ffestiniog, ready for the National Art Gallery.

The military had two sites at lower Harlech, the main camp was situated near Pen-y-Waen, about two miles north of Harlech, where the Gwynedd County Council now has its recycling plant. There is a plan of the camp layout, and it seems quite large, but neither the number of permanent staff based there or the visiting troop compliment can be ascertained – nor, indeed, what other facilities were available there. It had a link with Trawsfynydd Artillery Camp, though it is not known whether the officers based at Harlech lived there or at the main camp in Trawsfynydd, or where the camp administration was based.

Those based there or who were there on courses made very little reference to the camp; one can only surmise that to a large extent it was run as a transit camp. The intakes were there for six weeks' training on the range before returning to their regiments fully trained in the art of anti-tank artillery warfare.

These kinds of camps were not very popular with the troops, which might explain the lack of information about them – for the troops, the sooner they left the better! Being so far away from any large towns and facilities, which they had come accustomed to in other areas, they looked forward to moving on. The nearest pub was two miles away, and at the time the area was very isolated apart from a few farms and private dwellings dotted here and there.

The area was developed after the war, and it is not known in what condition the Morfa Road was at that time, or whether it was just a track that the military had widened. The road is now referred to as Ffordd Newydd (New Road).

The land for the camp and artillery range had been commandeered by the military from its then owner, Lord Harlech. At the end of hostilities, he sold the land to the Deudraeth Rural District Council at an agricultural land price, with the proviso that if the land was not used for development by the council then Lord Harlech could rebuy it – but more on this later.

The anti-tank artillery range was located about a mile and a half to the south of the camp; its purpose was to train troops in anti-tank warfare. A railway track was laid from the main GWR railway from a point near the level crossing (close to the farm buildings of Cerrig y Gwaenydd). The track then went at right angles to the main line, entering Morfa Road slightly to the north of Morfa Garage. It continued across the road (the A496) to what is now the entrance to the Glan Gors housing estate. It then joined another track, which had its own locomotives used to tow mock targets for the gunners. This track extended as far as the perimeter of the Harlech Golf Course.

Every infantry regiment seemed to have their own platoons of anti-tank gunners; they had to be well trained and Harlech was one of the few places which could accommodate them.

There is a report of the 1st Battalion Welsh Guards sending a couple of platoons to Harlech in 1943 for six weeks' training. Another report dated 17 June 1943 describes a brigade commander of the 70th Infantry Brigade, as listed in their war diaries, visiting the Harlech Range whilst platoons

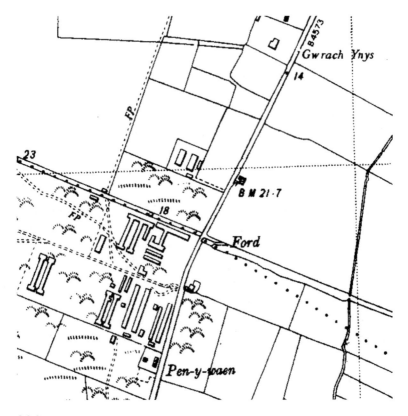

from his regiment were being trained. He was very pleased with the improvement shown in the results, especially as one platoon had achieved a 66% success rate in hitting the targets. In fact, their anti-tank platoons proceeded again to Harlech for a further three days' training in July of that year.

It is said that no single area of infantry firepower saw greater change and improvement during the Second World War than those relating to anti-tank warfare.

Another report stated that the Royal Artillery Training Camp was used by the 75th Anti-Tank Regiment prior to them going to Cairo to join the 8th Army. A recruit recounts his experience after his initial training. He was posted to the Royal Artillery and trained on two-pound anti-tank guns and later six pounders. After six weeks, he was posted to a camp in Scotland to fire the heavy guns and subsequently completed his training at Harlech before being posted overseas.

It has to be stated that the anti-tank training facilities at Harlech played a major part in the training of all anti-tank gunners and to their ultimate success in destroying enemy tanks.

What made this range unique was the fact that its transportation system connected directly to the main railway line; very few, if any, other ranges had such a link. Tonfannau Camp had a railway halt near its entrance, and Llwyngwril Burma Camp had the rail track running virtually through the camp, but without connections. This poses the question why such a link was made at Harlech. The local station and sidings were roughly half a mile away from the range, and one possible reason is that the locomotives could use the water tank facilities which were sited near the station.

The accommodation camp became less important as the war progressed towards its end, and the camp was utilised to hold Italian prisoners of war who were guarded by the Royal Pioneer Corps.

On 27 December 1945, the local Member of Parliament Emrys Roberts asked the Secretary of State for War what would happen to the anti-tank range at Harlech. He received the response 'no decision as yet' in a written answer.

In 1948, the rail track link was removed – its traces are still visible – and the site was sold to the local council by Lord Harlech, who received the agricultural value for the land. It was stated as part of the transaction that if the council did not develop the sites then Lord Harlech could buy the land back. The council did not develop the site – in fact, they sold it to a developer at a much higher price. It was claimed that Lord Harlech was displeased with what had happened and tried to enforce his claim to rebuy the land but failed on legal grounds. However, part of the money from that deal, to the author's knowledge, was used to lay a water main from Gellilydan to the Bont Newydd area and to connect all the relevant farms and properties to a piped supply. The farmers had fought a long battle for this and had won. This was more or less the last act of the Deudraeth Rural District Council before it was absorbed into the new Merioneth District Council.

On 19 October 1949, the government introduced the Town and Country Planning Act. During a debate on the 'National Parks and Access to the Countryside Bill' in the House of Lords, Lord Harlech made quite an important speech condemning the attitude of the War Department with regards to their building requirements. Part of his speech is given below – we, the general public, should take note of his remarks and be more particular in scrutinising official decisions:

> I have been a Minister of Works and I well remember that of all the awful builders and architects the worst are those of the War Office Lands Department. As I once said in another speech in this House, if you go round Army barracks, from Chelsea to Aldershot – the Army's archetype and capital – you will find that they manage through the centuries to combine the maximum of uglification of architecture with the maximum of inconvenience and discomfort to the soldier. That is the long-standing tradition of the War Office Barracks Department and the War Office Lands Department. Why is this? It is because anybody who is any good as a sapper

gets command of an army corps, if he is no good he goes to the Barracks Department. And that Department will not brook any civilian assistance or advice.

In that respect the War Office is quite different from the Air Force, if you go to Cranwell or Sandhurst you will see the contrast. You will see it also in the Admiralty establishment. But wherever there is a trail of the War Office Lands Department and the War Office Barracks Department, you will find what I have described. Even in their temporary camps it is the same. During the war they had the whole of Morfa Harlech for an anti-tank range. Under pressure they have given up a proportion of it, but they retain some, and it is still a place of Nissen Huts. There seems to be no idea of making even the temporary camps blend into the countryside and be such as to give the Territorial who goes to train there a sense of amenity or decency. Of all Government Departments, the War Office is the one to be trusted the least to erect buildings in a national park. That is the Department that needs to be watched...[11]

---

[11]   Hansard.

Llanbedr, Merioneth

FROM BEING AN obscure village, Llanbedr gained prominence during the war as the home for an RAF aerodrome that changed the life of the locality entirely. At the beginning of the war, there was an enormous expansion of the RAF, and naturally more airfields were required. As a matter of policy, navigation and gunnery training schools were located in northern areas of Britain, where it was thought they would be comparatively safe. The old counties of north-west Wales came under close scrutiny for suitable sites, with seven locations eventually being chosen: Valley, Mona, Bodorgan/Aberffraw, Llandwrog/Caernarfon, Penrhos, Llanbedr, and Tywyn, the two last named being within our own area of Merioneth.

The author worked on the construction of the Llanbedr aerodrome, which created a lot of work for the locals, with the additional income generated being of benefit to the community. Fleets of buses from Blaenau Ffestiniog, Porthmadog and Barmouth carried workers to Llanbedr. Site No. 1 was the main administrative centre; it was on the edge of the village and had been part of the Hafod y Bryn land. The author recalls some of the workers: Evan Francis from Dyffryn, Roberts from Tremadog, Evans the Golf from Criccieth (he was also a part-time golf pro), Roberts the Joiner from Barmouth, and a Mr Meadows, who was the general foreman. Mr Robey, the cashier for Mowlem (the firm of London-based contractors), was the most important person on the site, which has now been developed as a holiday park.

Massive American Caterpillar earth movers removed all the sand dunes and flattened everywhere to create the runways; it was tragic to see the wild rabbits trying to scurry away from the machines before being engulfed by them, and hundreds were killed in this way.

The aerodrome became operational on 15 June 1941 under the control of Valley; both sites played a role in guarding the Irish Sea from enemy air operations and providing cover for convoys. The first aircraft to be housed at Llanbedr were six Ansons used for training, but they were quickly replaced by Spitfires of 74 Squadron and a little later of 131 Squadron. Llanbedr could claim to be host to other types of aircrafts too, including Lightnings, Mustangs, Thunderbolts and Typhoons. Lysanders were used in early 1943 by the United States Army Air Force's (USAAF) 2025th Gunnery Flight for bombing practice on targets off the nearby coast.

Llanbedr was also host to a training team for unmanned planes, and this work continued after the war. The team also worked closely with artillery regiments based in the area by flying their planes with drogues attached for anti-aircraft practice. There was one instance when a pilot radioed his base for them to tell the gunners to shoot at the target and not the plane, and also to let them know that he had a wife in Barmouth and he wanted to see her again!

An interesting artefact from the period still remains buried in the beach at Harlech and has been baptised the 'Maid of Harlech'. In September 1942, owing to engine trouble, the pilot of a Lockheed P38F Lightning made an emergency landing on the beach near Harlech, having failed to reach the runway at Llanbedr. The pilot, Lieutenant Robert Elliot, was able to walk away from the plane unscathed, and it has remained there buried in the sand ever since. The plane was on a training flight from an aerodrome in Shropshire, and the incident was witnessed, through the window of his home in Harlech, by Dr Gareth Williams, who was then a child.

An interesting Welsh character based at Llanbedr was Squadron Leader William Ross, a native of Abersoch. He joined the RAF in 1929 and trained as a wireless operator. He later saw service in Iraq, Palestine and India. Returning to the UK in 1936, he completed an observer course and two years later qualified as a pilot. In 1940, he took part in the Battle of Britain. He came to Llanbedr in 1942 for a tour of duty, which meant flying to meet USAAF B24s off the coast of Ireland and guiding them on the remainder of their flight to Valley Airfield. Another Welshman claimed the first kill for Llanbedr. Flight Lieutenant Roy Harries, a flight commander in 131 Squadron, shot down, in conjunction with another pilot, a JU88, which was seen to crash into the sea. Harries eventually became the top Welsh fighter pilot of the war, with an official score of twenty victories to his credit.

The village benefited from the influx of military personnel, and the local children were more than happy at being allowed to visit the camp cinema on a Saturday morning – this, indeed, was a luxury for them. The RAF also had a house on the Cwm Nantcol Road converted into a hospital. This was located about 500 yards away from the Victoria Hotel.

Llanbedr also had its own Royal Observer Corps; they were based on the little hill above the village. The names of two corps members have come to light: Mr John Jones (Llanbedr) and Mr William Davies (Pensarn). Along with others, it was they who manned the post. They had to learn to recognise and record any planes flying overhead during each twenty-four-hour period. Among their families, it became something of a parlour game to test their ability and knowledge with cards showing the various shapes and silhouettes of planes, which were designed to help them memorise and recognise the various makes and models.

Llanbedr Airfield closed in 2004 with the loss of 130 jobs; this was a heavy blow to the economy of the area. Various suggestions were made as to its future use, and the future of the site has become a long drawn-out battle. In August 2011, a certificate was granted to Llanbedr Airfield Estates for use of the airport to test and develop unmanned aerial vehicles. In 2012, permission was granted to turn the airfield into a yard for dismantling airliners, whilst in 2013 the Welsh government included the site within the Snowdon Enterprise Zone.

Paths to Glory

IT IS WITH pride that we talk about our mountains and how they guarded our valuable art treasures during the war. Unfortunately, during the same period, these same mountains were the cause of many tragic accidents, mostly to aircrew, who, for various reasons, were unable to recognise the dangers that these mountains held for them.

Statistics show that, between 1940 and 1945, over forty mainly British and Allied planes were lost in this region alone:

1940 – 3
1941 – 8
1942 – 8
1943 – 6
1944 – 12
1945 – 3

Most of the recorded crashes could be classified and accounted for in various categories, but as with all accidents, there were reasons for them. One obvious explanation is the height of the mountains in north Wales and the often poor visibility, with clouds obscuring the peaks. Coupled with low engine power (preventing planes from climbing out of trouble), accidents were bound to happen – and they did.

Some accidents were caused by inexperienced pilots, most of whom were extremely young. There were a few instances of them showing off with dire results. Some accidents were caused by pilots having difficulty in flying their damaged planes, problems with navigation, shortage of fuel, and crew injuries. But worst of all was the influence of Mother Nature, who could change flying conditions in the mountains within minutes. A few of the main crashes in our area, which may be of general interest, are listed below.

1940

- In September, a Dornier 215 was shot down by a Spitfire over Trawsfynydd. Despite the death of one of the crew – 26-year-old engineer Unteroffizer Gustav Pelzer – there was considerable satisfaction in the local community; it was, after all, an enemy plane. Pelzer was buried at Pwllheli, and was the first enemy combatant to be buried in north Wales. At the end of hostilities his body, was reinterred at the German War Cemetery in Cannock Chase, Staffordshire (Plot 7, Row 8, Grave 192).

1941

- On 26 September, a Supermarine Spitfire X4843 piloted by an Australian trainee pilot – Sergeant N. W. Mowat, RAAF – hit the peak of Aran Fawddwy, Bala. The wreckage was not located for two days. On impact, the pilot's body had been thrown thirty yards away from the wreckage. A subsequent court of enquiry established that the aircraft was fifty miles off course but was unable to explain why.
- Engine failure caused a plane to crash on a hillside in Llanbedr; all crew members survived.
- Late on 21 March, the reality of war came home to the community of Blaenau Ffestiniog, when a Wellington Bomber R3288 crashed on the Crimea Pass, killing all but one of the crew of six. Based at RAF Norton near Nottingham, it was scheduled to take part in a raid on the submarine base at Lorient, a port in the Bay of Biscay. When near the French coast, heavy clouds obscured the crew's vision and their radio malfunctioned; they lost contact with the rest of the flight and were unable to locate their target. The captain

decided to abort the operation and return to base, ditching their bombs in the Channel.

A Messerschmitt plane intercepted them. In the ensuing battle, the Wellington crew saw the enemy plane going down in a steep dive caused by the damage they had inflicted upon it. During the skirmish, the navigator had lost his bearings and was unable to set a course to their base. They had to rely on visual sightings, if and when available. To adopt the words of a popular American song by Harold Adamson and Jimmie McHugh, it was a case of: 'We can still carry on. Comin' in on a wing and a prayer.'

They tried to locate airfield beacons or any light to establish their position, but to no avail. The situation was getting serious: fuel was low, and they had to find a landing place urgently. Breaking through the cloud they saw a light below (it transpired later that the light was from the railway shunting yard at Blaenau Ffestiniog). Seeing the outline of a mountain in front of him, the pilot tried to gain height and make for a gap in the dark mass. In fact, what he saw was the peak at the top of the Crimea Pass – the northern ridge of Moel Farlwyd.

They almost made it, but luck was against them, and the aircraft disintegrated on impact with the rocks of Moel Farlwyd.

The police were informed of the incident at midnight. On attending the scene with the local GP, Dr J. W. Morris, and an ambulance crew, they could not find any survivors in the main part of the wreckage; they noticed that the rear gun turret was completely missing. On impact, the rear turret, complete with the tail gunner, had broken off completely from the main airframe and rolled away. The tail gunner was knocked unconscious and also sustained an injury to his leg. When he came to, he realised that he was a prisoner in the turret.

Rescuers located the turret some fifty feet away with the still dazed tail gunner trapped within. Recounting what had happened some time afterwards, the tail gunner – Sergeant Peter Martlew – remembered hearing a language that he did not recognise and thought that they must have crashed in France or Germany. What he had actually heard were the rescuers speaking Welsh. He proffered his gun to them as a token of surrender, but soon came to realise that he was in safe hands and back in the UK.

It took about three hours to get him to the local memorial hospital, where his injuries were confirmed as a fractured right leg and severe bruising. He remained at the hospital for six weeks, where he was treated as a VIP, receiving numerous local visitors. He was commissioned in 1943 and left the service in 1946 as a flight lieutenant.

- On the 26 June, two bodies were recovered from a German Junkers JU88 which had crashed into the sea in the Barmouth area.
- In August, a Wellington bomber R1068 crashed on Ffridd Rhosfarch above Pennal. All crew members perished. A memorial was erected to them at Pennal, which reads:

TO THE MEMORY OF SIX MEMBERS
OF THE R.A.F.
WHO DIED FOR FREEDOM WHEN THEIR
PLANE CRASHED ON "FFRIDD RHOSFARCH"
17 AUGUST. 1941.

P/O. GEORGE JOYCE MATHEWS.	OLVESTON. BRISTOL.
SGT. JAMES F.P. STUART.	ONTARIO. CANADA.
SGT. HERBERT GEORGE MOLE.	KEW. SURREY.
SGT. ALLAN JACKETS.	HULL.
SGT. JOHN FRANCIS MOORE.	LIMERICK. IRELAND.
SGT. GEORGE HEWISON.	NEWCASTLE-ON-TYNE.

Faithful unto death

1942

- On 28 May, prior to being shipped out to the Middle East, Wellington Mk. 1C, HX433 of No. 1443 (Ferry) Flight based at RAF Harwell near Didcot was carrying out a fuel consumption flight when it crashed into the north-east face of Mynydd Moel (2831 ft) near Dolgellau killing all six crew members. Weather conditions were given as good, with cloud cover of between 4 and 7/8ths cloud. The court of enquiry later heard that the aircraft was some 20° off course when it flew into the mountain, and the crew may have become disorientated in the clouds.

- On 9 August, the pilot of an RAF Hawker Hurricane was killed when his plane crashed on Allt y Ceffylau, between Cwmorthin Quarry and Plas Cwmorthin, Tanygrisiau, Blaenau Ffestiniog.

- On 22 October, three Spitfires from RAF Llanbedr were on a formation flying practice flight. They were reported 'as overdue at base', and the Aberdyfi Home Guard was asked for information on any sightings of the aircraft. An extensive but unsuccessful search was carried out, and it was thought that all three aircraft had crashed into the sea. Two days later, a local farmer reported seeing wreckage. Apparently, the Spitfires had encountered thick cloud, and before they could climb out of it, they struck the western slopes of Tarrenhendre Mountain above Dolgoch Ravine, Pennal.

1943

- On 19 November, a Wellington Bomber LB185 was on a training flight from a coastal command unit based at Withybush near Hereford. With a crew of two pilots, a navigator, a front gunner, and two rear gunners/wireless operators, it crashed on a rocky outcrop on the summit of Moel y Croesau (1500 ft) in the Cwm Prysor region near Trawsfynydd.

  The flight had followed a routine pattern until their radio

failed and thick fog was encountered. After a six-hour flight, and with their fuel supply running low, they reduced height to try and visually locate their position. Within minutes, the Wellington hit the summit of Moel y Croesau. Whether they were on their correct course or had become totally disorientated by the fog is not known.

Four of the crew died on impact, and the rear turret was catapulted from the main fuselage landing about a hundred yards away. Its occupant, Sergeant Alex Sinclair, survived and was able to extricate himself. He walked to the main body of the wreckage and saw his dead colleagues. He heard a shout and saw that his co-gunner had been thrown out and was buried deep in a peat bog unable to move. Sinclair, though he had no idea where he was, informed him that he was going to get help.

He wandered aimlessly in the darkness and eventually came across a fence. Following it, he came to a rough track leading to an empty building where he rested for a while. He then resumed walking along the track until he reached Bwlch Gwyn Farm at 7 a.m., some four and a half hours after the crash.

The occupants, Mr and Mrs Roberts, were amazed to hear a feeble knock at the kitchen door and were a bit hesitant in answering. They were shocked to see an injured airman standing in the doorway seeking help. Mr Roberts quickly made his way to report the crash and to seek assistance at the Royal Observer Corps post near Trawsfynydd Railway Station. The military at the nearby artillery camp were informed, and a medical officer came out to give Sinclair first aid. The mountain rescue team at Llandwrog attended to the needs of the other gunner, who had a fractured spine. Both were taken to the Royal Naval sick quarters at Pwllheli, where Sergeant Sinclair was treated for internal injuries sustained from the battering received in the fall of the turret.

In 1964, Alex Sinclair returned to Trawsfynydd to thank

the Roberts family for their help and also to show his respect to his comrades at the crash site.

- On 26 December, an Avro Anson Mk. 1, EF953, Flight Training Command, No. 9 Observers Advanced Flying Unit flying from its base at RAF Llandwrog, Caernarfon, flew into Bwlch y Llan near Barmouth in low cloud, killing all four crew members. A shepherd, Goronwy Owen of Gellfechan farm, had the onerous job of carting the bodies down to the town.

- On 31 December, a Wellington Bomber Mk.1C, X9666 crashed in low cloud on the high ground above Trefri Fach Farm, two miles from Aberdyfi. Three of the five-man crew survived.

1944

- On 9 February, an RAF Mosquito crashed near the summit of Aran Fawddwy, Dolgellau; there were no survivors. A memorial was erected at Rhydymain to commemorate the incident. A wrecked aero engine forms the salient part of the monument and records the names of the airmen who were killed: Flight Lieutenant P. Riches, DFC and Flight Officer M.O. Slonsky.

- During their stay at RAF Llanbedr in 1943–4, the American Air Force lost at least six aircraft as a result of crashes which had occurred in the immediate area.

- On 8 July, a Boeing B17G Flying Fortress of the 569th Bomb Squadron based at Framlingham, Suffolk, made a forced landing at Morfa Airfield, Tywyn. The plane with fifteen crew members was returning from North Africa and during the flight had veered off course and was short of fuel. The crew had hoped to land at RAF Llanbedr, where the runway was able to accommodate them, but unfortunately they had to land at Morfa knowing that its runway fell short of the B17's requirements. The plane touched down and continued ahead to the end of the runway, overshooting and coming to rest near the railway line with its tail perched over a brick building. An engine caught fire, damaging a wing and destroying the aircraft.

The pilot deserved praise for his superb handling of the plane landing without any casualties. School children from the Corris area who attended Tywyn Grammar School related how they had heard about the crash and hurried to the scene. Though the plane was under military guard, they managed to collect souvenirs from it.

1945

- On 6 February, a Lancaster Bomber Mk3, NE132 crashed on Rhinog Fawr east of Harlech killing all seven crew members.
- Following the end of hostilities in Europe, the Americans began to return home, some to leave the forces, others to wait and retrain for the conflict with Japan. Most of the troops were taken home by sea, but some Air Force personnel were able to return by plane. On 8 June 1945, a B-17G Flying Fortress 44-8639 of the 511th Bomb Squadron, 355th Bombardment Group, was flying from Polebrooke, Northants, to the States via RAF Valley, Anglesey.

With a crew of ten and ten other air force personnel on board, they approached Valley in poor visibility. The crew requested a course which RAF Valley transmitted to them. For some unknown reason, the aircraft flew on a reciprocal course (the correct course but in the wrong direction) which took them inland towards Dolgellau. Later, the crew realised their error and began to turn to starboard in order to head seawards. Before they could complete their turn, the aircraft struck high ground close to the summit of Craig Cwm Llwyd on the southern side of the Mawddach Estuary, almost directly opposite Barmouth Harbour. The plane careered along the crags for over a hundred yards before finally coming to rest. Those not killed on impact were engulfed in the ensuing fire, and there were no survivors.

Eyewitness

Ken Jeffs BEM, a past coxswain of the Barmouth Lifeboat, recounted his memories of the crash on 8 June 1945, which he witnessed as a 14-year-old lad while playing on the beach opposite the Sailors' Institute in Barmouth. Ken had come from school and, as was his custom, had visited the quay to inspect the boats before going home. On this early June evening, the estuary was covered in very heavy mist and visibility was virtually nil.

Whilst mooching about, he heard the drone of an unseen, unidentified heavy aircraft circulating in a clockwise fashion over the estuary. He stared into the mist but to no avail; all he could hear was the continuous drone of the plane engines, which suddenly stopped. He realised that the plane must have crashed into the mountain on the Arthog side of the estuary.

Ken, full of bravado and eagerness to see the accident site, ran across the Barmouth Bridge and made his way to the scene. He was not the first person there; a local farmer, Robert Ieuan Lloyd, had already reached the site. What they saw was a mass of metal still burning fiercely. The plane's engines had rolled down the slope demolishing stone walls in their path. Edwin Lloyd was helping his uncle on the farm and recalled the crash:

> On that day there was quite a thick low mist. We heard the
> drone of a plane and eventually saw it; it seemed to travel very
> slowly and we could easily see the identification numbers on its
> side. Moments later we heard the crash and it was a frightening
> experience. I immediately made my way down to Arthog to raise
> the alarm and notify the authorities.

In the *Cambrian News* of 9 May 1995, Robert Lloyd recalls that he was working on the farm when he saw the plane travelling towards the mountain and he realised that it was not going to clear it. He heard the explosion and saw what can only be described as a river of fire flowing down the slope. During another explosion, he saw what he thought was someone being thrown from the plane, but in reality it was part of an engine.

There was nothing they could do. Little did they realise that twenty American airmen had perished in that blazing inferno. Later, a party of American officers visited the site to prepare a report on the crash.

The Sequel

In 1994 – forty-nine years later – Mrs Muriel Andrews and her son Richard, on holiday from Cambridge, were staying at the Wavecrest Hotel, Barmouth. After their evening meal, they took a stroll towards the harbour, as was their usual practice during their stay. Whilst enjoying the walk along the promontory (or, to be correct, the new embankment leading to Ynys y Brawd), their view suddenly changed. Both saw something descend from the sky until it was a little above house height, then cross the river and disappear behind trees on the southern, Arthog side of the estuary. The 'something' appeared to be very large, was grey and silent, and was also a very, very eerie sight.

Mrs Muriel Andrews subsequently wrote:

> It reminded me of an old grey bomber coming in to land as it disappeared as silently and suddenly as it had appeared. It was a thundery evening with an electric feel to the atmosphere with a high cloud cover, but this was definitely not a cloud.

One could not blame readers for taking this account with a pinch of salt. Mrs Andrews could well have hallucinated or misinterpreted a natural phenomenon, but for both her and her son to do so simultaneously, on the same subject, and to see the same thing, is a different matter altogether. Phenomena of this kind are not unique, but they lie beyond the realms of explanation or verification.

The author remembers the 'incident' well. By a strange coincidence, he and his wife Gwyneth were celebrating an anniversary with a family dinner party that summer and had asked Mr and Mrs Eric Jarman, proprietors of the Wavecrest Hotel, for a suitable menu. One morning, Mrs Sheila Jarman called and said that she was making a special dinner that evening for a guest and that beef Wellington was on the menu. Would we like to join the guest to see if it was acceptable for our party?

It was Eric Jarman who related to me the events that had 'upset' the Andrews, and this gave me the opportunity to meet them and hear of their extraordinary experience the previous evening. They recounted to me what they had seen; it was remarkable that both of them had seen the 'aberration'. Mrs Muriel Andrews remembered seeing similar planes during the war around her home in Cambridge. As the object glided on towards Arthog, Muriel had broken the silence, shouting, 'They are going to crash.'

I found them still in shock and perplexed about the incident; they were ordinary, solid, down-to-earth people and not ones who might be inclined towards publicity seeking. They asked if I knew of any airplane crashes in the area. I had a vague knowledge that an American plane had crashed just after the end of the war on the southern side of the estuary, but did not at the time know much about the incident except that it had flown in from Cambridge. They were not to know then that they had witnessed a scene which had happened at approximately the same time forty-nine years earlier.

They returned to the hotel, where both Sheila and Eric Jarman noticed that they were in a nervous and fraught condition; Muriel's arms were covered in goose pimples. Eventually they were able to recount to the Jarmans what they had seen.

Mathew Rimmer, a 15-year-old local youth, had explored and researched the site and had obtained the details of all on board the plane. He was intrigued when he heard about the Andrews's experience and contacted them for further information.

Mathew was subsequently instrumental in placing a memorial plaque on the site naming all who had perished. The stainless steel plaque depicting an engraving of a Flying Fortress was mounted on a nearby stone wall, in the place where it had been demolished by one of the engines rolling down the hill from the crash site. The plaque was designed and provided by Avesta Steel, Sheffield, and the chairman of Gwent County Council, Councillor Jim Kirkwood, who had established links between the company and the Rimmer family. A piece of debris on site has written on it: 'Twenty men died here. Please show Respect by Taking away Nothing But Memories.'

A dedication service was held on the 50th anniversary of the crash, attended by the Rimmer family, a representative of the American Air Force from RAF Valley, a British Legion padre, a bugler (Phyllip Pryce), and Bob Crabbe, who is the standard bearer of the Barmouth British Legion.

In 1996, Mathew Rimmer took the Andrews family to the site to see the plaque. In her account of the visit, Muriel stated:

> To those of us who lived during and experienced the war, it all seems like yesterday. With sheep grazing peacefully nearby and a lark singing it was difficult to imagine a scene of violence, fire, and sudden death, but this simple memorial to 20 young men who died on a lonely Welsh mountainside on their way home to their loved ones will serve as a reminder to so many of such sadness that should never be forgotten.

Even in 2014, the crash scar on the mountainside is still visible, a reminder to us all of the sacrifice these brave men made in giving of their lives for our freedom.

Lest we Forget.

Bevin Boys

THE BEVIN BOYS were young men conscripted from all over the UK to join the armed forces but who, after registering for military service, found that they had been directed to work in the mines. Between December 1943 and 1948, some 48,000 of all men conscripted were deployed on such work as Britain was desperate for coal to fuel vital wartime industries. As it was impossible to import coal, a greater number of miners were needed, not only to meet the increased demand but also to replace experienced miners who were serving their country.

The Bevin Boys were named after Ernest Bevin, the wartime Minister for Labour and National Service, who had the idea to conscript workers into the mines. None of the conscripts knew why they had been selected for the pits rather than the services, though the selection was said to be impartial and carried out by an independent body. Some said that weekly draws were undertaken by one of Bevin's secretaries. Ten digits (0 to 9) were placed in a hat, and the digit drawn. All conscripts with a National Insurance number ending in that digit were then directed to the mines unless they were highly skilled or were deemed to be physically unfit for mining. In announcing the scheme, Bevin made the following comment:

> We need 720,000 men continuously employed in this industry. This is where you boys come in. Our fighting men will not be able to achieve their purpose unless we get an adequate supply of coal.

Be that as it may, many believed that the Bevin Boys

comprised left-handed men, who 'could not fire a Lee Enfield .303 rifle', and those who were flat-footed; in both cases, it was said, there was a tendency to say 'send them to the mines'. Whether this is true or not is unknown, but it made the chosen conscripts feel like second-class citizens. They felt that having offered to 'fight for their country', their selection to be miners made them feel undervalued.

The Bevin Boys were first given six weeks of training (four off-site, two on) before working in the mines. The work was typical coal mining, largely a mile or more down in dark, dank tunnels. Conscripts were supplied with helmets and steel-capped safety boots; although 'conscripted', the Bevin Boys were not issued with uniform and generally they wore the oldest clothes they could find. Many had to suffer unwarranted taunts that they were avoiding conscription, which was then mandatory for all young men in Britain. As many 'conscientious objectors' were also directed to work in the mines, the Bevin Boys were regularly stopped by the police checking to see whether they were avoiding conscription.

The programme was wound up in 1948, but unfortunately the Bevin Boys did not enjoy the rights given to others who had served in the armed forces, most notably the right to rejoin the jobs they had left on being called up. The Boys were not recipients of any honour or decoration for the valuable service they had given to 'King and Country', in spite of Winston Churchill's promise that 'the miners would be able to stand as equals with the fighter pilots, merchant navy and the soldiers for recognition of their efforts' – gallant but empty words!

It was not until 1995 that their contribution was fully recognised in a speech by Queen Elizabeth, some fifty years after VE Day. The conscripted miners had to wait until 2008 to be honoured with an official badge from the government.

Recently, a memorial to the Bevin Boys was unveiled at the National Arboretum at Alrewas, Staffordshire, by the Countess of Wessex.

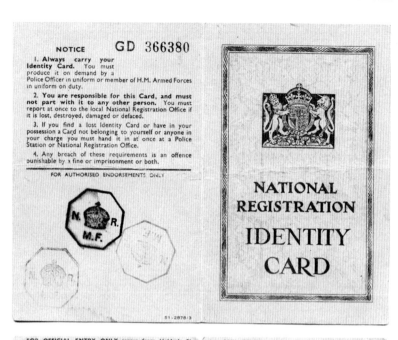

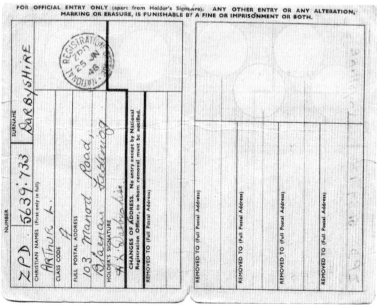

Identity Cards had to be carried at all times. Shown here, the card that was issued to the author after his demobilisation from the Navy.

"Nid wyf yn rhy hen— oni ddylwn tybed?"

Teimla llawer o ddynion ar ol ymneilltuo nad oes bellach alw am danynt. *Dyna gamgymeriad.* Y mae gan Brydain orchwyl ar gyfer pob dyn iach a chryf yn y gweithfeydd mawrion er mwyn creu MWY o ddrylliau, MWY o danciau, MWY o eroplenau, MWY o longau. Nid yw o bwys a oes ganddo brofiad blaenorol mewn gweithfa. Trefnwyd i roddi hyfforddiant i bob un—ac y mae'r tal yn dda.

Ewch, ysgrifennwch neu gofynnwch ar y teliffon am gyfle i drafod y pwnc yn Swyddfa Leol y Weinyddiaeth Lafur a Gwasanaeth Cenedlaethol, a gosodwch eich enw ar y rhestr am waith a ddyry i'n bechgyn yr Arfau at ymosod ac at sicrhau buddugoliaeth bendant.

Eich Dyledswydd YN AWR yw

ISSUED BY THE MINISTRY OF LABOUR AND NATIONAL SERVICE

"I am not too old – perhaps I should?"

This is a poster by the Ministry of Labour asking for retired men to consider going back into industry to help increase the production of munitions and armaments etc.

Your duty now is war work

Defensively Equipped Merchant Ships (DEMS)

OVER THE YEARS, very little publicity has been given to those from the navy and army who served as gunners on defensively equipped merchant ships (DEMS). The first gunnery training course took place to train the officers of merchant ships in 1939, and it was in that year also that the Admiralty established the DEMS organisation.

The armaments fitted to merchant ships varied, but there was usually a 4-inch deck gun at the stern (depending on the size of the vessel) and a 13-pounder gun (3-inch shell) usually at the bow, mounted so it could be used against U-boats and surface raiders in conjunction with the usual anti-aircraft guns.

Weapons such as these required trained personnel, and they were initially manned by the army's Royal Artillery. In 1941, personnel serving on merchant shipping were formed into a new regiment, the Maritime Anti-Aircraft Regiment Royal Artillery, which was eventually organised into six regiments containing a total of 14,000 men including officers.

Reservists and new entrants were recruited from the Royal Navy and Royal Marines, and numbers were also boosted by the addition of 150,000 merchant seamen trained and qualified as gunners. All servicemen serving on board DEMS ships had to sign on as members of the crew and therefore came under the jurisdiction of the master of the vessel. As such, military personnel could visit neutral countries without risk of internment. When leaving the ship on shore leave in neutral ports, gunners would have to forsake their military uniforms and don civilian clothing.

In 1943, a number of WRNS personnel (the Women's Royal Naval Service, also known as the 'Wrens') were appointed as boarding officers. Their role was to inspect ships in harbour, deliver sailing orders, check guns and ammunition stores, and generally keep an eye on the gunners. Normally, the ship's second mate would have been designated as the gunnery officer and would have received gunnery training; a non-commissioned officer would be in charge of the gunnery crew. These men served on the Malta, Atlantic and Arctic convoys and provided a sterling service in conditions that can not easily be described. On the Arctic convoys, they had to endure extreme weather conditions, and despite the constant threat of hostile aircraft and U-boat attacks, they continued to carry out their duties. Their vital service was conducted without publicity or thanks from the general public, which to a large extent was totally oblivious of their existence.

The writer had occasion once to stay a night at a DEMS transit centre in Southampton; to this day he has not forgotten that experience. The building was huge, cold, and miserable – a proper doss house in the true sense of the word. In fact, a mortuary would have been a more apt description of the place. To think that these gunners, after a hazardous voyage, had to put up with such a place made me very thankful that I belonged to another branch of the navy.

One of Barmouth's well-known personalities, Hugh J. Rowlands (a practising solicitor in the town), was drafted into the DEMS as a gunner in 1941. Commencing his naval career at HMS *Glendower* in Pwllheli (a naval training establishment on what would later become a Butlin's holiday camp), Hugh completed his gunnery course and spent the rest of the war sailing on merchant ships. Among the artefacts kept at the Barmouth Sailors' Institute are some motley old documents belonging to Hugh, which can be seen hanging on a wall; they

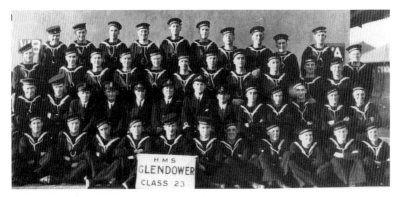

Class 23 of HMS *Glendower*, February 1941.

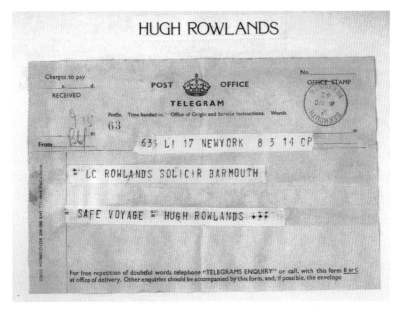

Copy telegraph sent by Hugh John Rowlands from New York to his office at Barmouth.

consist of a telegram sent by him to his office in Barmouth saying that he had arrived safely in New York, a harbour pass for Stranraer, and an American harbour pass for New Jersey. It is interesting to note that in one of these passes he is listed as a gunner and in the other as a deckhand. Also displayed is a newspaper 'world weather chart map' on which he plotted the

Stranraer and New Jersey Port Security Passes issued to Hugh John Rowlands

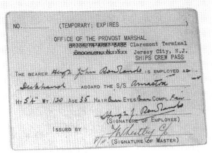

World weather chart map on which he plotted the route of his ship to America and then North Africa.

route of his ship to America and then North Africa. There is also a photograph of his training class at HMS *Glendower*.

Whilst in Stranraer, Hugh served on HMS *Shepperton*, one of the stern-loading boats ordered by the Southern Railway in 1933 for use on the intended Dover–Dunkirk ferry route. She was taken over by the military in 1939 and commenced service as a minelayer in the English Channel, eventually seeing service as a troop transport between Stranraer and Larne. It seems that Hugh's American pass was issued whilst serving on HMS *Amastra*. This again was a merchant navy boat, a Raspan class merchant aircraft carrier (also known as a MAC), and had been converted in 1943. She operated as an Atlantic escort throughout the war.

It is said that Glyn Roberts, later of Beehive, Barmouth, but originally a native of Rhiw, Blaenau Ffestiniog, and a schoolmate of the present writer, was also in the DEMS, and that at one period both he and Hugh J. Rowlands were serving on the same ship. This, however, can no longer be confirmed.

It is very likely that there were others from this area who served with the DEMS, but unfortunately their names are not known to us.

Combined Operations

A BOOKLET PUBLISHED in 1943 by His Majesty's Stationery Office, *Combined Operations 1940–42*, gives the reasons for the formation of this unique union, but before the story of the marines in this area is explored, it is well for younger readers to understand the reasons why it was established. This is explained in the foreword to the booklet:

> The term combined operations is vague and does not convey more than a general meaning, yet their scope is precise and definite – a combined operation is one in which two or more Fighting Services co-operate in order to strike the enemy with the maximum of effect at a chosen place and a chosen moment.

The Combined Operations Command was formed from officers and other ranks of the three fighting services. Its primary function was to provide amphibious warfare training, which comprised offensive actions from small raids to large assault landings. It was also the task of this command to plan and execute raids on the enemy coast.

On the material side, the new amphibious warfare was a complicated business and had many aspects. Machines of war and special types of assault craft, both large and small, as well as other devices for the discomfiture of the enemy, all had to be studied and produced. On the human side, such warfare necessitated the closest spirit of co-operation in all who waged it.

The Combined Operations Command was concerned with these and many others aspects. It produced the craft and the weapons, but above and beyond all else, it sought to foster the spirit of co-operation in all fighting men, united as they were by the danger and glory of their calling. In so doing, it created in combined training centres sailors–soldiers, airmen–sailors and airmen–soldiers who had a complete understanding of each other's methods and problems.

The Combined Operations Command had its own troops, of which the commandos formed a part, but many other troops also passed through their hands. These included not only British and Dominion troops, but also American troops and those of other allies: the Czechs, the Poles, the Norwegians, the Dutch, the Belgians, the Fighting French – in fact, any nation contributing to the Allied campaign against Nazi Germany. The motto of those who played a role in the command's success was 'United We Stand'.

The commando or special service troops were to be amphibious; this meant first and foremost that they had to learn to cooperate with the Royal Navy. Schools for this purpose were established in various places along the British coast so that the men might become familiar with the way of life, customs, habits and outlook of sailors. They had to be able to get in and out of small boats in all kinds of weather and to swim, if necessary, in full equipment with firearms held above the water. They also needed to be familiar with portable weapons, from rifles and tommy guns to three-inch mortars and anti-tank rifles. In addition, they had to be able to carry and use high explosives and know how to hunt tanks and their crews. These were just some of the things that a commando had to learn if he was to become proficient in his chosen trade of war. Moreover, it was not just the tools of this trade that he had to master, but his mind as well. A commando had to become not only a specially trained soldier, but also a trained individual soldier; being self-reliant and self-confident formed an integral and vital part of his mental and moral make-up. To achieve these mutually dependant qualities, the men, on entering the depot, were treated as far as possible as individuals. They were required to do everything for themselves; it was not for them to await orders from their officers or their NCOs. They had to do the sensible, obvious thing just because it was the sensible and obvious thing to do.

They developed a way of life first taught to them when they joined the British Army as recruits; nearly all of them came to the commandos having already passed the rigorous training undergone in the army. The specialised commando training, with its emphasis on individual initiative, was superimposed on to this foundation.

A typical example of a training exercise might be the following. A troop (sub-units of a commando unit are known as troops) would parade at, say, 3 p.m. and be told that the next parade would be at 6 a.m. the following morning at a location that might be 60, 70 or sometimes 100 miles away. How each commando got to that place was his own affair. The difficulties he might encounter, the shifts to which he might be put to carry out this order, did not matter. What did matter was that he was present at the appointed time and place.

The author bore witness to the importance placed on these appointments while he was serving on HMS *Effingham* in Dartmouth during 1943. A marine commando coming back from leave arrived at Kingswear Station, Devon, but somehow missed the ferry from there to Dartmouth. The next ferry was not until the following morning, but his leave expired at the usual 23.59 hours, which meant that he had to reach his destination by that time. In his best uniform, he swam a distance of at least four to five hundred yards across the River Dart – a deep, fast-moving tidal river. With the blackout regulations in force, visibility would have been poor, and once in the water it must have been extremely hard to maintain one's sense of direction.

His comment on arriving at the other side was that his CO would not have accepted his explanation on how he missed the ferry; his job as a commando was to be there at the appointed time, which he had achieved.

When not engaged in active operations, the commandos

continued their training. They lived for the most part in billets and received no extra pay, but were allowed 6*s.* 8*d.* a day with which to keep themselves. In the maintenance of discipline, petty punishments were as far as possible avoided; they had not been abolished altogether, but they were infrequent and the necessity for their infliction did not often arise. The man who committed too many small crimes suffered the final penalty – he was forced to leave the commandos and all efforts to be given a second chance would be in vain.

The residents of the coastal belt of Merioneth can be proud that this marvellous body of men did most of their training on our shores and terrain.

The Royal Marines

THE ROYAL MARINES Prayer.

O Eternal Lord God, who through many generations has united and inspired members of our Corps, grant your blessing, we beseech you, on Royal Marines serving all around the globe. Bestow your crown of righteousness upon all our efforts and endeavours, and may our laurels be those of gallantry and honour, loyalty and courage. We ask these things in the name of Him whose courage never failed, our Redeemer, Jesus Christ. Amen.

The author has to admit a bias towards the Royal Marines as he was attached to the Royal Marine 601 Flotilla for a period in 1944 while stationed at Langley Camp, Hampshire. The landing crafts were moored at Buckler's Hard and he has many happy memories of those dedicated men.

In his book, *The Royal Marines in Wales*, Anthony J. Perrett notes 'it was probable that there have been Welshmen in the Corps since its formation in 1664 and it might have been assumed that possibly half of the two new regiments raised in 1690 came from that Principality and commanded by the Earl of Pembroke'. The marines have had a presence in south Wales for most of this period, but it was only at the outset of WWII that they ventured into our area, which they did with complete thoroughness. The area between Tywyn and Barmouth was taken over for their training on amphibious crafts, and five camps were built. Starting from Tywyn, these were Matapan Camp, which was located at Ynysymaengwyn, the home of the Corbett family; then Gibraltar Camp in Llanegryn; Burma Camp in Llwyngwril; Iceland Camp at Fegla in Arthog; and

Front entrance and gate posts of the old Matapan Camp still visible today

finally Crete Camp in Barmouth. It seemed that the position of the camps was chosen to mark the progressive acquirement of skills gained by the trainees.

Matapan would have been the reception camp for the marines, though most of the intakes had already been trained to a high standard and some would have already seen action.

The whole concept of the various camps was to ensure that the men were trained in conditions they would most likely meet. The coastline of west Merioneth was ideal training ground for amphibious crafts, with its open beaches, sand dunes, shale, muddy estuaries, and vicious currents, all of which would help to make the marines proficient in the art of beaching their crafts intact at a required point.

Though the marines have always had a role within the Royal Navy, the marines as such did not usually do any seamanship, and they had to be taught the rudimentary skills of navigation and even how to steer a boat. Each of the camps listed specialised in one aspect of those requirements which would later benefit them when they landed on enemy coasts. At the end of their training, they received the coveted red Combined Operations badge consisting of an anchor for the navy, a gun for the army, and the eagle wings for the air force, which they would proudly sew on their uniform to signify that they were now part of Combined Operations.

The main house of Ynysymaengwyn was taken over as the officers' mess; brick buildings were built in the surrounding woods and Nissen huts erected on the lawns, though in 1963 the main house was deliberately burnt down as it was considered unsafe. There now only remains the concrete foundations and a part of the guardhouse by the entrance. Today it is the Ynysymaengwyn Caravan and Camping Park.

The troops arrived in the station and were then taken by trucks to Matapan Camp, not knowing exactly what the future held for them. The NCOs told them that this was the first camp of five camps in which they would stay, and that their wish for sea service would be granted. After training they would become crews of landing crafts – it soon became clear to them that it was not going to be an easy posting.

Readers may ask why it was called Matapan. It looks as if the authorities found the Welsh name a bit of a tongue twister, especially for the non-Welsh speakers, and opted for a simpler name. At the time, a naval battle between the Royal Navy and the Italian Navy had just taken place at Cape Matapan off the south coast of Greece. The Royal Navy had gained a decisive victory, with the Italians losing five of their warships, and to commemorate the event the camp was named after the naval encounter.

Entrance into the camp was through two large square, stone-built pillars, upon which the gates were hung. A large imposing ornate capping (possibly of carved sandstone and currently painted) was mounted on the top of each pillar, and this depicted, on both front and rear faces, an image of an elephant with a howdah carriage on its back. Old photographs of the property show that the gates and elephants were an original feature of the house many years before it became an army camp.

An interesting artefact still remains visible today on the nearby Talyllyn railway bridge by Cynfal Farm. If you look carefully, you can see where a marine has carved his name on the slate coping stone above the bridge: 'Marine P. Stratton, 1943, 282 Squad'. He probably spent hours sitting and scratching his name on it whilst off duty, having no money – as was usual among most of the lads then – to go to town.

Matapan was for kitting out, selection, and assigning to the various jobs for which they had been chosen. Those selected as coxswains of landing crafts were given intensive training and then moved on to Gibraltar Camp. There they were given intensive courses on signals and seamanship and had to complete an assault course and infantry training – though they were probably well versed in that before coming to Matapan. Some were selected as mechanics and sent to Hayling Island for specialised training, but the majority would be deckhands. They all found the course to be harder than anything they had gone through before; the knowledge which they had to assimilate covered everything: aircraft recognition, use of Browning machine guns, and how to look after the Ford V8 engines which powered the crafts, including a course on general maintenance. After a week, it would be time to pack their belongings and move to Gibraltar Camp at Llanegryn for further training. Their kits were placed in trucks for conveyance to their new camp, but the troops had to march there.

Gibraltar Camp was situated at Peniarth, and when the War Ministry commandeered it, the owners were Colonel J. F. Williams-Wynne and his wife. The colonel at the time was serving in the Far East, and a marine brigadier, accompanied by another officer, arrived at Peniarth to tell a shocked Mrs Williams-Wynne that the house and grounds were to be requisitioned for the use of the marines. Soon the ground saw the rapid erection of brick buildings and Nissen huts to form a large camp; it had a gymnasium, a cinema/theatre, and most important of all a parade ground. The commander and his staff were accommodated in the main house, and it became the largest of the five marine camps in the area. A nearby house was taken over as a hospital. The officers used the main driveway to the house whilst the troops used another drive.

The course at Gibraltar Camp would end, but the troops had to undergo eyesight tests for night vision and undertake a simple test in seamanship, morse and semaphore, with the best squad being presented with a shield. They then moved to Burma Camp at Llwyngwril. The name of the village was a bit of a tongue-twister to most of the men, but they overcame this by calling it 'Little Willie'.

The aim of Burma Camp was to train officers and men in AA gunnery, including use of such weapons as Oerlikons and Bofors guns. The camp co-operated with the RAF at Llanbedr, which flew the drogue-towing aircraft for the practice shooting.

Burma Camp was split into two as the Great Western Railway bisected it. The camp was not ideally situated as there was little in the way of entertainment in the locality, and there was very little to do to relieve the rather barren nature of the area. Burma had its own cinema, but the main source of entertainment was at Tonfannau Camp, where excellent theatrical shows were available.

Whatever thoughts the men had about the tough course at

Gibraltar Camp were soon shattered at Burma. The CO was a stickler for perfection, the instructions were more advanced, and, as one session finished, the next would start immediately afterwards. There was more emphasis on seamanship, winds, tides, compass settings, navigation and piloting, and then they would be marched up the hills for semaphore instructions. Discipline was strict, but as old sweats they were used to that, and at the end of the course they gained their naval berets and had pleasure in sewing the Combined Operations badge on their shoulder, denoting that they were properly trained. Whilst at Burma Camp, the coxswains visited the Royal Electrical and Mechanical Engineers (REME) Camp at Tonfannau for a three-day course on maintenance of the V8 engines – the author can also vouch that these engines were temperamental.

The book *Royal Marines in Wales* recounts how a young officer stationed at Burma Camp made a request for leave. On being asked by the adjutant why he wanted leave at that particular time, knowing full well that preparations for D-Day were of the utmost importance, the officer stated that he wanted the leave to play cricket. The adjutant himself had not had any leave for six months and was therefore not very sympathetic to the request, which was refused. However, within two hours a signal came from HQ containing the following message: '2nd Lt Trevor E. Bailey will be granted leave to play cricket at Lords'. Older readers will remember Trevor Bailey as an England Test cricketer.

As usual at the end of the course at Burma Camp, the troops had to leave, and the same routine was upheld: kit on trucks and march to Iceland Camp in Arthog.

Iceland Camp was probably situated in the most beautiful area of the Mawddach estuary, and it is little wonder that the site was known as Artist's Valley. In 1902, a developer from Cardiff, Solomon Andrews, bought a large estate from Jane Jelf-Reveley (connected with Caerdeon Church) situated in the Arthog/Fegla area for £8,500. It comprised seven farms, some of which were sheep farms with grazing rights on the slopes of Cadair Idris. Andrews's intention was to develop the area as a tourist resort, and in his dreams he visualised the area as being a rival to Llandudno and Aberystwyth. Incidentally, at the same time, another entrepreneur, Arthur McDougall, the self-raising flour magnate, had similar ideas for Fairbourne, as both men saw the opportunity of making money from the new tourist trade. Properties were built in both areas, but their owners' dreams were never realised.

Development took place at Fegla. Nine houses were built near the estuary and named Mawddach Crescent, though the end house later collapsed due to subsidence. Similar problems are believed to have been the cause of Mr Andrews's dream never being realised. For more information about the Fegla, readers are advised to read Bernard O'Connor's book *The History of Mawddach Crescent*. The Crescent was occupied by various artists, but all that changed in 1941 when architects, surveyors, engineers and contractors came to transform the coastal area completely – military camps were built and virtually all beaches were made secure against invasion. Contractors and the Pioneer Corps got to work building concrete blockhouses linked by rows of tank traps known today as dragon's teeth. Gigantic steel poles were stuck into the ground to dissuade enemy aircraft from landing, and all were bounded by barbed wire. Virtually all beaches from Dyffryn through to Fairbourne and Tywyn were subjected to this treatment, as it was believed that the estuaries and the shelving coastline could attract enemy landings.

At this time, Mr Roberts of Fegla Farm was informed that his land would be requisitioned for the use of the military, but he could stay on in the house and farm the land that was not required for military use. The eight families in Mawddach Crescent were also given similar notices to leave, but one lady, Miss Beatrice Carr, refused to go because of her father's age and frailty. Such was her determination that she went to the War Office in London, dressed in her British Red Cross commandant uniform. She demanded attention and won her case; three other families had partial reprieves as well. The military took over, moving into all the top floors and a few of the ground floors of the Mawddach Crescent houses.

The ground floor of No. 2 was the galley (cookhouse) and the men's dining hall, the upper floors being sleeping quarters. The first floor of No. 3 was the senior non-commissioned officers' (SNCOs) sleeping quarters. Originally, the ground floor of No. 8 was to be the officers' mess, with sleeping quarters on the first floor. The connecting walls in the second floors had doors knocked through to allow access to all properties. Eventually, Bryn Celyn cottage, 400 yards upstream, was requisitioned as the officers' mess.

Two grey-pebble concrete sentry boxes were erected on either side of the access road by Fegla Farm, with a guardhouse in the adjoining field. Today, the sentry boxes are part of the landscape even though they have the same tendency as the Tower of Pisa – they lean heavily to one side!

Numerous concrete bases can still be seen today; they are laid on both sides of the track leading to Mawddach Crescent. They were the bases for a variety of Nissen huts, which comprised a guardhouse, stores, ATS quarters, a dining hall, ablutions and a sick bay. There were about fourteen bases on the wooded hill east of Fegla, where other Nissen huts were located. A large cinema was also built and a NAAFI at the bottom of the hill, where the troops could relax.

The training at Iceland was very arduous, with fall in at 5.30 a.m. and a five-mile walk and run before breakfast. However, at long last the marines had what they wanted: boats. These were not exactly what they had pictured, with rowing races across the Mawddach in boats resembling pontoons. When doing route marches, a favourite ploy was to fill one's water bottle with beer bought the previous evening in the NAAFI. This welcome change was appreciated, but it wasn't long before the ploy was found out, and one morning on parade, the order was given to empty all water bottles, and all the beer just disappeared into the ground. Those guilty of having beer were punished with

"Beth am dani, FERCHED?"

Gwyddoch mai'r Fyddin, y Llynges, a'r Llu Awyr biau'r hawl gyntaf ar y *dynion*. Ystyr hyn ydyw mai chwi'r merched raid ddyfod i'r adwy gyda gwaith "munitions."

O ran hynny, mi fyddwch yn falch o allu cynorthwyo i droi allan arfau i'ch brawd, i'ch gwr, i'ch cymdogion. Bydd yn bleser eistedd i orffwys ar ddiwedd diwrnod dygn a gallu dweud, "R'wyf *finnau* wedi gwneud fy rhan!"

Peidiwch poeni os na chawsoch brofiad o waith diwydiannol o'r blaen. Gellir eich hyfforddi mewn byr amser mewn swydd a fydd yn wirioneddol waith rhyfel ac yn helpu eich gwlad. Peidiwch ag oedi funud. Ewch i'r Employment Exchange, neu gellwch sgrifennu neu deliffonio yno, a dweud eich bod eisiau helpu.

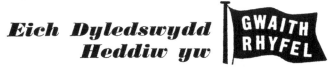

Eich Dyledswydd Heddiw yw GWAITH RHYFEL

ISSUED BY THE MINISTRY OF LABOUR AND NATIONAL SERVICE

What about it Girls?

This is a poster by the Ministry of Labour asking for women to volunteer for munitions work to fill posts vacated by men who had been called up to the services.

Your Duty Today is War Work

247

three extra parades. A dangerous incident happened when a delivery of hand grenades had been unloaded from the train at Barmouth Junction (as it was called then) on to an army truck; one of the boxes fell off the back of the lorry and its contents were strewn across the road. The railway staff were not allowed to touch them, and Iceland Camp was informed so they could send appropriate personnel to deal with the situation.

Iceland was the base where marines got to practise on real boats, and very soon they came to realise why the Mawddach had been chosen for their training. They had to negotiate a course under the railway bridge, which had a very fast current running beneath it. Great care also had to be taken when steering under the bridge not to run aground on the shallow bar guarding the entrance to the estuary. To make matters worse and more realistic, trainee fighter pilots from the nearby air force base made mock attacks on the boats and used them as imaginary enemy targets.

The run ashore to Barmouth was enjoyable, but this entailed walking over the bridge, which incurred a toll of 2*d*. The troops tried to overcome this by going over in groups, and when passing the pay booth someone would shout, 'The last man will pay.' But this did not last long; it is believed that eventually the toll was lifted for the troops of Iceland Camp.

Perhaps today's younger readers will think that the way the armed forces were treated would not be tolerated in today's world. One marine recalls how he bought four doughnuts from the NAAFI in preparation for a route march that he knew he would be on, placing two into each of his ammunition pouches. After marching for a period, they had a break and he decided to eat one of his doughnuts. Unfortunately, an officer saw him and told the sergeant to put him on charge for 'eating without permission'. On returning to camp, he was given '7 days pack drill' in full marching gear, one hour every evening! This punishment was hard labour, I'm told.

Training continued until the last day at Iceland. They all had to go over the assault course, which in itself was very hard, but to do it in full battle order was another thing. Starting from the beach, they climbed up ropes to the top of the cliff. Once there, they had further obstacles to overcome: ditches two yards wide and nearly three yards deep and crawl-through tunnels with thunder flashes being ignited all the time. When they eventually covered the course, they had to rope down the cliff and run to the finishing point. By now, they would be covered in mud and truly exhausted.

After all this, they left Iceland for HMS *Effingham* in Dartmouth, Devon. HMS *Effingham* was based at the Royal Naval college there. The author, after he had completed his own commando training at HMS *Northney*, served on HMS *Effingham* for six months prior to the Americans taken over the base.

In the author's naval experience of the Combined Operations Service, men were drafted (posted) for a period not exceeding six months and then redrafted to other units. This meant that one could not develop true friendships with your mates, who never became more than merely acquaintances. It was believed, though never seen or confirmed as an order, that this was a deliberate policy. In the event of action, if one saw a friend injured or killed, it was thought that this would impair the efficiency of the person's fighting ability, whereas for an acquaintance it would be just a case of 'bad luck, Jack'. This was never promulgated officially, but it was acted on. When meeting old shipmates, the comradeship of the past had become just a vague memory, and now both were virtually strangers to each other.

It was during the period of serving on HMS *Effingham* that I was ordered, together with another fellow petty officer, Jan Dudley, to go to Slapton Sands, which was between Kingsbridge and Dartmouth. Our instructions were to make secure and report the British craft beached on the sand. It was a hot day in April and walking on the beach with our equipment was hard work as the sand underfoot was not firm but consisted of very small pebbles; as you walked on it you sank a couple of inches. No information had been given to us of what to expect, and when we reached our destination one could see a fleet of American ambulances lined up and emergency vehicles around the place with their personnel. We secured the British boats and returned to our base at Dartmouth.

It was not until about forty years later that I heard the full story of the tragedy which had occurred there. Exercise Tiger was a massive exercise involving tank-landing crafts, swimming DD (duplex drive) Sherman tanks, soldiers, sailors, and all the paraphernalia needed to forge a bridgehead on the beaches of Normandy in the long-planned invasion of Europe. Slapton Sands was very similar to Utah Beach in Normandy, which would be the designated landing place. The exercise took place on the 28 April 1944 – two hours after midnight. Suddenly, nine German E-boats appeared; they had located the movements of the force and had come to investigate. Having located them, they fired their guns and torpedoes and virtually decimated the flotillas. Over 900 servicemen were killed or drowned, and the incident was classified as 'top secret'. The reason for this, it was said, was to avoid the German High Command putting two and two together and linking Slapton Sands with the very similar Utah Beach in Normandy.

It is well worth recording that the Americans lost only 200 men on the D-Day landings on Utah Beach, and as mentioned earlier, it took forty years for the full story to unfold. A Sherman tank recovered from the sea at Slapton has been placed as a memorial to those Americans and British servicemen who lost their lives there.

Crete Camp, Barmouth

Of all camps held by the marines in the area, Crete seems to be the one with the least information about it. The location of the camp is quite well known, and its purpose was to teach seamanship and navigation to the troops. There is no record of weekly intakes from Iceland to Crete; after completing their training at Iceland Camp, troops were sent directly to the south coast. The progression seemed to finish at Iceland, and one can only assume that both camps worked in conjunction with each other – that is, Iceland would send troops over to Barmouth for instructions on how to handle boats. However, Crete Camp had quite a large presence in Barmouth; twelve four-storey houses in Porkington Terrace – almost the entire row were requisitioned (the houses were built in pairs with a narrow gap between them), although some of the residents were allowed to remain in situ, living on the ground floors.

One of these was Miss Olive Johnson of Bod Idris, No. 4 Porkington Terrace. Miss Johnson was one of the leading lights of the Barmouth Debating and Literary Society and a very popular figure in the town.

The army constructed walkway bridges on the fourth floor between houses, providing access between them. These houses were occupied largely by marines, instructors and administration staff, but there were also some ATS personnel billeted there. The view from Porkington Terrace overlooks Barmouth Bridge, and they could see the troops coming over it from Iceland. There used to be a rule that troops marching over a bridge had to break step.

Interestingly, my father, who was a carpenter and joiner, travelled every day with others from Blaenau Ffestiniog to work on the conversion of Porkington Terrace. One local Barmouth joiner is also remembered, a Bob Pugh, who later joined the Royal Navy and met up with the author at Devonport Barracks in Plymouth.

As stated previously, the toll for the bridge at that time was 2*d.* per person, and it is doubtful if the military would have paid for the passage of troops across the bridge on a daily basis. Probably an agreement would have been made with the county council to waiver the toll for military personnel.

On the open land opposite Porkington Terrace was a steep gulley. This led down to the estuary shore through a small tunnel-like gap under the railway line and emerged close to the old lifeboat station; originally, this old access had been used to convey craft to the area for repairs. On this piece of land, Nissen huts were erected to accommodate landing craft operations. A NAAFI was located near the lane leading to the Panorama Walk, and higher up was a cluster of Nissen huts. The marines were a unit unto themselves, and they kept well apart from the OCTU. They were only concerned with the landing craft training – square-bashing and assault courses were to be had at the other locations.

Sketch of the camp at Llangwril drawn by Capt R F Tebbutt during the war

Burma Camp, Llwyngwril. Pencil sketch by Captain R. F. Tebbutt.

Royal Observer Corps

THE OBSERVER CORPS (later the Royal Observer Corps) was formed in 1925 and made up of civilian volunteers who had given up their spare time. They wore RAF-style uniforms – though originally just the basic overalls – and came under the jurisdiction of RAF Strike Command.

Under the command of a Commandant Observer Corps (usually a serving RAF air commodore), the volunteers were trained by full-time professional officers. In 1941, King George VI approved the use of the prefix 'Royal', and henceforth the Corps was known as the Royal Observer Corps (ROC). This was in recognition of their work during the Battle of Britain.

In the early 1930s, the Observer Corps began expanding throughout Britain. Posts were organised in various towns and linked to a group centre, which would pass information through to Fighter Group Headquarters and the sector operation rooms of Fighter Command. The Observer Corps was the 'eyes and ears' of the Royal Air Force, as their motto – 'Forewarned is Forearmed' – indicated. By the outbreak of WWII, the Corps's presence extended throughout the country, with posts in our area at Abersoch, Porthmadog, Barmouth, Tywyn, Aberangell, Blaenau Ffestiniog, Trawsfynydd, and Llanbedr.

The Observer Corps's greatest contribution was during the Battle of Britain. The information they obtained supplemented the crude radar system of the time, which was not very effective in inland areas. The observers were a vital link in the chain of information which enabled British fighter planes to successfully intercept German bombers. During this battle, the Luftwaffe started to attack the radar stations, which, if damaged or destroyed, would blind the RAF. However, with the help of information from the Observer Corps, fighters could be airborne with at least twenty minutes to spare – the time required for them to reach their optimal flying altitude. Observation posts and control centres were manned continuously from 3 September 1939 until May 1945.

In the beginning, many observation posts were only glorified garden sheds, but these were eventually replaced by substantial brick buildings. Later on in the war, specially designed observation posts were introduced: usually two-storey structures with an open-top observation platform above a small crew rest area. Quite a few were equipped with special radios and aerials, which meant that distress calls from aircraft could be received. With such radios, it was also possible to transmit the position of the ROC post to a distressed aircraft or a course for it to steer to the nearest airfield.

To prevent crashes on high ground, a scheme was devised code-named 'Granite'. This applied mainly to ROC posts in mountainous areas similar to ours. When the clouds descended below 1,000 feet, the ROC centre would be informed, and all posts in the group would be given the instruction 'Stand by for Granite'. This meant that in daylight red flares would be placed at each corner of a thirty-foot square; at night, just the one flare was used. When low-flying aircraft came into the sector, the code word was given and the post would light the flares. This could be done independently if the post considered that an aircraft was flying into danger.

The constant vibration on planes and the shock of heavy landings caused problems with the radios and other instruments. The writer recalls that, at the beginning of the war, his brother, on completing his degree course in physics at the University of Wales, Bangor, was directed to work for a well-known radio valve manufacturer in London. At that time, the filaments in the valves were so delicate that they were not able to withstand the rough conditions under which they had to operate and had a high failure rate. Fortunately, the research team on which my brother worked was able to resolve the problem.

It is said that over 7,000 British and Allied aircraft were saved through the work of the ROC. The Corps also monitored enemy aircraft movements, plotting their courses and passing on the information to their control centre. In 1941, a dispatch from Air Chief Marshal Sir Hugh Dowding stated:

> It is important to note that at the time [July to September, 1940] they [the Observer Corps] were the whole means of tracking enemy raids once they had crossed the coastline, their work was quite invaluable, without the air raid warning system we could not have operated and inland interception would rarely have been made.

The vital work of the ROC continued throughout the war. By 1945, there were over 1,500 posts controlled by some forty centres.

In 1944, during preparations for the invasion of France, there was a request for volunteers from the ROC to perform aircraft recognition duties as 'seaborne observers'. Over 1,500 volunteered, and 796 were accepted. They joined the Royal Navy and were given the rank of petty officer (aircraft identification). They continued to wear their ROC uniforms with 'SEABORNE' flashes sewn on them. During the D-Day landings, two observers were allocated to all participating US naval vessels and defensively equipped merchant ships (DEMS). The observers assumed control of each ship's anti-aircraft batteries, with the intention of reducing the high incidences of friendly fire between allied vessels and aircraft. In the last paragraph of his letter to the Corps, Air Chief Marshall Trafford Leigh-Mallory states:

> The work of the Royal Observer Corps is quite often unjustly overlooked and receives little recognition, and I therefore wish that

the service they rendered in this occasion be as widely advertised as possible and all Units of the Air Defence of Great Britain are therefore to be informed of the success of this the latest venture of the Royal Observer Corps.

In June 1945, the ROC stood down, and over 2,000 volunteers were invited to attend a final ceremony at RAF North Weald, Essex. Part of the ceremony entailed the dedication of a new ensign (this being the Royal Air Force ensign defaced with the ROC badge in the fly in place of the RAF roundel). The ceremony concluded in a march past, with Lord Beatty taking the salute. This was the only time the ROC marched together in their uniforms. In 1947, because of the Cold War, the ROC was again reformed and went on to perform nuclear war analysis and provide a fallout warning service. It wasn't until 30 December 1995 that the ROC stood down for the final time, marking the end of a record seventy years' voluntary service in defence of the realm.

Wartime booklets

Tywyn

THE OLD URBAN district council of Tywyn covered quite an area and included Aberdyfi. Virtually all the area was utilised by the military during the war years, and according to locals about eight military camps were located there.

An interview with Sir Meurig Rees of Escuan Hall, Tywyn, provides some interesting recollections of the time. Sir Meurig, who is a former Lord Lieutenant of Gwynedd and a past chairman of the Royal Welsh Agricultural Show, provides an account of his life and tribulations as a farmer during that period, and also his impressions of wartime Tywyn and how it affected him and his farm.

Sir Meurig remembers the building of Tonfannau Camp, and what makes it interesting for him is that his late wife was brought up in the farm neighbouring the camp. He thought that about 250 persons were employed there, which provided a significant boost to the local economy.

The biggest change seen was in the life of the town, which lost its tranquillity and sense of identity. When it came, the army bulldozed through the local way of life, with military police and pickets patrolling the streets every night. Overnight, a seaside town changed into a garrison town.

Five camps were established around the town area. Neptune Hall was taken over by the Royal Service Corps (now called Logistics); the Royal Marines were at Llanegryn and Peniarth; the RAF and the RAF Regiment were at Morfa; and the Royal Artillery was at Tonfannau. There were also marines at Llwyngwril and Ynysymaengwyn, and last but not least, there was the Tywyn Home Guard.

As a farmer, Sir Meurig was in a key industry, and the slogan at the time was 'Dig for Victory'. Many a farmer, after a hard day's work, had to report for duties with the Home Guard, and probably had to do a stint of patrolling and guarding of vital bridges. The farmers were ruled by the War Agricultural Executive Committee, which directed them to increase production and to put a percentage of land down to potatoes and grain. This was back-breaking work, as use of tractors was not yet widespread, and much of the labour was carried out with the help of shire horses, which themselves had to be fed, watered and groomed afterwards. For every acre of land planted, the farmers received £20, probably the first subsidy ever given to farmers.

Petrol and food were rationed, and cars were few and far between. Those that were on the road had their headlights masked so as to comply with blackout regulations.

In the period 1939–45, Escuan Farm consisted of 360 acres of pasture and had a pedigree herd of Welsh Black cattle. The cattle were bred for rearing beef calves and to provide milk. There was also a mixture of sheep, hens and pigs. The farm grew its own crops – oats, barley and mangolds (a root vegetable) – for stockfeed. It was Sir Meurig's job to mix the rations: chopped straw topped with a three-inch layer of chopped mangolds and then home-milled oats topped with linseed and left overnight to moisten. This provided a good mix on which the stock thrived.

At Escuan they had to grow five acres of potatoes, which had to be dyed blue to avoid any being traded on the black market. They were stored on the farm until the following year when they would be ready for planting. The back-breaking task of lifting the crops would be shared with German and Italian prisoners of war, together with land girls. During haymaking, British soldiers also came to help; they welcomed the break from their army duties, and several of them would have had farming experience. They were not paid but were very happy to sit down to a meal of home-made ham and chips after their day's work.

258

Tywyn was a quiet Welsh-speaking community, but the war changed all that. The influx of new residents, be they service personnel or civilians doing essential work, changed the community in a way that can still be seen today. Wartime migration caused the town to become anglicised, a process that has continued to this day. The latest census indicates that more than half of Tywyn's present population were born in England, and another portion claim an English-only identity. Only 34% of the local population claim a Welsh identity, and the statistics are similar in other seaside towns in the area.

Tywyn has had a Territorial Army presence since the beginning of the last century; their HQ was a corrugated iron hall: Neuadd Pendre. This was the home of the Terriers, part of the 7th Battalion of the Royal Welch Fusiliers. They bivouacked around Neptune Hall for their summer training.

For most of the last century, the armed forces had a significant presence in the area. It was a major training ground for amphibious landings in the Second World War and was considered a strategic war base. Abandoned pillboxes can still be seen along the coast to the south of the town. However, the links with the armed forces came to an end when the Joint Service Mountain Centre at Morfa Camp closed in 1999.

On the south side of town, Neptune Hall stands out. It has now been converted into flats, but during the war it served as an officers' mess. Neptune was the camp where the Royal Army Service Corps (now a part of the Royal Logistics Corps) did their training, but it eventually became an internment camp. The RASC was a unit on its own and had nothing to do with the marines stationed in Tywyn.

They trained on landing crafts, the area's shale beach, muddy estuary and sand dunes being the ideal environment to train in for the Normandy landings. The DUKW (Duplex Utility Karrier, Wheeled), an American, two-ton capacity, six-wheeled truck, could operate on land and sea. Other vehicles included Alligator tanks, Buffaloes, Weasels, and Terrapin armoured transport vehicles. It was said that occasionally the DUKWs were taken over to Abersoch for their crews to gain handling experience in sea conditions. In addition to the *Camroux III*, there were two other ships, one named *Drake* and a tank landing craft, anchored at Aberdyfi for the use of the army.

The DUKWs were capable of transporting tanks right up on to the beach; it is said that the Sicily landings had only been possible through their use. They could carry goods and equipment off large ships out at sea and bring them into land. They were as large as a bus on the road, but when loaded they appeared low in the water. It is interesting to note how the vehicle got its name: the 'D' stands for the year of manufacture (1942), the 'U' denotes utility, the 'K' front-wheel drive, and the 'W' refers to the craft's six-wheel dual-driving axles. The first training on DUKWs took place in Ayrshire in the winter of 1943/4 and then at the Tywyn Amphibious School in January 1944. The DUKWs were also used on the Rhine crossing, and to a large extent nearly all their personnel were trained at Tywyn. The 536 Company of the RASC trained at Tywyn, and each company was composed of platoons of thirty DUKWs numbered A1–A30, B1–B30 etc.

On D-Day, 6 June 1944, during the ferrying of materials on to Sword Beach, a signal was sent at 0900 hours to the effect that twenty-three DUKWs, fully laden with ammunition, had landed, but that three had been damaged by mines and underwater obstacles. Later in the war, when the crew of a DUKW were transporting troops across the Rhine, a young soldier asked a crew member where they had come from; he was told that they came from Tywyn and would be returning there on completion of the crossing. The young soldier was quite upset, as he came from Tywyn, but he had to continue on to fight the Germans. However, the DUKW team were concerned that their next landings would probably be on Japanese-held territories or even Japan itself.

Morfa Camp opened on 8 September 1940 and consisted of three grass runways. It contained the usual Nissen and Maycrete buildings and control tower, although these have all now been demolished. The base was established as an air co-operation base for the Royal Artillery anti-aircraft practice camp based at Tonfannau. U Flight was equipped with Queen Bees (a type of radio-controlled Tiger Moth) and C Flight with Hawker Henleys. Their prime job was to tow drogues so that the anti-aircraft unit at Tonfannau could practise shooting at them. Sir Meurig recalls 'that the sound of firing was continuous all day. Planes from the Morfa Airfield were being used to tow drogues (a kind of windsock), whilst the anti-aircraft gunners practised firing at it. One could see the puffs of smoke emitted from the cordite.'

The unit became part of the 631 Squadron and was eventually deployed to Llanbedr. Morfa was then transferred to 22 Group Technical Training Command. The airfield personnel helped the emergency services to deal with aircraft crashes throughout north-west Wales. The aerodrome closed on 25 July 1945. It became an army camp and subsequently an Outward Bound school, whilst the grass runways were utilised as sports fields.

On 21 October 1975, Mr Dafydd Elis-Thomas MP (the Plaid Cymru Member for Merioneth) asked in the House of Commons why the Secretary of State for Defence no longer permitted civilian aircraft to land at Morfa Camp, Tywyn. In a written reply, the Secretary (Mr Robert C. Brown) said: 'The airstrip adjacent to Morfa Camp, Tywyn, has not been needed for Service purposes since Tonfannau Camp, Tywyn closed in 1969. It has been recently surveyed and declared unsafe for normal use and may be used only in emergency by aircraft designed to land on agricultural ground.' It has been said the airfield was prone to being waterlogged.

Tonfannau Camp had a more or less open door to local residents, who were allowed into the various entertainments and concerts by ENSA. Dances were also held in the camp and attracted quite a large crowd. Sir Meurig remembers what was called the 'Liberty Buses' plying to and from Newtown and Aberystwyth to bring the girls in.

Like Barmouth, Tywyn saw its promenade taken over by the military. All houses were commandeered, the larger dwellings being used as the officers' mess and ATS quarters, while Gwelfor served as the military hospital. A NAAFI complex with a cinema and ballroom came into being. The dance halls were apparently very popular and it was said that you could dance every night of the week. Neptune Camp had a dance hall with its own thirteen-piece band, while the marines at Llanegryn's Gibraltar Camp had their own entertainment. Sir Meurig confirms that girls were also ferried to these camps on dance nights.

During this period pub hours were quite different to what they are today, with stop tap at 9 p.m. in the town. However, this was easily overcome by belonging to a mess, where you could drink all night. With around eight military camps in the area, queues at the cinemas were enormous, obliging them to screen two shows per evening. The army hired the

DUKWs at Tywyn Beach – photograph courtesy of the *Daily Post*

Congregational chapel as a canteen, and here lads could relax and play dominoes etc., with refreshments most probably served by members of the church.

In December 1946, Emrys Roberts, the MP for Merioneth, asked a question in the House of Commons regarding the number of establishments still occupied by the War Office in the county of Merioneth. In a written reply, the Secretary of State for War gave the following particulars for the Tywyn and Aberdyfi areas, demonstrating that there was still an overwhelming military presence in the locality:

Tonfannau – 200 acres
Beach Camp – 6½ acres
Corbett Avenue Camp – 4½ acres
Gwalia Camp – 2 acres
Matapan Camp – 57 acres
Miniature range – ¾ acre
Morfa Camp – 20 acres
NAAFI Hut – ½ acre
Neptune Hall Camp – 1,275 acres
Unnamed training area – 338 acres
Recreation Ground – 18 acres
Rifle Ranges – 80 acres

The Secretary of State's reply also noted that Tywyn's church hall and Congregational chapel were still being leased, but made no reference to the Outward Bound properties in the area or the parts of Cadair Idris that came under Admiralty jurisdiction.

A reminder of the diversity of personnel based at Tywyn can be seen at the cemetery, where twenty-six WWII servicemen and one servicewoman are buried. Of these, seven are from the RAF, five from the Royal Canadian Air Force, two from the Royal New Zealand Air Force, two from the Royal Artillery, three from the Royal Welch Fusiliers, and one from each of the following: the Military Police, the Welsh Regiment, the Royal Engineers, the Pioneer Corps, the Royal Australian Air

Force, the Women's Auxiliary Air Force, and a member of the local Home Guard who died whilst on duty. The local police occurrence book contains the following entry for 24 August 1941:

> Sudden Death
> PS. W. Rowlands reports the sudden death of one John Griffith Roberts of 2 Glandysynni, Bryncrug, whilst on Home Guard Rifle Practice on the Rifle Range.
> At an inquest held 25/8/41, Verdict, Death from Heart Failure, probably through excessive heat and unusual exercise.

As indicated, the inquest was held on the day following the death. During his research work into this book, the author sent an email to the Gwynedd Coroner's Office querying the position with Inquests during the war, especially in large cities where casualties would have amounted to several hundred per night. The response was that during WWII the system of Coroners' Enquiries and Inquests was largely suspended and very few Inquests were conducted into military deaths.

It is not generally realised that over 1,600 members of the Home Guard died on duty during the conflict. It is also worth noting that all war graves are the responsibility of the British Commonwealth War Graves Commission, and it has to be said that all the graves are kept in immaculate condition by them.

Even today, Tywyn still retains vivid mementos of the period. Although most of the camps have been converted by now into caravan sites and holiday homes, local people still recall their wartime names. On the coast to the south of the town, old pillboxes can still be seen, as can the concrete anti-tank blocks further north at Fairbourne. Time spent amongst these relics helps one to imagine the wartime atmosphere of the past.

Tywyn well remembers the fallen, with buildings for the benefit of the community erected in their honour: the Memorial Hospital, the Memorial Institute, and the porch of St Cadfan's Anglican Church – the main locus of remembrance each

The Tywyn Home Guard comprised men from the Tywyn district including Bryncrug, Abergynolwyn and Llanegryn.

Armistice Day. Today, the hospital is no longer under threat of closure, but unfortunately the Memorial Institute has a 'For Sale' sign on it.

Bryn Paderau Memorial Park was created by a local businessman Mr Roy George Middleton, MBE. This Park induces the feeling of homage to the fallen. The English translation of the park's name 'The Hill of Prayers' signifies that it has to be treated with reverence and respect and a reminder that all the names on the stone were flesh and blood, who gave their lives to ensure our freedom and way of life – we should never forget that supreme sacrifice.

Recently, Sir Meurig officially opened the renovated and modernised 'old Territorial Hall' as a community hall – Neuadd Pendre. Over the years, the building has had many different uses. From the time when it was built in 1912 for the Territorial Army, it has been used as a drill hall and small-bore rifle range, and been used for weapons training and sports and social activities. In later years, the hall has hosted whist drives and bingo games, served as a meeting place for various committees, and as a resource for the general use of the community.

A Wurlitzer theatre organ has now been installed in the newly renovated hall. Owned by Mr John Smallwood of Tywyn, he has generously granted the permanent loan of the organ to the people of Tywyn under the custodianship of the local town council. The American-built organ is a three-manual, nine-rank organ and was originally installed at the Granada Cinema, Woolwich in 1937. The 600 plus organ pipes and other instruments are contained in two chambers behind the stage. Neuadd Pendre can be proud of its acquisition, which is a fitting reward for a hall which has witnessed and survived such a tempestuous period of local history.

Bryncrug LDV (Home Guard)

by Ieu Thomas, Bryntirion, Bryncrug

SOON AFTER THE Second World War broke out, it was essential for all local men and women to register for active service, but farm and quarry workers were exempt.

A unit of the Local Defence Volunteers was formed in Bryncrug. A few months later, uniforms were delivered to Mr Edwards's house at Y Bont, where those registered to serve had to collect their suits. A measuring tape was unavailable, so they had to take what fitted them best. There were denim jackets, trousers and cheese-cutter caps without badges. LDV bands were worn on the left arm. Their boots arrived much later.

The assembly point was at the Old School, and the organising officer came from Tywyn. The commanding officer was Mr Helm, who lived at Hillsborough Terrace, Tywyn, and his deputy was Captain Tommy Rowlands, the painter. At their first meeting, they promoted Griffith Lewis to sergeant and his brother Morris to corporal; they were experienced soldiers having both served in the First World War. The medical officer was Dr Marshall Lloyd of Tywyn.

During the initial training at the school, they used broom handles to practise with, until they were later issued with rifles. Several months later, the LDV became the Home Guard, by which time the uniforms, overcoats, boots and gaiters had arrived. Most of their training was carried out in the Rhydyronnen Valley, defending the Tywyn Water Supply and Treatment Works.

During one night-time exercise, it was suspected that an invasion was imminent, with an alarm being raised that a tank could be seen near Cynfal Farm. The full LDV company went to investigate, but they soon realised that they were mistaken. A small hedge fire from earlier in the day had reignited and cast a shadow over a harvest binder, which had been mistaken for a tank.

There were also mock invasions held for a whole weekend between two villages, Bryncrug and Abergynolwyn. The Bryncrug wives used the Old School to prepare meals for their soldiers, but the medical officer would not eat at Abergynolwyn cookhouse and ordered his meal at Bryncrug. During one of these exercises a young soldier was very reluctant to take orders from the corporal, who showed him his two stripes and was told to obey. During another of these exercises, a soldier (not to be named), who was going over a fence at the time, had a narrow escape when a bullet just missed his head!

In the corner of Maestegfryn field there was a circular lookout post pointing towards Tywyn Road (where the AA Box used to be). Built of sandbags it had a corrugated roof and was at a higher elevation than the surrounding hedge. Guard duties changed every two hours. The gun used at the post was a Browning automatic, and Llewelyn Thomas was in charge of it, but it was never fired. He took the gun home with him, cleaned it thoroughly, and replaced it back in its canvas cover.

There were two men in the village that belonged to the ARP. They patrolled the village at night to check that no lights showed from the windows. An initial warning would be issued, with a fine for a second offence.

As youngsters during the war years, we would search for discarded drogues – some had been hit by shellfire and some had become loose from the towing aircraft and fallen to earth.

The drogues, which were made from very fine canvas material, were used for numerous purposes, and they were well worth looking for.

At the time, a large garage for housing buses at Bryncrug was taken over as a NAAFI store for the area, but this attracted rats to the village, which took some time to eradicate.

***

Similarly, the author recollects that in this period flour used to be delivered to the bakeries in large white cotton sacks, which were very much sought after by the womenfolk as they could be used to make various garments for children. Occasionally also, discarded parachutes were somehow acquired, and these again would be used to good effect, adding a little to the meagre clothes ration.

Aberdyfi

ABERDYFI IS A small seaside village situated on the mouth of the Dyfi estuary and is the most southerly port of the old county of Merioneth. Ship building and fishing played a prominent part in the history of the village, which, in its heyday, with a population of less than 1,000, was a prominent port for the export of slate and oak bark from the south Merioneth area.

Few will be unfamiliar with the song 'The Bells of Aberdyfi' ('Clychau Aberdyfi'), which refers to the sound made by the church bells of the legendary kingdom of Cantre'r Gwaelod. Mythology relates that Cantre'r Gwaelod, off the coast of west Wales, was protected from flooding by dykes, with sluices being opened at low tide to drain the land. There are varying accounts of why the land was lost to the sea. Some say a maiden named Mererid neglected her duties and allowed the well to overflow, others that a drunken prince forgot to close the sluice gates against the incoming tide. Legend has it that the church bells of Cantre'r Gwaelod can still be heard ringing out today in times of danger.

Like other areas of Merioneth prior to WWII, Aberdyfi had suffered a decline in the fortunes of its traditional industries, but the coming of the war brought new life and hope to the village. Its influence far surpasses its size, and it is fair to say that whilst Aberdyfi is a small village, its name is well known throughout the country for its contribution to the world of sport and leisure. It has two railway stations and once had a ferry service to cross the river Dyfi to Ynyslas; it was probably the advent of the railway that forced it to close. The eighteen-hole golf club is also world renowned, with many famous players being members.

Another important event in the history of the village was the establishment in 1941 of the first ever Outward Bound school. This, again, is a unique institution which has grown worldwide. Its founders, Kurt Hahn and Lawrence Holt, with the support of the Blue Funnel Line, made sure that Hahn's ideas, formulated at Gordonstoun School, Scotland, would be followed.

Their inspiration was to give young seamen the ability to survive severe conditions at sea by teaching them confidence and perseverance and instilling in them the tenacity to withstand harsh and extreme conditions. Captain Freddie Fuller (John Frederick Fuller) took over leadership of the school in 1943. He was serving on the Blue Funnel Line and had had the horrendous experience of being torpedoed twice. After one of these incidents, he had taken command of an open lifeboat for thirty-five days without losing a single person; for this he was awarded the MBE. He served the school well until his retirement in 1970.

It is not known what contribution, if any, the school made to the war effort. It has been said that both the RAF and the Sea Rescue Service completed a training session at the school, but this has not been confirmed.

The Aberdyfi lifeboat has operated for nearly 150 years and has had an illustrious history since the time it was established by the RNLI in 1853. Cardigan Bay has been – and still is – well served by its lifeboat service. The following list gives the location and type of boats which serve the area:

Aberystwyth – Atlantic 85
Borth – D class [1B1]
Aberdyfi – Atlantic 75
Barmouth – Mersey D class [1B1]
Criccieth – Atlantic 85
Pwllheli – Mersey D class [1B1]
Abersoch – Atlantic 75

The Aberdyfi lifeboat has taken part in many rescues, and sadly some crew members have paid the ultimate price. The present boat, an Atlantic 75 (which it is hoped will soon be replaced by the newer Atlantic 85), is housed in the boathouse by the jetty. It is launched using a lifeboat tractor and currently averages twenty-five emergencies annually. Call-out records from the war are no longer available, but one can be sure that every emergency call received was answered. Aberdyfi was served by conventional lifeboats until their withdrawal in 1964, when it became a permanent inshore lifeboat station.

The old boathouse, Traeth Dyfi, dates from 1837 and was used by three different lifeboats until it was converted into a bakery in 1886. Lessons learnt during the war years have been incorporated into the structure of the Aberdyfi Search and Rescue Team, which provides permanent search and rescue cover throughout the year. It is part of the North Wales Mountain Rescue Association and covers an area from mid Wales to Cheshire, including Aberdyfi, Abergynolwyn, Llanberis, north-east Wales, the Ogwen Valley, and southern Snowdonia. Their nearest neighbouring search and rescue group is the Aberglaslyn Mountain Rescue Team, which is a registered charity and covers north-west Wales and the north of Snowdonia. The Aberdyfi team is staffed by around thirty volunteers and is funded almost entirely by voluntary contributions. The team is permanently on call.

The story of mountain rescue began in the RAF Llandwrog Airfield, Caernarfon, during WWII. The task of searching for and rescuing survivors generally fell on the senior medical officer of the nearest RAF Station to the accident. Flight Lieutenant George Desmond Graham was the medical officer at RAF Llandwrog, and he was also a keen mountaineer. Posted to Llandwrog in 1942, he had organised an unofficial voluntary group to assist with search and rescue. Flight Lieutenant Graham pestered the Air Ministry for equipment and training for his group, but his pleas initially fell on deaf ears. By the time his pertinacity bore fruit in 1943, his rescue activities had already saved ten lives. In July of that year, the RAF Mountain Rescue Service was created and Graham's team was reorganised. He is credited with the prominent role in the creation of the Mountain Rescue Service and was later awarded an MBE for his efforts. The Mountain Rescue Association have erected and dedicated a memorial to Flight Lieutenant Graham in Carlisle Cathedral.

The Mountain Rescue Service[12] was officially based at Llandwrog from 1941–5 and at Llanbedr, Merioneth, from 1945–9. In their early days, the RAF's mountain rescue team was involved in what could be termed a local tragedy. On 22 October 1942, three pilots of the RAF 41 Squadron were killed when, in bad weather, their Spitfires flew into the side of the 2,077-foot peak of Tarrenhendre, about seven miles to the north-east of Tywyn. An air search found the wreckage two days later, and a team went up to the peak to retrieve the remains and carry them down the mountainside, where they would then be transported to Barmouth. The following day another party was sent to retrieve the wreckage of the aircraft for inspection.

The year 1950 was when the first civilian search and rescue teams were formed. While the role of the RAF's mountain rescue teams was initially to rescue aircrews whose planes had come down in the mountains, they became increasingly involved in the rescue of civilians out climbing or walking. It was clear that a civilian counterpart to the RAF's teams was required, and it was at this time that the Aberdyfi Search and Rescue Team came into being, along with similar organisations elsewhere.

***

---

[12] A unofficial mountain rescue team (mrt) existed from 1941 but was formalised as the RAF Mountain Rescue Team in July 1942.

Recollections of the late William Selby Davies

The author is indebted to Councillor Mrs Megan Reynolds of Vanner, Aberdyfi, for permission to publish the recollections of her father, the late William Selby Davies, who served as an engineer on the *Camroux III* when she was based at Aberdyfi.

'With Leycakes and Jam'

'Mr Davies, would you like to go to Aberdyfi to take the post of second engineer on the *Camroux III*?' said George Wood, my chief engineer. We were on a small ship called the *Camroux II* in Blyth, Northumberland. I was second engineer, and, until a month ago, I was also the ship's machine-gunner. Then the Royal Navy allocated two seamen from a defensively equipped merchant ship to our vessel, and I was relieved of the job. George had taken me by surprise. A few weeks before the war, I had taken my two children to Blyth. They were happily settled there, and I didn't want to go to west Wales and leave them in what was practically the front line, as Blyth was a submarine base and liable to be bombed at any time. 'I don't think I can go, George,' I said, 'not with the children up here.' 'Give it a thought, Bill,' he said, 'and if you don't like it, I'll see to it that you come back here.' I decided to give it a try.

I was paid off the next day and came down by the night train. This was a very nice firm to work for. We travelled first class at their expense, and they allowed subsistence money as well when travelling. They also paid for any taxis used. I had to change at Newcastle upon Tyne. When I entered a first-class carriage four young men followed me. Along came an angry guard and ordered us out. The four young men left, but of course I stayed put. The guard approached me and said, 'What about you?' I said nothing and pulled out my ticket. 'Oh, OK, sir, sorry,' he said. I was now a sir. There was no heating on trains at this time, and the lights were dim and the curtains strictly drawn.

After travelling all night, we arrived at Machynlleth still

in the dark. Remember, we had double summer time then. I had to wait some time for a train to Aberdyfi. Somebody in a house across the road from the station was selling tea and sandwiches, which were very much appreciated. Finally, the train arrived and I was on the last stretch. It was getting light and I was quite enthralled by the views along the way. I had been told that Aberdyfi was a small town, but that it had two stations and that my destination was the second one. When I got out at Aberdyfi, I had no idea which way to go. I approached the porter and said that I understood there was a small ship here and could he direct me to it. He pointed towards the jetty, which was out of sight, and said in a very north Welsh accent, 'You see that balloon there? It is fast to the ship.' So I set off, carrying all my possessions along the railway lines. It was rather rough going, and when I saw the ship I went over the wall about where the post office is now and proceeded along the road.

There was no one on deck when I went on board. I went down the companionway. There were four men chatting in the galley, and the chief officer was washing his feet in a bucket. I asked if the captain was on board. He was not. And when I told them who I was, I was told that the chief engineer was in his room. I went along and found him asleep on his settee. The next day I signed on, was warned about talking outside, signed a secrecy paper, and had my fingerprints recorded. I was appalled at the state of the engine room, and the signs of neglect on the main engine and subsidiary machines. I learned that the previous engineer was only interested in drinking. He was also very lax at the controls because he had put the engine on full ahead when it should have been on full astern and caused a lot of damage in Fishguard Harbour.

To me, this was luxury: to be able to take off my clothes, get into pyjamas, and go in my bunk and sleep. I hadn't been able to do this for four years! And a proper full-sized bath and hot water! Luxury indeed.

Aberdyfi at this time was a very busy place. The jetty was

three times the size that it is today. We were alongside the jetty and so was the training ship belonging to the Outward Bound Sea School. At anchor in the river were *Golden Valley* and a Dutch ship. There were thousands of troops training for the coming invasion of Europe. There were many six-wheeled amphibian vehicles called DUKWs. They were used to train drivers to take men aboard from one of the anchored ships and land them ashore. There would be four men and an instructor aboard, and each man had to do the circuit until he was proficient. One could change the tyre pressures on the DUKW while travelling to compensate for soft or hard surfaces. There were also six-wheeled vehicles without propellers that travelled the water by rotating their wheels. And there were also six-wheeled vehicles that would roam the hills and could climb at incredible angles.

Our first operation following my arrival was to monitor some shelling from Ynyslas. Two days later, we had to take divers up to near Aberdaron to try and recover some unexploded shells from the sea floor so we could find out why they hadn't gone off. During these trips it became obvious to me that the main engine was in urgent need of an overhaul. The chief engineer agreed that we would do some work whenever we were likely to have some free days without operations.

All the windows in Aberdyfi were criss-crossed with sticky tape, but many had been broken by explosions on Ynyslas beach when they tested things like cordite mats and Bangalore torpedoes. One fine Sunday afternoon, shortly after my arrival, I decided to take a walk up the hill. I looked down at Happy Valley and thought it was very beautiful. I sat down and tried to draw a picture of it. It was really beautiful. I carried on up the hill and came to a little farm. I found out later that it was called Bwlch. I could see some tables set and some people eating in an otherwise empty hay shed. I suddenly felt that a cup of tea would be very nice. I sat down at a table and soon a very pretty young lady approached. 'Hello,' she said. 'Hello,' I replied. 'May I have a cup of tea, please?' 'Yes,' she said. 'Would you like bacon and eggs and fried bread followed by some leycakes and jam?' Would I? 'Yes, please,' I gasped, in case she changed her mind. The meal served in the hay barn was superb. When I got back I told the lads what I had found and learned that they often went up to Mrs Jones for a meal. From then on, I, too, was a regular visitor to Bwlch, summer and winter.

Shortly after, I had a consultation with the captain. He was of the opinion that we were likely to be in Aberdyfi for the duration of the war and that it would be a good idea to get my children here. He did all he could in the way of giving me leave to get them down. I was very fortunate to get them settled comfortably. The people took such good care of them that it seemed my worries were over, and a great weight was off my mind. I should have mentioned that, when the war started, everything had been arranged to send them to Canada to stay with my brother for the duration, as I was going to join the Royal Navy, but the Germans torpedoed the SS *City of Benares*, which was loaded with children, so no more children were sent.[13]

One of our operations about this time involved anchoring a buoy out in the bay with a very high balloon above it. Halfway between the balloon and the buoy was suspended a dummy aeroplane made of chicken wire and three-ply. It looked very realistic and was designed to test proximity fuse shells from Ynyslas. The shells did not have to hit the plane but exploded at their nearest point to it. This was achieved by using the Doppler effect principle. Each shell had a small radio transmitter and receiver in the nose that was switched on as the shell left the gun and also a self-destruct mechanism in case it didn't go off. I dismantled one once to see how it worked. Even I sinned.

---

[13] The SS *City of Benares* sailed from Liverpool on 12 September 1940, bound for the USA and Canada. Amongst the passengers were ninety evacuated children (aged between 5 and 15 years). Some 600 miles and five days out from Liverpool, she was torpedoed and sunk by a German U-48 submarine. Of the ninety children on board, only thirteen survived the ordeal. After this incident, no further attempt was made to evacuate children overseas.

There was a rocket launcher on the ship. It was not used often, but when it was used, all hands had to be undercover, and afterwards most of the ship had to be repainted. It was replaced by a twelve-pounder gun in mid 1944. We were all very well known in the town and took part in whist drives, dances, social evenings etc. that were held in the church hall. I had an unusual job for a seaman, for every time we came in I had to climb on to the roof of a big warehouse owned by a local businessman and twist the ship's telephone wires around the main GPO wires. Sometime later there was a proper plug fitted on the jetty for us. We all loved the place – and not only the place. Five of us married local girls, one a Borth girl, and one a Machynlleth girl. As Christmas 1943 approached, it was decided to arrange a party for the local children. The word 'local' took on a rather wide meaning in this case, as they were welcomed at the church hall from as far away as Tywyn and Machynlleth. For two or three weeks before, most of us were busy making toys. My contributions were puzzles, and I made a dozen or so ring-and-string puzzles. We had games, a dummy donkey, some comedy, songs, dances, and some nice things for all the children to eat and drink. I well remember carrying a little girl about eight years old who couldn't walk. I wonder if any of those children, now past middle age, will remember. Sometime later a local lady invited the crew to a dinner party in a local cafe as a thank-you gesture. There was a tray of loose cigarettes on the table, and I was able, surreptitiously, to put some explosive ones amongst them, with hilarious results.

EPILOGUE: A week later I came out of chapel, opened my cigarette case and found only one cork tip. I lit it and walked on. Then it exploded, to the amusement of passers-by.

We did a lot of work for the RAF testing station at Aberporth. One task, which lasted several days, was to test underwater jet propulsion. First a launching frame was bolted to the ship's side and was used to lower the torpedo into the water. Then a balloon carrying a cine-camera and a man in a basket underneath was stationed high above the ship. This way, one was able to photograph the movements of the torpedo underwater. This took several days, as they could not take instant photos as today but had to take the camera back to base for the photos to be developed and printed. On the last day, it was decided to conduct the test using a different rate of power, and the torpedo was launched several times with disappointing results. Finally, the Royal Navy officer in charge decided to double the charge. The result was quite frightening. The initial impulse shook the ship. The torpedo travelled a few yards under the water then shot into the air. It did a few zigzags over the ship with a terrific roar and then dived back into the water. There was a mad scramble to get undercover – as a professional coward, I went down the companionway without touching the steps!

We had to make several trips to obtain fuel oil. Once we went to Barry. The place was crammed with American troops, many riding back and fore along the streets. Petrol did not seem to be a problem to them. We went to Swansea. It had been bombed and was a scene of desolation. We also went to Fishguard. One dark and stormy night, four of the balloon crew were returning aboard. On reaching their quarters, they noticed that one of their party was missing and went back to look for him. Remember, there were no lights anywhere. One of them noticed a torch alight under the water. The man had fallen in and swallowed water so could not shout. They got him out rapidly and he was none the worse after a rub-down.

Twice during my time in Aberdyfi I had to take the temporary position of chief engineer on ships in the North Sea when there was no other chief available. It involved taking a night train either to London or back up to the North, to Tyneside or Blyth, and a return to the old routine of sleeping, or rather trying to rest, fully clothed and with a lifejacket on.

Probably our most dangerous operation was to dispose of some dodgy ammunition in the bay. Some ammunition had been captured by the forces and taken to Aberporth for analysis. There had been a fire at the base, but luckily it had not reached the ammunition dump, or there might have been a hole where the base used to be. Lorries took it very gently to Cardigan, from where we were ordered to take it out to sea and dump it. So, with great difficulty because of the bends in the river, that's what we did.

I had to take one of the ship's motor boats to help steer the ship round some of the bends. It was quite tricky because I not only had to pull her round but also had to avoid getting run over. The crew loaded the ammunition, ever so gently. At this time I was racking my brains trying to find an excuse to ask for compassionate leave, but couldn't think of one. We proceeded downriver and out into the bay, and the cargo was disposed of safely. Everybody heaved a sigh of relief.

One day, a farmer who lived not far away came to the ship in great distress. It appeared that the threshing outfit had come to his farm that day and, as practically all local men were away in the armed forces, he wanted to ask the captain if he could get permission to ask for some volunteers to help. He was invited aboard to see him but was too afraid to come down the gangway as the ship was moving slightly and so was the gangway. He got his permission and several of us volunteered to go, but we were liable for instant recall by three blasts on the siren. The work was familiar to me, having being brought up on a farm. To the others, who had never handled a pitchfork or a sheaf-cutting knife, it was hard labour, but we got his corn threshed in the end. We had a ship's dog named Tim who could climb vertical ladders – really vertical ones like those found in jetty walls. When the farm dogs threatened him, he calmly walked up a ladder to the top of the rick, much to the surprise of the farm dogs. They looked up at him with an expression that seemed to say, 'How the heck did you do that?'

Doing the farmer's threshing was not our only venture into the realm of community service. One day, our Captain George Barns was approached by the secretary of the golf club. It appeared that the drainage ditch on the course was overflowing. Due to the layout of the course, it could not drain naturally but had to be pumped over the dunes. They could not start the engine that worked the pump, and they could not find anybody to see to it. The chief engineer went along to see what was wrong with it and started to take it apart. As one of us had to stay on board at all times, I was asked to go and carry on with a part overhaul over the next two days. So we got the engine going and the ditch pumped out. For our services, our captain was made a life member of the club. I was fortunate enough to meet my wife here,[14] and we got married on 25 October 1944. I asked the captain if I could have a few days off, and he said I could take as much time as I wanted, so we spent a week wandering around Newport and district. We managed to buy a nice house, but we were never able to live in it because for several months we could not get vacant possession. It was necessary to find suitable alternative accommodation for the tenants before we could insist on them leaving. My wife was able to buy some reasonably good furniture at auctions and we were able to store it in a shed.

Unfortunately, my wife's mother fell ill with creeping paralysis and she had to take care of her, but the crew were all too willing to help. The boatswain (pronounced 'bosun') took charge of the operation. Of course, it was his job to take charge. As some of the pieces were rather big to take up the stairs, it was decided to take them in through the windows. One of the DEM lads was quite a good carpenter, so he was detailed to take out an upstairs window while two others were to rig a boom and tackle in a higher window. Two others were to come with me to load the furniture on to the lorry that we had borrowed. By the time we arrived, everything was ready, and all the pieces were hoisted up and inside in a slick and seaman-like manner.

Probably our most spectacular operation was when the rocket ships came. To prepare for this, several lorryloads of

[14] William Selby Davies was divorced and lived with his two children in Blythe, Northumberland.

rockets were brought to Aberdyfi and stored in a large shed used by the balloon crew, which was built near the entrance to the jetty. It was demolished after the war, and there's now a boat park where it used to be. The rocket ship was long and rather flat. The rockets, about a thousand of them, were carried aboard, one man carrying one rocket at a time, and each was installed in its own projector, which was set at an angle of about 45°. Now the ship had more firepower than a cruiser. The first firing was arranged for Christmas Day. The inhabitants of Aberdyfi were warned to keep indoors. After a few trials to obtain the best positions, all seemed ready. It should be remembered that it was necessary to aim the whole ship at the target. Our ship had about eight WAAC girls on board, a cinematographic section. There were two cine-cameras on tripods ready. Unfortunately, most of the girls were lying on the hatch, greenish in the face and making frequent trips to lean over the ship's side! So, after about two minutes' tuition, some of our crew had to try to operate the cameras. The rockets were fired about twenty-five at a time on to the mudflats above Aberdyfi. The firing was most spectacular. Afterwards, I was asked to go on board. The vibration caused by the rockets going off nearly always resulted in some damage. This time it was the pump that transferred fuel oil from the tank that had cracked, and they had no power for lighting or cooking. I was able to rig up a temporary supply system for them using an empty five-gallon oil drum and a rubber hose, and they were very pleased. There followed a week of preparations, and on New Year's Day there was a repeat performance with another rocket ship. Forty-five years later, the changing currents removed some of the surface of the mudflats and revealed many rockets, so the army bomb disposal teams came and gathered them, surrounded them with sandbags, and blew them up.

One Saturday afternoon, I was asked to take six army officers to Ynyslas to watch a football match. I used one of the ship's motorboats. When they came back after the match I found I could not start the engine. The army officers had to be back by a certain time, so one of the sergeants at the base offered to take us across in a six-wheeled amphibian. I agreed and left the boat moored safely in Ynyslas. Those vehicles were steered by applying a brake to one side, which slowed down that side and caused it to veer in that direction. The driver was going all over the place, sometimes halfway up the dunes. One of the officers remarked that he had never been in one of these before; the driver replied that he had never driven one before, which to me seemed obvious. Just before we got to the river, there was an awful clatter from the engine and then it stopped. This was rather lucky for us because if it had stopped five minutes later we would have been in the river and could have been swept out to the bar and beyond. We were able to signal the ship and were taken across by another motor boat. We towed back the one with the faulty engine the next day.

A team of electronic experts were with us once for several days. We would sail out into the bay. They would rig up complicated aerial arrays and reflectors. The aim was to try to make the enemy think that the invasion was coming to the north of France. Another group was trying to improve methods of interfering with enemy communication using a battery of revolving variable condensers. They were also experimenting with showers of tiny bits of aluminium foil, all the same size. No doubt, all this in a small way helped to win the war.

The end of the war in Europe took one by surprise, although it was now fairly obvious what the result would be. As we were not likely to have an immediate operation, I was given a week's leave. So my wife and I went to Birmingham on the night train. On leaving the station in Birmingham, we could see flags flying, bands playing, and Scottish pipers proud-footing it in the streets. I asked somebody what it was all about. 'Where have you been?' he replied. 'Don't you know the war is over?' Birmingham was en fête that day – and that night. So was every other town probably. People were riding on the tops, bonnets and wings of cars. The streets were so crowded, the cars could only crawl. Complete strangers were embracing each other.

There were thousands of troops, seamen and airmen of many nations celebrating in the streets. There was a bonfire in front of the main post office. All sorts of things were thrown on it: wooden benches from the parks, old frames, tyres, and I saw several policemen's helmets thrown on as well. And it went on all night. It was a time for rejoicing. But the Japanese had still to be beaten. They held out for nearly three months more. The first atom bomb was dropped on Hiroshima on 6 August 1945 and the second dropped on Nagasaki three days later. The Japanese surrendered, and that was the end of the war. Now it was over, we all felt relaxed. But we couldn't just pack up and go. There were many things to be disposed of. Two different size balloons, drums of rubber solution, lorries, ammunition, rockets, shells etc. – not to mention the dummy aeroplane that was given to me personally. As I had nowhere to keep it, it was discarded on council land. I kept my mouth shut in case they asked me to move it or pay rent. It lay there for years, and then they finally destroyed it.

But the people of Aberdyfi were not going to let us go like that. A gentleman named Mr Jones, affectionately called 'Banjo Jones' because he was a wizard with the banjo, arranged a professional concert for us as a kind of parting gift. There were actors, singers, and comedians from London. Mr Jones, who escaped from Jersey just before the Germans occupied it, gave us a wonderful demonstration of what beautiful music could be played on a banjo. One act was billed as a 'surprise item'. To everyone's surprise, three of the balloon crew came on stage, dressed in oilskins, sou'westers and sea boots, and they sang in beautiful harmony a tune called 'If I were a Blackbird'. They had a standing ovation. They could have gone home to Cornwall a week ago but had stayed on at the arranger's request.

We left Aberdyfi on 5 November 1945. We proceeded to the Tyne, where the ship was converted back to a cargo ship. To me, who had gone to Aberdyfi rather against my will, it was the end of an era, and the beginning of another very happy one.

The Long Watch

We were in London; I was the 2nd engineer on the MV *Camroux II*. We had taken on a cargo of scrap iron for Middlesborough from Cox and Danks Depot and were almost ready to sail when my chief engineer, George Woods, received a telegram stating his mother had died. He contacted head office and was granted compassionate leave. But there was a problem; they could not find a temporary replacement chief. It was suggested that I be asked if I would take over as chief and take the ship to Middlesborough and back to London. It was pointed out to me that it was quite illegal to go to sea with only one engineer on board. It was also pointed out that it would be a feather in my cap if I took over. It would be quite a responsibility to be the only engineer on board; when leaving and entering harbour, there was a great deal of manoeuvring to do with the main engine. There would also be several auxiliary engines running, a degaussing generator to combat magnetic mines, two generators for power on deck and for lights, and also a compressor. Also one had to be constantly in the engine room when in convoy, as the ship often had to adjust its speed to keep its position in the convoy. I decided to take it on.

We proceeded to Southend, which was a convoy control area, to wait for a northbound convoy. We had thick fog the next day, and it lasted for four days. No great strain for me as there was only one generator running for lights and charging batteries. The convoy assembled during the next two days, and we weighed anchor and sailed. Two days later, we were well up the North Sea in two lines of ships travelling in a swept channel, when a destroyer sailed down the convoy flying flags which, when decoded, required all captains to check a certain paragraph in the convoy control manual. This paragraph described how to carry out a certain manoeuvre. What had happened was that they had received information that mines had been laid in the swept channel during the night, and it was necessary for the convoy to carry out this manoeuvre in order to proceed along the now mined channel until it was swept again. The procedure was for each ship, when it reached a certain point, to turn outwards. The ships on the starboard line turned starboard and sailed southwards outside the convoy. And the ships on the port side turned to port and sailed southwards outside the convoy. When they reached the end of the convoy, they were to close up into two lines. After about five hours, this manoeuvre would be repeated and we would sail north for about two hours. We did this for two days. That meant we were going back and forth over the same stretch of water for two days. It was a little worrying, as we were a sitting target for aircraft and E-boats, but we were not attacked once, which was rather unusual as we seldom had a passage without an attack of some kind. The weather was overcast, which may have accounted for it. We finally arrived at our destination. Five days in the engine room.

Friendly Fire from the British

I can't remember the date of this happening, but it was probably about November 1942. We were sailing north in convoy and had to make a small manoeuvre as the tail of the convoy had drifted to the west of the swept channel by a strong westerly current. To regain the channel, we had to steer east and pass a port-hand buoy. The sun had set a while ago, but there was a red glow in the west which was reflected in the east, and there were some dark clouds.

We were just rounding the buoy when we heard a bomber approaching from the east; we could just make it out against the sky. Every ship within range fired at it (and many out of range too). There were loud cheers, which soon stopped when we saw it was a British plane. Our gunners were questioned at the enquiry and said that it was the destroyer escorts that had brought it down. They were told that they could not say that.

The Three Musket-Dears

How I had the job of machine-gunner thrust upon me for six months during the war needs some explaining. When the war started, I was on a ship called SS *Chelwood*, and we were issued with two twin Lewis guns and two Royal Navy men to operate them. By the way, we had balloons and Holman bomb throwers too. I was fascinated by the way the Royal Navy men stripped and reassembled them, and I asked if I could watch. They were only too pleased, and under their tuition I practised until I could do it quite well. In fact, each of us was able to do it blindfolded. Sometime later, I moved to another ship, the *Camroux II*. After the Dunkirk evacuation, all guns and Royal Navy men were taken from us for obvious reasons. After a while, they gave us rifles. When machine guns became available again, the bosun was ordered to a London gunnery training establishment to take an MG course. He came back and, according to him, knew all about it. The next day, a brand-new Lewis gun was delivered in separate pieces in a wooden box in its original grease. He had no idea how to assemble it. As he looked in dismay at all those bits, someone said, 'Why don't you ask Bill? I think he might know something about it.' The captain asked if I could assemble it, and I said I could. He told me to carry on. It was easy, and after I had finished, I fired a burst. The captain said I would have to go on a course. The course was funny for me because I knew it already, but tried not to show it. During the next few weeks, I took courses in operating Marlin and Hotchkiss guns. The gun that we finally had was a Hotchkiss. This gun was very good; it could fire one shot at a time.

It was mounted on a post on the poop. When I remarked that one felt very vulnerable standing there during air raids at sea, which took place quite often, I was asked to design a shield. This I did, and an engineering firm made a good one, two thicknesses of steel and a slit for the gun, and it could be swivelled all around. One day, we had come down the North

Sea in convoy, and we were the first of four small ships to leave the convoy and turn into the Thames. There was an air raid in progress, and due to the weather only the bigger ships could use their guns; I think the guns of the other three ships must have been inside somewhere out of the spray. But I had made a canvas cover for the barrel and breach and another for the ammunition roll. So with two quick flicks, my gun was always ready. Two of the enemy planes came towards us and dropped two bombs. Both missed, but the first plane carried on past our port side. Generally, one only had about six seconds when a plane was in range of our guns. I aimed well in advance, and it flew into my bullets. They smashed into the engine and cockpit, and it came down just ahead of us. Though I had fired at several, and I'm sure had hit some of them, this is the only one I succeeded in bringing down.

The Message

The female dispatch rider wheeled her motorcycle on to the wharf, lifted it on to its stand, and approached the ship. She looked very smart in her uniform and with her goggles pushed up on to her forehead. She walked up the gangway and asked to see the captain. We were at Rosebank Wharf, Fulham, in a small ship called the *Camroux II*. We had discharged our cargo and were preparing to sail, and it was about 7 a.m.

The message she brought was disconcerting to say the least. It appeared, so the message from the Admiralty said, that, under cover of a heavy raid on London during the night, the Germans had dropped a large number of acoustic mines into the Thames, and that nine ships had already been sunk. We were to proceed to the convoy control area at Southend to await a northbound convoy. But we, as a diesel-engined ship, were to leave the convoy as soon as we left the Thames and to proceed independently using the inshore route. The reason for this was that the thud of the diesel engine was more likely to set off an acoustic mine than a steam engine, so no diesel-engined ship was allowed to sail in this convoy. The journey down the Thames was rather nail-biting. The main engine was used as little as possible. When the engine was needed to provide steerage way, either the chief or I would go down to the engine room and, very gingerly, and half expecting a big bang, would start the engine at dead slow ahead. More ships had been sunk during the morning. As we went past, we could see the upper works of some, the masts of others, and some that were just wreckage. We had to wait two days for the convoy, which was lucky for us as there was bad weather in the North Sea.

Two days later, on a Sunday morning, I had come off watch at 8 a.m. By 9 a.m., I was lying in my bunk, fully clothed as usual and with my life jacket on, and reading a newspaper a few days old. Suddenly, there was a terrific bang. The correct thing to do was to get out and up on deck rapidly. But the ship was vibrating so much and tossing me about in my bunk that for a while I could not get out. When I did get on deck, the first thing I did was to put a machine gun and some ammunition in one of the lifeboats, which of course were hanging outboard on their davits. Then I went in to the saloon and switched on the automatic radio that would send out a continuous SOS signal. I was responsible for this radio set. It now seemed we were not going to sink immediately. The whole ship was a shambles. The wheelhouse, which had concrete slabs around and on top of it, had collapsed, but the three people inside it had managed to get out. The main engine was cracked in three places. The propeller and its shaft were badly damaged. The compressor, generator, and pumps were all broken. The windlass was shattered and both anchors had gone out to the full length of their chains. We were now anchored to the bottom. We had been blown up by an acoustic mine. As we lay there, we could see several contact mines drifting down the channel. Bad weather had torn many from their anchorages, and the wind and currents caused them to drift to the west. I got the machine gun out of the lifeboat and fired at some of them, but although I hit them not one exploded. It was necessary to hit on the top of a horn to set them off. I had to stop shooting when they came too close or I might lose my head. Soon a destroyer arrived from the convoy, which was about ten miles to the east of us, in answer to our SOS. Men came aboard to help us. Then the destroyer was blown up by two contact mines and was sinking rapidly. Before long, another destroyer arrived to take the crew off the sinking one, including survivors from a sinking ship the previous night. Then an American tugboat named *Courser* arrived on the scene and put a towline on the *Camroux*. The anchor chains were cut with an oxyacetylene torch and left at the bottom of the sea. We were towed to the most convenient port, which was Grimsby. It took six months to repair the ship and get her to sea again.

***

Aberdyfi Home Guard

Like other places, Aberdyfi had its own Home Guard company. Lying at the southern end of the county, Aberdyfi and Tywyn were aligned with the Machynlleth area and were part of the 3rd Battalion of the Merioneth Home Guard. Their history is well recorded in the eight diaries which have been deposited in the Merioneth Archives in Dolgellau. They make interesting reading, and the impression they give is of a very well-organised and trained force who were a credit to their uniform. Considering that they were in reality civilians dressed as soldiers, they did an excellent job of work, and the area can be extremely proud of their achievements. One has to concede that one platoon of Home Guard is very similar to one in another district, but not always so; different terrain meant different approaches. The Aberdyfi Company seems to have had very good leadership, and the troops were taught basic military tasks efficiently and thoroughly. The company had around fifty personnel and were led by a captain, a lieutenant, and a sergeant. Their official reports are clear and concise. Some of the reports and messages are interesting and are listed below:

B Company – 54 total comprising 2 Lieutenants and one Sergeant
Duty report, Section Leader A. E. Jones
All volunteers reported for duties at 9.45 p.m. All lamps lit at barricades, visited No. 2 Patrol at Abertafol Hall at 11.30 p.m. Patrol reported seeing search light in an easterly direction at 12.55 a.m. Nothing further to report on this watch.

No. 1 Patrol – 1.30 a.m. to 5.00 a.m.
Trefeddian Observation Post 1.30 a.m. to 5.00 a.m.
Nothing to report.

July 2 1940
A special duty of 8 men with rifles, bayonets and 40 rounds of ammunition were sent out, 4 to the east and 4 to the west of Aberdyfi on the main road, returning at 12.00 p.m.
Nothing to report.
All rifles and ammunition checked. OK.

25th July 1940
10.30 p.m. message received from M. M. Jones, Police Station that a telephone message had come from Ynyslas that a bright light was visible near the National School on the side nearest the Church and had been seen for 20 minutes.

Blackout regulations were strictly adhered to and enforced, especially in an area as sensitive as the port of Aberdyfi. It was very important that no lights be shown as there was every possibility that a German U-boat could be lurking in the bay or even waiting for a signal from the shore.

Saturday, September 7th 1940
4.10 – Order from O/C battalion, giving Code Watch; Company to stand by at 5.00 o clock.
5.10 – 46 members of the Company standing to.
5.20 – Company distributed through the village.

6.50 – Orders from O/C, Company be instructed to keep in touch with H/Q. Utmost vigilance necessary. Members to be ready to report at short notice. Landings are expected under smoke screen which will be mixed with Poison Gas. Volunteer Jenkins assumes telephone duties and will assemble Company if necessary.
7.45 – Company dismissed.

Sept 16th
Aircraft reported, also the sound of bombs dropped in the estuary, reported by the 10.00 a.m. Patrol.
Rifles and ammunition returned. H. Green

Tuesday, Sept. 24th 1940
9.45 – Air raid warning – Purple
10.35 – Air raid warning – White
11.29 – Air raid warning – Purple
11.40 – Air raid warning – White

Monday, 7th October 1940
Message as follows:
'Office of origin Lancashire Police Headquarters.
Escaped from a military camp at Selthwaite near Bilverston at 15.15 today, Franz von Werre, Oberlieutenant in German Air force, speaks good English, 26 years of age, 5ft 7ins, 10 stone. Fair hair, blue eyes, fresh complexion, clean shaven, no lobes to ears. Dress, Blue shirt, no hat, jacket or overcoat. Light blue German Air Force trousers, dark boots or shoes.'

15th August 1941
Mines are constantly being washed up the shore, and leave severely alone, warn police.

Tues, 2nd Sept. 1941
Platoon No 1. Shot second round, Adjutant in attendance. Plane shot down in estuary opposite Brynerthyn, advised Training Reg. Tywyn. Tywyn aerodrome officials took over.

Sept. 1941
Special Notice to Inlying Piquet. Should any message being a single word such as 'Ebony' or 'Emergency' or 'Belgrave' be

received [by the Inlying Piquet] on the telephone, the Company Commander or whosoever is acting on his behalf must be informed immediately.
W. H. Green Lt

16-2-42
Major Jones Evans, Acting Captain William H. Green. Message received from 2nd in Command, 3rd Merioneth Battalion as follows: 'A person [man or woman] is going round the H. G. Headquarters making enquiries for supposed "security purpose" and bears a pass or certificate signed by Major Simpson. Should anyone bearing such a pass present themselves here, they are to be put under arrest immediately and H.G. headquarters notified. W. H. G.'

22nd Oct. 1942
3 Spitfires took off from Llanbedr near Harlech at 11.30 this morning, and have disappeared,
forward any information which may have any bearing on their disappearance to the H.Q.
[see photo of Memorial Stone Pennal]

A more humorous entry:

Having stoked the fire with two shovelful of coke from the metal bin, Pt. Eaves discovered three rounds of .303 ammunition in the third shovelful. We stood by for an explosion in case any rounds had been put on the fire, but as nothing happened it is clear those were the only 3 rounds dropped into the coke bin.

The local company had quite a few of what were called Trident practice messages. These provided practice at taking down messages for the men. They were assessed on their ability to write them down clearly and accurately, noting the time they were received and taking any action deemed appropriate. Often the messages did not have any significant purpose or sometimes even make sense. A few are listed here:

10-3-41 Trident Practice Message, 22.10.
A message should be like a maiden skirt, short enough to be interesting and long enough to cover the essentials.

Trident Practice Message 26th March.
It is arguably to witness the unparalleled embarrassment of a harassed pedlar, sitting on a cobblers chair gauging the symmetry of a peeled pear, potato or pomegranate with tranquillity and ecstasy.

Trident Practice Message April 21st 1941, 23.10.
4 beautiful blondes with blue eyes are proceeding along the promenade at a leisurely pace. Please advise necessary action.

Trident Practice Message, 15th May 1941.
Don't look now but 100 parachuters just landed on the coast. Am sending out archers and cross bowmen, please send me 1,000 arrows feathered No. 9 mark 11.

Trident Practice Message, 2nd June.
Six German E-boats operating in Aberdyfi Bay, green flares have been seen at sea level; report immediately if orange flares are seen.

Trident Practice Message, 11th June.
A good sentry is alert – suspicious and inquisitive.

Trident Practice Message, 13th June.
Everyone must realize that the responsibility for training largely rest with himself.

Another Trident message which caused a stir was the following:

Trident practice Message received which in view of its obscenity and ridiculous as a practice call, we are not recording it in the log book. In view of the nature of the message we suspect a hoax and phoned Tywyn 327 to verify the source.
Your action in not recording on the log book the Trident Practice

Undated photograph of the Aberdyfi Home Guard.

Message received is appreciated; you showed more common sense than the sender.
W. H. Green 1st Lt

19th June
Water taken in the correct spirit is a good drink.
W. H. Grccn, message ends.

6th July
The road block two miles north west of Aberdyfi harbour has been demolished by German AfV. Send 1 Platoon with 3" mortars, 2 CMG immediately to Penhelig Hall Station.

The comradeship and fellowship in the Home Guard was very apparent. *Dad's Army* on TV conveyed the humorous side of the corps, but it was not all fun and games. On the whole, though, every Home Guard man enjoyed the experience of being a part-time soldier or what might be termed in modern-day parlance a citizen soldier.

The following are the names of those who served in the Aberdyfi Company of the Home Guard, part of the 3rd

Battalion of the Merioneth Home Guard. It is not known if the list is complete:

Lt Col. M. I. Jackson, Morawel; Capt. Evans Jones; Lt W. H. Green, Sea View Terr.; Lt J. G. L. Farrar, Trefri; Sgt A. E. Jones, Bryniau Uchaf; Cpl J. W. Lloyd, Penhelig Terr.; Cpl E. O. Williams, Evans Terr.; Cpl A. Green, Moranedd; L/Cpl J. Davies, New Houses; L/Cpl Tom Davies, Penhelig Lodge; L/Cpl H. O. Powell, Gwendon

Privates: J. E. Baines, Trefri Lodge; P. Coughlin, New Houses; W. D. Davies, Nantiesyn; E. R. Davies, Vanner; R. Davies, Copper Hill St.; E. Davies, Morlais; B. Evans, Copper Hill St.; B. Edwards, Terrace Road; O. Edwards, Church Street; W. Eves, Mount Pleasant; J. H. Evans, Fronheulog; E. J. Evans, Tynewydd Farm; E. Fowles, New Street; D. J. Griffiths, Moranedd; M. Griffiths, Copper Hill; A. Green, Moranedd; S. T. Green, Bryn Cottage; D. G. Greenland, Penhelig Terr.; A. L. Galbraith, Crychnant Farm; J. B. Hughes, New Houses; O. Hughes, Penhelig Terr.; E. J. Hughes, Maes y Glyn; W. Hughes, Nantiesyn; Tom Jones, Tainewyddion; A. E. Jones, Bryniau Uchaf; A. N. S. Jones, Abergroes Farm; W. B. Jones, Copper Hill; J. M. Jones, Fronheulog; R. D. Jones, Nantiesyn; G. P. Jones, Dyfi Bungalow; T. Jones, Bodafon; J. G. Jones, Sychnant Farm; M. I. Jackson, Morawel; T. James, Central Pharmacy; M. James, Glandyfi Terr.; D. J. James, Glandyfi Terr.; J. W. Lloyd, Penhelig Terr.; R. T. Lewis, Copper Hill; O. Lloyd, Nantiesyn; R. G. W. Lewis, Glanrafon; F. Morris, New Houses; E. G. Owen, The Hall; John Parry, Copper Hill; F. H. Teal, Hafodarfor; T. Thomas, Penhelig Terr.; H. G. Welby, Tregonwel; J. Wisby, Bodfor Terr.; E. Williams, Evans Terr.; S. W. Williams, Evans Terr.

3 Troop 10 (IA) Commando, X Troop

THE X TROOP is possibly unique in the annals of British military history. Its inception was the brain child of Lord Louis Mountbatten (later Earl Mountbatten), Chief of Combined Operations, and its formation was authorised by Winston Churchill. During the pre-war era, many German and Austrian refugees had come to Britain. They were mostly of Jewish descent and had suffered under the oppression of the Nazi regime, which as a matter of ideology wanted to annihilate and exterminate all Jews.

All these refugees had appeared before alien tribunals and had been classified as refugees from Nazi oppression. Whilst many wished to fight Hitler's regime, they were not allowed to enlist and fight in the British Army but could only join as non-combatants in the Pioneer Corps. This was the first unit to accept aliens as recruits.

It soon became apparent that these people had special skills and a sense of duty far beyond the norm; they had seen their homes and families torn apart and their possessions confiscated for no other reason other than the fact that they were Jewish. They had had to suffer the indignity of wearing armbands to denote that they were Jews, and all this left them with a burning desire to be more than passive non-combatants. They could and would contribute their skills to the best of their ability in order to defeat Hitler's Germany. These men were well educated intellectuals, not riff-raff, and they wanted to exploit their skills and expertise to help the Allies to victory, and the establishment soon came to realise this.

In 1942, when the X Troop was formed, 350 refugees volunteered for 'dangerous duties', with eighty-six being chosen initially. It was Churchill who suggested that they be called the X Troop. As we all remember from our algebra lessons at school, x represents the unknown quantity.

The aim was to train the men chosen to the highest standards in commando skills. They were mostly between 18 and 25 years of age and were all able to speak German fluently. An Army Council Order decreed that, to avoid recriminations, especially if they still had relatives on the Continent, recruits must be given new identities, adopting British names and documentation to safeguard their original identities. The men could choose any suitable name with the exception of 'Smith', as this was a name that some of them had difficulty in pronouncing.

Members of the X Troop would be attached to other elite troops, either in the front line or behind enemy lines, and would perform intelligence, interrogation and reconnaissance tasks, singly or in small groups.

They came to Aberdyfi in September 1942. Only the local policeman, Mr Davies, shared their secrets; locals had an inkling but kept quiet. They were billeted in local private homes and, surprisingly, the locals and the troops became good friends. They were able to entertain the village with dances, lectures and a mixture of social events; in fact, two of the troopers married local girls.

The troop's commanding officer was from Caernarfon: Bryan Hilton-Jones, a Cambridge modern language graduate and fitness fanatic. His father and grandfather had been local doctors practising in Harlech. The troop's training included field craft, camouflage, map and compass reading, marching, rock climbing, demolition, street fighting, firing of British and German weapons, wire cutting, obstacle crossing, day and night patrols, infiltration, housebreaking, lock picking, swimming fully clothed, observation, signalling, and boating. Some later earned their wings as parachutists. At this time, the men could not attain commission rank. When this rule was abolished in 1944, eighteen of them became officers.

Though they were a unit on their own, '3 Troop' were part of the 10th Inter-Allied Commando, which at that time consisted of the following groups: the Dutch in Porthmadog, the French in Criccieth, the Polish in Fairbourne, the Norwegians in Nefyn, and the Belgians in Abersoch.

The CMWTC (Commando Mountain Warfare Training Camp) was at Llanrwst, and the HQ of No. 10 [IA] was at Harlech. The HOC (Holding Operational Command) was at Wrexham Heritage Camp, the present-day site of Ysgol Morgan Llwyd. The commandos also trained in Snowdonia, especially in the area near the Watkin Path. The Cambrian Coast was considered to be ideal for the training of amphibious boats etc. '3 Troop' were also known as the 'British Troop', and although the 10th Commando Unit was trained to fight as an entity, the '3 Troop' acted as an exception.

The war record of '3 Troop' is beyond praise. They served in the Italian and Adriatic theatres, took part in the invasion of Sicily and Normandy, and participated in the advance from the Maas to the Elbe. They served with distinction, though unfortunately twenty members of the troop were killed and twenty-two wounded.

Few commanders gained the respect and admiration of their troops, but Bryan Hilton-Jones commanded by example and with inspired leadership. He was severely wounded in action and was awarded the Military Cross. From the beginning of the war until 1944, all officers were British. As previously stated, the rules were then changed, but by this time 'X Troop' had proved their worth in action. Nevertheless, decorations were scarce, mainly because attached troops seldom qualified for awards. However, one corporal, Ian Harris (born Hans Ludwig in 1920), received the Military Medal.

An imposing memorial was placed in Penhelig Park and suitably inscribed; the residents of Aberdyfi had not forgotten their friends. Sir Meurig Rees of Escuan Hall, Tywyn, and a former Lord Lieutenant of Gwynedd, unveiled it on 15 May 1999 – a fitting monument in an ideal setting. The wording on the memorial states: 'For the members of 3 Troop 10 (IA)

Commando who were warmly welcomed in Aberdyfi while training for special duties in battle 1942–1943. Twenty were killed in action.' A plaque on the sea wall provides further information:

> The British Army Commando Troop consisted of eighty-six German-speaking refugees from Nazi oppression who were given fictitious names and identities as British nationals for their own protection and effectiveness. Commanded by Major Hilton-Jones, MC, their duties were reconnaissance, interrogation and intelligence. Deployed singly or in small groups, they rendered distinguished service in the defeat of Hitler's Germany.

In 1943, Major Hilton-Jones was second in command of the whole of the 10th Commandos, and, whilst still in Aberdyfi, he married Edwina Hughes, a Caernarfon girl. In due course, they were blessed with their first child, a son named Gavin.

Bryan Hilton-Jones first joined the Royal Regiment of Artillery in 1939 and later became involved with the commandos. He took part in the D-Day landings in Normandy but was severely wounded in the stomach and taken prisoner by the Germans. The first news his wife had of him was a broadcast by Lord Haw-Haw from Berlin listing names of prisoners captured, and Bryan was amongst them. She received a letter from him in December 1944 stating that he was a prisoner; he had been hospitalised by the Germans as his condition was extremely critical, but he was eventually released by the Americans and returned to England. It was predicted that his injuries would prevent him from being able to eat normal food again. However, he made a remarkable recovery and was able to eat well again and pursue his love of mountaineering. He was invalided out of the army and joined the Foreign Office, but left to work for ICI before he and his family moved to Spain. Tragically, both he and his two daughters were killed in a car accident near Barcelona in 1970. In his brief history of 3 Troop (IA) Commando (25 April 1946), Major Hilton-Jones said:

This band of 'enemy aliens' volunteers earned for itself a not unflattering reputation. The achievement of which was in no small measure due to the sincerity and wholeheartedness put into his service by every member of the 'Troop'. For them perhaps more than for many others it was a question of self-respect and self-justification.

Ynyslas

Ynyslas does not form part of the Merioneth coastal belt, lying across the Dyfi estuary in Ceredigion. Nevertheless, owing to its close proximity to Aberdyfi, the research work carried out there during WWII inevitably impacted on the Merioneth village.

Ynyslas had a research facility and was one of those 'hush-hush' places. Official information is very scarce, but it is said that the facility played a vital role in the development of rocketry and many of the by-products which came from it such as home insulation and even pacemakers.

The unit was a top-secret missile research facility and had been selected by the Air Ministry to become a missile testing site. Several houses were commandeered by the military and, at one time, the *Camroux III*, anchored at Aberdyfi, provided billets for thirty army officers. The *Camroux III* had completed a detailed survey of the foreshore of Ynyslas, which was later squared off into grids. Each grid was allocated a target reference for the rockets, and this was used to test their accuracy. The ship also used a rocket-testing bed with a thousand rockets, each with its own projector placed aboard. The banks of twenty-five rockets were fired simultaneously on to the mud banks and their landing sites recorded. The *Camroux III* also assisted with the experimental development of radio and radar, as well as with various underwater propulsion systems. It seems that Ynyslas was operational right up until 1946, when testing facilities were transferred to the MOD site at Aberporth.

The above information is taken from 'Heritage of Wales News', the blog of the Royal Commission on Ancient and Historical Monuments of Wales.

The *Camroux III* pictured at Smiths Dock in 1935.

Bryan Hilton-Jones in family group shortly before he and two of his daughters were tragically killed in a motor accident.

Bryan Hilton-Jones in his Army uniform.

Women's Voluntary Service (WVS)

THE WOMEN'S VOLUNTARY Service (WVS) was founded in June 1938 by Stella Isaacs, GBE, the dowager Marchioness of Reading and Baroness Swanborough, in response to the government's request for support in their Air Raid Precautions Act of 1937. They had set out objectives for the WVS, which were 'the enrolment of women, for Air Raid Precaution Service for Local Authorities, to help to bring home to every household what air attack may mean and to make known to every household in the Country what it can do to protect itself and the Community'.

As one would expect, most of the senior posts were held by women who the dowager knew or trusted, and they therefore tended to be from a specific social class. As the WVS was a voluntary organisation, this wasn't a major problem initially, as no one held any specific rank or post. One could be appointed a group leader for a specific task, but on completion of that task become part of another group under another leader working on a different task altogether.

When war was declared, the WVS had around 165,000 members, but by 1943 this had increased to over one million. Uniforms were not supplied initially, but a badge was issued in 1938, and in June 1939 an overcoat and cap were made available, which could be bought for a given price. However, by 1940 instructions had been given that WVS members in responsible positions, especially those in contact with the civil authorities, be asked to wear uniform on official business.

It is very hard to define the work of the WVS. One literally could say, 'When wanted, they would be there.' Their work covered every aspect of life in wartime. Perhaps the first instance where they acted as a working unit was when they helped to organise the evacuation of children from the cities to safer places in the country. They were responsible for the removal of about one and a half million children, and took responsibilty for the logistics of the process. For instance, all children had to be screened to ensure that they were clean and properly clothed and had with them gas masks and other requisite items. Members of the WVS had to personally escort them to their new destinations, either by train or car, and transfer them into the care of the local WVS unit, whose members also acted as billeting officers to house them in appropriate homes. Obviously there were problems, and the WVS had to deal with them – especially the effects that the upheaval of leaving home had on the children.

Mention has already been made of the WVS manning canteens etc. It has to be borne in mind that all their work was done on a voluntary basis and that most of the members were either middle-aged or older. They gave sterling service and one which the service lads appreciated – a 'cup of char' was welcomed at all times. Perhaps the general public did not realise the efforts and sacrifices these ladies had to bear to help those less fortunate than themselves.

The WVS were also involved in organising salvage collections and were active in giving aid to bombed-out families and in helping them to find temporary accommodation. They manned information centres to give details about 'bombed-out' places, they provided rest centres and mobile canteens, gave general support to civil defence operations, and even acted as ambulance drivers. They were a source of comfort to many anxious families after an air raid, and they were able to help, advise and guide families through their anguish and to help them recover. The following article appeared in the *Barmouth Advertiser* on 1 March 1945:

BIRKENHEAD APPRECIATION

Letter to Council

Mr D. H. Davies, LL.B., Clerk to Barmouth Urban District Council, has received the following letter from the Mayor of Birkenhead and Chairman of Birkenhead Education Committee:

'Now that official evacuation is over, the Birkenhead County Borough Council and the Education Committee desire to express their gratitude to the people of Wales for all they did for Birkenhead children throughout a long and anxious period.

We would thank the Billeting Officers and the members of the Women's Voluntary Service whose difficulties we realised, without, we are afraid, being able to do all we would have liked to solve them; the Directors of Education and the Welsh Teachers, who so readily extended to our children the educational facilities which have given Wales its renown, and above all, the foster parents, who not only housed the children but extended to them a warmth of personal affection of which we had ever recurring proofs.

We wish to place our appreciation on record and it is our hope that the future lives of our children will be markedly influenced for good by their experience of country life and by the personal relationships which they have established during the years their home town went through the most trying period of its history.'

Winston Guthrie-Jones with his mother Marie Guthrie-Jones near The Last Inn, Barmouth.

I WISH TO MARK, BY THIS PERSONAL MESSAGE, my appreciation of the service you have rendered to your Country in 1939.

In the early days of the War you opened your door to strangers who were in need of shelter, & offered to share your home with them.

I know that to this unselfish task you have sacrificed much of your own comfort, & that it could not have been achieved without the loyal co-operation of all in your household.

By your sympathy you have earned the gratitude of those to whom you have shown hospitality, & by your readiness to serve you have helped the State in a work of great value.

Elizabeth R

Queen Elizabeth (the royal consort and later the Queen Mother) issued an official letter in which she thanked those people who had taken in evacuees. It was an open letter, but the names of many of those being thanked had been inscribed in the lower left margin of the letter or on the official envelope itself. It was a nice gesture which I am sure was appreciated. In 1966, the name of the WVS was changed to the Women's Royal Voluntary Service (WRVS), and on its seventy-fifth anniversary it was changed again to the Royal Voluntary Service.

Memories Galore

THANKFULLY, TODAY'S YOUNGER generation have no clue or idea as to what life was like during the war. Virtually everything was rationed and, if not rationed, it was very scarce. The concept of 'rationing' was introduced by the government at the start of the war, and the idea behind it was to ensure that everybody had a fair share of what was available. Rationing of 'basic foodstuffs' was introduced almost immediately. Petrol was high on the list, but at that time few had cars – there were fewer than six private cars in the Manod area of Blaenau Ffestiniog and only a few vans being used by businesses. In those days, most goods travelled by rail, so to the average person petrol rationing was no great hardship. Whilst passing the Cambrian Garage on the way to school one morning, I noticed a new Morris 8 priced at £110 on display in the garage showroom. Today, that sum looks ridiculously low, but even then only a few could afford it, and to own a car was a nigh on impossible dream in those days.

By 1940, all basic foods had been rationed: tea, butter, margarine, bacon, sugar, jam, cheese, eggs, meat, and even clothing. The method of rationing was quite simple: a person was allocated so many coupons, which could be redeemed for various commodities. Meat was rationed by price depending on the supply; the average amount was one shilling's worth every week, which equated to about a pound of meat in weight.

By 1942, austerity had become the norm – rice, dried fruits, tinned fruits, chocolate, sweets, biscuits, and soap were also now rationed. Offal and sausages were not generally rationed, but only the selected few were able to procure them. Nevertheless, by late 1943 sausages had also been added to the list.

Imported fruits had disappeared as ships were being used to transport vital war supplies; exotic imported fruits were a luxury, and the cargo space could not be spared. In my earlier book *Barmouth Sea Heroes*, mention is made of a young girl who had been given a bunch of bananas from her seafaring father. Her brother teased her because she didn't know how to peel them; she had never seen a banana before. Agricultural growers in Britain made tremendous progress in producing food, and making the slogan 'Dig for Victory' a reality was the norm for many. Allotments were provided, and people were encouraged to grow their own vegetables, which eased the rationing problems. To the author's recollection, no mention was made about coffee, and no trace of it can be found on any rations list. Had it been completely restricted owing to shipping problems or was it that most of the population drank tea?

On the positive side, the community came closer together, more willing and eager to help one another. 'Dunkirk spirit' came to the fore as the nation realised its difficulties and made a supreme effort to minimise and overcome them. Residents in the cities developed a new sense of humour, more often than not after an air raid, with even partially destroyed shops continuing to sell their wares, often with an appropriately humorous sign outside – 'More Open Than Usual', for instance. It was also at this time that the British art of 'orderly queuing' was born, something that has remained with us ever since.

To see literally hundreds of people moving at night into the London Underground stations in order to sleep in relative safety will remain with me always. They suffered the Blitz, the flying bombs, and later on the V-2 rockets. The drone of the V-1 flying bombs (commonly referred to as 'doodlebugs') was quite distinct, and their paths could be followed. When the engines cut off, they would then start to nosedive towards the ground in deathly silence. This was the calm before the storm. Seconds later would come the thunder of the explosion and the devastating shock waves and vibrations which followed. One watched them fall without knowing exactly where; on exploding, they would literally destroy complete streets. Under such conditions, it was hard to blame anyone for wanting to give up, but in fact the opposite was generally the case. A sense of humour bolstered people's resilience and got them through the bombs and the shortages, which by now had become a way of life. In the end, they knew that they would succeed and overcome the hardships and horrors of the Blitz.

One night, whilst I was serving in Chichester, an air raid was in progress on Portsmouth. I assumed that it was too far away to affect us and went to bed. However, unbeknown to me, a land mine was dropped nearby during the night. I woke up in mid-air, having been caught in the blast, and landed on the floor with a crash. This was a nasty experience, but at least I was alive!

During the war, there were five dominant characters which somehow held the public's and every serviceman's attention. These were Lord Haw-Haw (William Joyce), who had become a well-known radio voice, the disreputable spivs, and the fictional characters of Mr Chad, Kilroy, and Jane. Lord Haw-Haw was regarded as a joke, and though his information could sometimes be correct, he was never taken seriously. People certainly listened to him, and his programme, which began with the radio call of 'Germany Calling, Germany Calling', was well recorded, but his propaganda was never believed, and his programme was, on the whole, regarded merely as entertainment by the British population.

The spiv was a different creature, a product of the time. It is very hard to define what a spiv was, or to understand the origin of the name, but in times of need and shortages there is no doubt that the spiv came into his own. They were able to acquire almost anything for a price, and they would often sell illegal goods at street corners from an old suitcase – always, of course, watching out with half an eye for the police. In their world, everything was available for the right price, and it was at this time that the term 'black market' was born. Spivs generally seemed to be a breed of their own, flamboyantly dressed in loud clothing and ties and normally wearing a long brim felt hat. To a large extent, their attire showed their distaste for the dismal utility clothing almost ubiquitous at the time. The spiv could be classified as a small-time crook, a 'wheeler-dealer', someone who had managed to avoid call-up to the armed services on some pretext or other, and they were mainly to be found in the larger cities. Another term used to describe them was 'black marketeers', as they dealt in scarce commodities which they supplied without coupons – at a price, of course! Private Walker in the *Dad's Army* series is the stereotypical spiv.

The comedian Arthur English also adopted a spiv persona on TV for many years after the war. Despite living outside the law, spivs were believed by many to perform a useful public service. Locally, we had our own black marketeers, though these could hardly be classified as crooks; regulations could never cover every eventuality, neither could they be totally enforced. There was nothing stopping a person from breeding an extra pig above and beyond their quota and then selling it quietly at a good price to a prosperous customer. Similarly, butter could change hands at a good profit, but the buying public did not resent this dubious trade. In a crisis, one was willing to pay over the odds to acquire the odd necessity.

Mr Chad was a fictional character who appeared everywhere but who no one ever saw. He was always portrayed looking over a wall, showing the top half of his face and a large bulbous nose with his fingers protruding over the top. His comments were always to the point, and any free wall space was liable to have his caricature chalked on to it. It is said that he was 'born' in 1941 at a secret radar school in Lincolnshire and that initially he was an illustration on a blackboard depicting the effect of a capacitor in an electrical resistive circuit. From these inauspicious beginning, he developed into a form of cartoon character. Mr Chad was a commentator on shortages, and

311

his 'Wot, no …' slogans ('Wot, no char?', 'Wot, no beer/nylons/bananas?') brought a great deal of mirth to the population and were generally well received.

'Kilroy' was another slogan that appeared everywhere, and is occasionally even seen today. The full slogan was 'Kilroy was here', though this was more of an American creation than Mr Chad. Again, it is not known for certain how 'he' was born or came about, but it is said that the original Kilroy was an inspector checking work on tanks and double-bottomed ships under construction in American shipyards. To satisfy his employers that he was performing his work properly, he would scrawl on the various steel plates 'Kilroy was here'.

American troops, on seeing the slogan on their crafts, adopted it for their own use as a marker in unfamiliar territory – rather like a dog marking his territory. It has to be said that when one entered a strange place it was comforting to know that Kilroy had been there. Later in the war, Mr Chad and Kilroy became attached to each other in one cartoon.

Jane, a glamorous and curvaceous young lady, was a cartoon character in the *Daily Mirror*, and the pin-up of the troops. Jane did more than anybody to keep up morale; her daily antics were always anxiously awaited, and there was always a debate as to which item of flimsy underwear would be removed the following day. One always laughed over her antics; she kept the troops happy and was possibly the forerunner of the 'real' Page 3 girls.

Another memory which has stayed with me was seeing the body of a German sniper who had been shot. There was nothing

unusual in that except that in this case the sniper could not have been more than 16 or 17 years of age and had tried to disguise himself as a Red Cross worker. In another instance, one of the lads came across a dead German soldier who had been wearing a pair of jackboots. He retrieved them for his own use, making the comment that 'Dead soldiers don't want boots'. This philosophy may seem callous today, but those were the accepted values of the day, and it is wrong to judge events of that period by today's standards.

War is not a game – unpleasant and unexpected things happen, and one has to accept these and make the best of them. If the question is asked, was the war necessary and justified, the overall answer has to be 'Yes'. At the same time, however, one should be thankful for having survived it and not forget those who perished in safeguarding our way of life and heritage.

Appendix

The following list gives an idea of what was allowed per week on rations, although amounts often varied depending on supply:

Bacon and ham 4oz (equivalent to 3/4 thin slices of our pre-packed meats)

Sugar – 8oz

Loose tea – 2oz (there were no tea bags then; equivalent now to fifteen teabags)

Meat was controlled by price; on average the amount to be had was based on one shilling's worth, which equated to about 1lb of a cheap cut of beef. A lamb loin chop would weigh about 4oz, a pork loin chop around 8oz

Cheese fluctuated between 1 and 2oz (a pack of 200g is the equivalent of around half a pound or 8oz)

Marmalade, jam, treacle – 8oz per month

Lard – 2oz

Eggs – one per week, two occasionally, or a packet of dried eggs per month (suitable for scrambled eggs)

Sweets and chocolates – 8oz per month

Milk – 3 pints or one tin of milk powder equivalent to 8 pints
every 8 weeks
  Flour
  Biscuits
  Coal – 1 cwt per week per household
  Rice and dried fruit
  Soap – 4 coupons per month, with 1 coupon each for 4oz of hard
soap, 3oz of toilet soap, a 3oz pack of soap flakes, and a 6oz pack
of soap powder
  Tinned tomatoes and peas
  Sausages – not rationed prior to 1943
  Curtailment of gas and electricity
  Vegetables – not rationed as to a great extent they were largely
home-grown, though shortages did occur

Another restriction which the general public was asked to observe was in the use of bath water. It was asked that people fill their bath tubs to a depth of five inches only. King George VI was said to have had all the baths at Buckingham Palace painted with a line to mark this depth.

Clothing was also rationed from 1942 using a points system: sixty-six coupons per person per year, lowered to forty-eight in 1942, and again to thirty-six in 1943. All items of clothing were allocated a points value: sixteen points for a man's raincoat, fifteen for a woman's, eight points for a pair of trousers, seven for a pair of boots, five for a pair of shoes, and eight points for a skirt.

It was no wonder that spivs were able to generate trade by selling nylons to women. It should be added, however, that in large towns and cities residents could supplement their rations by going to a British Restaurant for a meal, and most factories had a works canteen which was able to supply workers with hot meals outside the rationing system. Country folk did not have these extra facilities, but did have opportunities to grow more of their own produce. It is hard not to wonder, when considering the abundance of food available today, whether the present generation could have coped with what was available then.

Local Defences

Air Raid Shelters

The influx of refugees from various large English conurbations was an indication that the north Wales area was seen as a reasonably safe place to live during the war. There were no nightly air raids, and air raid shelters were not a part of daily life in this area.

Other areas were not so fortunate, and the government quickly realised that the Germans were contemplating air raids on the larger towns and cities as a means of demoralising the population. As a consequence, protection, by means of shelters, had to be devised. Public communal shelters were constructed by local authorities for the use of pedestrians, drivers, and passengers etc., who had been caught outside during air raids. These shelters were intended to accommodate about fifty people; they had 14-inch thick brick walls with a 12-inch reinforced concrete roof above.

For home purposes, two types of shelter were mass produced and made available: the Morrison shelter and the Anderson shelter.

The Morrison shelter was a self-assembly kit to be used inside the home. Measuring 6 feet 6 inches long, 4 feet wide, and 2 feet 6 inches high, it had a solid steel plate, an eighth of an inch thick, on top, welded wire mesh sides and a lath type floor, and weighed some 5 cwts. It was designed to enable a normal-sized family to sleep in it at night and to give some protection from air raids and falling debris. When not in use as a shelter, it could double up as a normal table.

Morrison shelter

Morrison Shelter used as a dining table

Anderson shelter

The Anderson shelter was designed for outdoor use and could accommodate up to six people. Resembling a miniature Nissen hut, it comprised six curved and six straight panels of galvanised corrugated steel sheets. When bolted together, the curved panels formed the centre section, with the straight panels completing the ends, one of which was fitted with a door. The shelters were 6 feet high, 4 feet 6 inches wide, and 6 feet 6 inches long, and were designed to be buried at a depth of 4 feet in the ground and covered with a minimum of 15 inches of soil above the roof. The soil could then be planted with vegetables or flowers. The internal fittings were left to the discretion of individual owners, who were also supplied with

317

Stanton Air Raid Shelter

A picture of a pillbox taken in 1984 at Bennar Beach, Dyffryn Ardudwy. Reproduced by kind permission of Mr Hugh Roberts, Barmouth.

Home Guard observation post at Aberamffra, Barmouth. From inside, the post affords a clear view over Barmouth Bridge and the Mawddach Estuary. During the war it would probably have been continually manned until the threat of invasion had abated.

a manual handpump to remove water from the floor of the completed unit. Without doubt, both shelters reduced injuries and deaths from nearby bomb blasts and flying shrapnel. Both types were supplied by the local authority and were free if the family income was less than £5 a week. Otherwise, a charge of £7 was levied.

In 1984, Mr Hugh Roberts of Barmouth photographed a concrete construction at Rowen Farm, Tal-y-bont, Barmouth. This appears to be an example of a Stanton air raid shelter made by the Stanton Ironworks, Nottingham. They were made from steel reinforced precast concrete sections some 20 inches wide. At either end were flat concrete panels with a height of 7 feet in the centre. As far as can be ascertained, this structure was demolished in the summer of 2013. It may have been purchased post-war by the local farmer as a shed for storing feed or other farm implements. Many shelters suffered the inglorious fate of becoming henhouses.

Mawddach Crescent, Fegla, Arthog

Sentry posts still evident at the entrance.

Anti-Tank Measures

After the fall of France and other European countries, the lesson learnt by the British military authorities was that the key battles had been won by German tanks and their tactics. To prevent a repeat of such victories in the UK, it was vital that impediments be placed at strategic places to combat the threat of sudden tank attacks.

Towns and villages were protected by a series of concrete pillboxes and obstructions, while road blocks were placed at crossroads and bends in the road. The intention of these was to slow down and hinder any advancing force, thus giving the defenders the opportunity to concentrate their firepower in one direction. The defenders would have been armed with heavy and light machine guns, light mortars and rifles. They would have been drawn from the regular army or the Home Guard.

Heavy rail lines or steel girders were also bent, riveted or welded to form obstructions on main roads. The steel formed two uprights, one shorter than the other so that the top bar would be inclined at an angle of about 60° to the road, and they were known as 'hedgehogs'. These were inserted in prepared sockets on main roads, about 2 to 3 feet apart. The sockets had a cover on them, which allowed normal traffic usage to continue but enabled the barricades to be inserted quickly if and when they were required. The author remembers seeing these in position by the GWR railway bridge near the Wynnes Arms Hotel, Manod, during a Home Guard training session. Barricades of this type would raise up the front of any tank trying to pass through and would give defending forces the opportunity to fire at the tank's weakest point, its underbelly.

Talyllyn Pass, A487

Three stone-built tank obstructions remain visible to this day on the roadside between Dolgellau and Corris. They can be seen just below the summit of the Talyllyn Pass.

Bwlch Oerddrws, A470

Identical obstructions were built at Bwlch Oerddrws along the road between Dolgellau and Dinas Mawddwy.

Erected in 1940, the obstructions used locally quarried rock with mortar to bind. When completed, they stood some 6 feet high and 4 feet 6 inches square at the base, with the gaps between them infilled with rubble. They were situated so that both sides of the road were obstructed, from the slopes on the north side of the road to the valley below the road to the south. To cross the valley, the blocks descended a bank to a small stream at the bottom and then continued up the opposite slope as far as crags on a nearby hill. They run for a distance of some 75 yards. They were part of the Western Command stop line system, which covered a large area of Wales. In our area, the blocks were located to protect access to Liverpool, Birmingham and south Wales, and ran in a line from Rhyl to Machynlleth.

Talyllyn Pass,
A487 Road

Bwlch
Oerddrws,
A470 Road

Bwlch
Oerddrws,
A470 Road

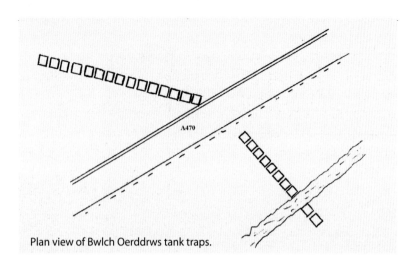

Plan view of Bwlch Oerddrws tank traps.

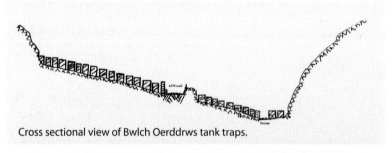

Cross sectional view of Bwlch Oerddrws tank traps.

A Hedgehog anti-tank device.

Fairbourne Anti-Invasion Defences

Fairbourne had hundreds of concrete blocks and pillboxes along its seafront. These were to stop any landings from the sea and can still be seen today. Dyffryn Ardudwy beach, further up the coast, was a prohibited area as the beach had iron stakes inserted in it to stop any German aircraft or gliders using it as a landing place.

Pillbox

Pillbox within a line of concrete anti-invasion defences

Military Mawddach: 20th Century Military Sites, Monuments and Artefacts around the Mawddach Estuary

Written by Graham and Jacky O'Hanlon, *Military Mawddach* is an illustrated fifty-four page guide to over fifty wartime sites and places of interest in the area, all of which are photographed and documented. The guide can be downloaded (for a small fee) from their website.[15]

The authors have kindly granted permission for me to list the following sites of interest with accompanying grid references:

Camps

Burma	SH582 092
Bronaber	SH715 319
Gibraltar	SH612 054
Iceland	SH631 148
Matapan	SH599 023
Morfa	SH579 011
Tonfannau	SH560 038

Observation Posts

Aberdyfi	SN597 967
Llyn Cregennen	SH658 144
Ynyslas	SN608 925

Pillboxes

Barmouth	SH623 157
Egryn (disguised)	SH593 198
Fairbourne #1	SH611 120
Fairbourne #2	SH611 125
Maentwrog	SH643 400
Tywyn Beach	SN593 969
Ynyslas	SN627 936

---

[15] www.mawddachestuary.co.uk/military_mawddach.html. Further information can be obtained from www.mawddachestuary.co.uk

Tank Traps

Bwlch Oerddrws	SH795 172
Bwlch Llyn Bach	SH751 133
Fairbourne	SH612 120
Llyn Gwernan	SH705 160
Happy Valley	SN656 994
Mawddach Estuary	SH646 156

Others

Beach Defences, Fairbourne	SH611 123
Bronaber Artillery Range	SN725 309
Harlech Anti-Tank Range	SH577 333
Llanbedr Airfield	SH570 261
Peniarth Medical Centre	SH611 060
RASC Amphibious School	SN580 999

All these defences were erected in haste during 1940, but the threat of imminent invasion had passed by the middle of 1941 when Germany invaded Russia.

Surcouf: the Mysterious French Submarine & the Barmouth Connection

ONE OF THE most intriguing and mysterious stories of WWII is the story of the French submarine *Surcouf*.

Today, it is almost impossible to disentangle fact from fiction, so many different accounts are given of various incidents involving this vessel that the truth has become lost in a deep watery grave. The submarine was named after a wealthy French privateer, Robert Surcouf, who harried English ships at the turn of the eighteenth and nineteenth centuries. Surcouf was a French hero adored by his countrymen for his success at besting the hated English.

Surcouf was better known as 'King of the Corsairs' (a corsair being an archaic term for a pirate). During his legendary career, he captured forty-seven ships and was renowned for his gallantry and chivalry. In his younger years, Surcouf[16] was heavily involved in the slave trade; transporting slaves between Africa and Réunion (a French owned island to the east of Madagascar) in the Indian Ocean. Although this trade was outlawed in 1794, he continued unabated and amassed a

---

[16]   A statue of Surcouf can be seen in St Malo, but there is no mention of his early days participating in the slave trade.

considerable fortune from his illicit slave trading. Welsh people can also be proud of him, as he was a Breton born in Saint-Malo in 1773. Educated by the Jesuits, Surcouf enlisted on a merchantman sailing to India at the age of fifteen, but upon his return to Saint-Malo he found that the French Revolution had taken place and that life had become very different in France.

He sailed to Mauritius, then a French possession, only to discover on arrival that France was at war with Britain. He served as first officer on the 44-gun frigate *Cybèle* and was promoted to captain when he expressed an ambition to become a privateer against Britain. At that time it was difficult to obtain authorisation and a 'letter of marque': a document issued by the French national government authorising a sea captain to sink and plunder ships which were enemies of France. A 'letter of marque' would normally allow the holder to retain a portion of his booty, but Surcouf set sail in the brig *Créole* (he had been given orders to bring back rice to Mauritius) having failed to obtain this document.

At sea, Surcouf encountered three English ships, forcing them to lower their colours (flags) after a brief encounter. The three ships were escorted back to Mauritius, together with their cargos of rice and maize, and Surcouf was welcomed as a saviour in the famished capital Port Louis. The seizure of these goods was declared legal, but since Surcouf did not have a 'letter of marque', the authorities confiscated the whole cargo, refusing to allocate a portion to Surcouf, the privateer or corsair responsible for its capture.

In May 1800, Surcouf took command of *Confiance*, a fast, 22-gun ship from Bordeaux which had been under repairs in Mauritius. He led a brilliant campaign and captured nine British ships. In October, his ship encountered the 26-gun *Kent*, a 229-ton Indiaman which, with passengers, had over four hundred souls on board. Robert Surcouf managed to take her intact.

Surcouf became a living legend in France, but in England he was regarded as a public enemy and had a price of five million francs on his head. In 1809, Napoléon Bonaparte personally offered him the title of captain and command of a frigate squadron, but Surcouf refused. His preference was for an independent command, to which Napoleon eventually agreed. Surcouf was made an officer of the *Légion d'Honneur* on 18 July 1804.

In February 1809, Surcouf arrived in France with a cargo of eight million francs. Robert Surcouf died in 1827, aged 53. In many respects, his life is reminiscent of a Welsh privateer from a century earlier, Henry Morgan, who was knighted and made an admiral in the Royal Navy and later became governor of Jamaica. Morgan was one of the most notorious and successful privateers of his period, and his exploits in the Caribbean, including successful raids on Spanish settlements, have become legendary. However, whereas Morgan had a reputation for being the most ruthless privateer ever to operate along the Spanish Main, Surcouf was noted for his firm but fair discipline and his humane treatment of prisoners.

To date, a total of five French ships have carried Surcouf's name, the submarine cruiser *Surcouf* being the third to do so. Launched in 1929, *Surcouf* was commissioned (brought into active service) in 1934. Weighing in at just over 3,300 tons, she was 361 feet long, making her at that time the largest submarine in the world. Equipped with two diesel engines and two electric motors, she was capable of eighteen knots on the surface and of ten knots when submerged. She had an operating range of 10,000 miles.

Her armaments comprised twin 8-inch guns in a single turret, fourteen torpedoes, and a 16-foot motorboat. A hanger aft of her conning tower housed a Marcel Berson-411 observation seaplane, capable of 110 knots and a range of 400 kilometres. In all, she was quite a formidable fighting ship.

The *Surcouf* was designed as a commerce raider, capable of seeking and engaging in surface combat. Because of this role, she was equipped with facilities to secure forty prisoners.

After commissioning, *Surcouf* had very little chance of showing her potential as a commerce raider; most of her sailing was done above water and mainly just to show the flag. She was plagued with mechanical problems and rolled badly in rough seas. Trim was difficult to adjust during a dive, with it taking over two minutes to dive to a depth of around forty feet. Without radar, this would have made her vulnerable to attacks by aircraft.

At the outbreak of WWII, she undertook convoy work, but had to return to Brest for repairs to her hydroplanes and rudder. In June 1940, when Germany invaded France, *Surcouf* was still at Brest awaiting repairs. To avoid capture, she sailed for Plymouth, limping across the Channel with a broken rudder and one defunct engine.

By the time France surrendered, *Surcouf* was safe in Plymouth, tied up to the old French battleship *Paris* astern of HMS *Revenge*. Fearing that the French might hand over their fleet to the Germans, the British launched Operation Catapult. This gave the French ships four options: rejoin the fight against the Germans, put their ships out of reach of the Germans, scuttle their own ships, or face being sunk by the British.

Most ships accepted these terms and surrendered their ships to the British authorities. The two main exceptions were the North African Fleet based at Mers-el-Kébir and other French Navy ships based in Dakar. Elsewhere, French ships were boarded by armed sailors and marines at various ports in Britain and Canada. The only serious incident occurred in Plymouth on 3 July, when a boarding party from HMS *Revenge* boarded both the *Surcouf* and the *Paris*.

The sentries on the *Paris* were taken by surprise. However, the first man down the ladder of the *Surcouf*, Leading Seaman Webb, was shot and killed by a French officer. He in turn was shot and killed by a British officer following behind Webb. Two other British officers were fatally wounded before the

Surcouf's captain bowed to the inevitable and surrendered. It is tempting to speculate whether the spirit of the old privateer Robert Surcouf had anything to do with the skirmish between the British and French. The *Surcouf's* crew would have known of his exploits and may have wanted to emulate his success in fighting the English.

The taking of the *Surcouf* increased tensions between Britain and the new Vichy government in France. Tensions mounted still further when a hospital ship carrying members of *Surcouf's* crew who had chosen to be repatriated to France was attacked and sunk by a German U-boat. Rather than point the finger at Germany, the collaborationist government in France blamed Britain for their deaths.

Fourteen crewmen on the *Surcouf* and one officer, Louis Blaison, opted to stay in Britain and join the Free French Navy. The *Surcouf* herself was refitted and handed over to the Free French in August 1940. In the interim, it appears that the fourteen crewmen who had chosen to stay and fight Hitler's Germany were stationed in Barmouth, with ten of the sailors being billeted in a boarding house kept by Mrs Caddie Owen of Moss Bank – wife of the local barber Jack Owen.

It is not known why they came so far from their base – Barmouth being at least 270 miles from Plymouth – at a time when travelling was so difficult. It has been suggested that they might have been billeted locally to keep the crew isolated from those who had elected to return to France, though they would have encountered other sailors loyal to Vichy French in Barmouth at the time. Local residents remember the *Surcouf* crewmen holding parades and roll calls every morning on the old recreation ground at the north end of Barmouth where the council houses now are. It is not clear what they did for the rest of the day. Mrs Owen's son, Tommy, remembers them well, particularly their peculiar taste in food. Nevertheless, the question of why they came to Barmouth has still not been satisfactorily answered. Was it to rendezvous with somebody? Who paid for their quarters?

It is possible that they had been granted leave, but then one cannot envisage how they would even have heard of Barmouth, let alone want to stay there when the attractions of London were so much nearer. Also, the fact that they organised parades and roll calls suggests that they were in Wales on official duty. Barmouth, though, had no naval facilities, and it remains a mystery what these duties might have been. Like so many things about the *Surcouf*, what is known raises plenty of questions, but clear-cut answers are not readily available. What is certain is that like all soldiers and sailors in a foreign country, the crew of the *Surcouf* left their mark in Barmouth. Even today, photos of the sailors can still be found in the town, and local residents recall many of their names.

After the refit, *Surcouf* was transferred to the Free French Navy, and Louis Blaison was appointed her commander. The tension between the French and English persisted, with each side making accusations that they were spying for the Vichy government. On one occasion, the British even accused the *Surcouf* of attacking their ships.

The Royal Navy was reluctant to recommission the *Surcouf*, as her complement of around 110 to 130 men was the equivalent to the normal crew of three British submarines.

By coincidence or calculation, the British decided to place a liaison team on board the *Surcouf*. This consisted of a sub lieutenant, a leading signaller, and a telegraphist, all of whom would presumably monitor the activities of the submarine and report back to the British authorities.

Subsequently, the *Surcouf* was sent to the British base at Halifax, Nova Scotia, and given the task of escorting trans-Atlantic convoys. In April 1941, whilst docked at Devonport, she was damaged by German bombers and was taken in July of that year to the United States Naval Shipyard in Portsmouth, New Hampshire. After a three months refit, she continued to New London, Connecticut. The American authorities had not recognised the Free French government, so it is difficult to understand why they allowed the *Surcouf* to be repaired in their yards.

Surcouf left New London on 29 November 1941 to return to Halifax. Here she picked up an admiral from the Free French forces and took him to Quebec City. Rumours were circulating that *Surcouf* was going to liberate the French overseas territory of St Pierre and Miquelon from Vichy control – and this is exactly what happened. On 24 December, in conjunction with the Free French corvettes *Mimosa*, *Aconit* and *Alysse*, *Surcouf* took control of the islands for the Free French without resistance.

This was an action that had major repercussions in America. The American Secretary of State, Cordel Hull, had only recently concluded talks with the Vichy French government in which he had agreed to respect the neutrality of French possessions in the western hemisphere. He threatened to resign unless President Roosevelt demanded the restoration of Vichy control over the islands. The president contacted General de Gaulle to discuss the situation, but, as might be expected, any suggestion that de Gaulle relinquish his newly won territory was met with a resounding 'Non, Non, Non'. Faced with this fait accompli, Roosevelt quietly dropped the matter.

According to one unconfirmed report, President Roosevelt sent a destroyer to St Pierre on 1 January 1942 to restore it to Vichy control; it is also alleged that the *Surcouf* fired on the destroyer killing two American sailors. There is no supporting evidence to suggest such an incident ever occurred, though it is of course possible that the authorities were able to hush it up.

Later that month, de Gaulle ordered *Surcouf* to the Pacific, triggering rumours that she would attempt to liberate Martinique from Vichy control. Her official orders, however, were to head for Sydney, Australia, via Tahiti.

After leaving Halifax on 2 February 1942, the *Surcouf* headed for Bermuda to take on supplies. This was her last port of call, which she left on 12 February, bound for the Panama Canal. After leaving Bermuda, however, she was never seen again.

The fate of the *Surcouf* has never been confirmed conclusively. An American freighter, the SS *Thompson Lykes*, steaming from Guantanamo Bay, reported hitting and running down a partially submerged object on 18 February, which scraped her side and keel. They heard voices but continued ahead without stopping, thinking they had struck a German U-boat.

The incident was reported to the Panama authorities, but there were no other reports of U-boats in the vicinity. The captain of the freighter may have been aware of this, but nevertheless decided to continue. It has to be assumed that the object which the *Thompson Lykes* struck was the *Surcouf*, although subsequent inspection of the freighter showed little sign of damage. It is possible, therefore, that the Surcouf did not sink immediately, but was able to continue towards the Panama Canal. If the *Thompson Lykes* incident did sink the Surcouf, then her wreck currently lies in water some 3,000 metres (9,800 feet) deep.

However, it may have been another incident, the following day, that was responsible for the French submarine's demise. Records of the American 6th Heavy Bomber Group, operating out of Panama, indicate that they sunk a large submarine on the morning of 19 February 1942. Their reports show that two A-17 and one B-18 aircraft were deployed, dropping eight bombs on the submarine. However, no German U-boats were recorded as being lost on that date, so it is more than probable that it was the *Surcouf* that the American Air Force attacked and sunk. The people of Cape San Blas, some fifty miles east of Panama, said that several bodies had been found and buried in their town.

A French inquiry also came to the conclusion that the submarine had been sunk by 'friendly fire'. In his book *The French Navy in World War II*, Rear Admiral Auphan states:

'For reasons which appear to have been primarily political she was rammed at night in the Caribbean by an American freighter.' General de Gaulle in his memoirs had little to say on the subject, save that the *Surcouf* was 'sunk with all hands'.

In memory of the *Surcouf* and those who lost their lives, a memorial was unveiled on 23 September 1951 by General de Gaulle on the quayside at Cherbourg. The names of all 130 French members of crew are listed, together with the three members of the Royal Navy liaison team: Sub Lieutenant Roger John Gilbert Burney, Leading Signaller Harold Frank Warner, and Telegraphist Bernard Gough.

It is virtually impossible to determine the exact reason why the *Surcouf* sank. Rumours abound, and there has always been a suspicion that – as Rear Admiral Auphan remarks – the French submarine was sunk for political reasons. If the admiral was right, then the ramming of the *Surcouf* by the *Thompson Lykes* was a deliberate act, albeit one that failed to sink the *Surcouf* immediately. As a result, the heavy bombers were called in to deliver the 'coup de grâce'.

However, no conclusive proof either way has ever come to light. Whether the true cause of why the *Surcouf* sank is ever proved beyond reasonable doubt largely depends on whether the submarine's wreck is ever found and investigated. Only then will Robert Surcouf's soul finally be laid to rest.

The Truth Revealed by Robert Ifor Roberts

Following the controversial capitulation of France in May 1940 and the decimation of the British Army, many units of the French forces, in particular French naval ships and personnel, fled to Britain.

In Barmouth, a large contingent of French sailors arrived and was billeted in numerous hotels and boarding-houses, including my home, Llys-y-Delyn. I was sixteen at the time and sitting my school-certificate exams at the local County

School. As I had studied the French language as one of my school subjects, I welcomed the opportunity to put this facility (such as it was!) to good effect, and soon forged a cordial relationship with our French guests, particularly with two of the younger sailors, Gilles and Andre. Few of the French matelots could speak any English.

I quickly gained in confidence and facility in French and on at least one occasion was called to the Admin. Office, two doors away from Llys-y-Delyn to assist with interpretation between the billeting staff (a young British Army officer and his ATS typist/secretary, both non-French-speaking) and various French personnel on some very minor matters. Relations between the French sailors and the local population were initially very cordial and many long-term friendships were cemented.

Shortly after my 17th birthday on 3 July 1940 – a most significant date in world history for reasons which at that time I had no inkling - I was in our downstairs sitting-room with our French friends, where a card game was in progress. Suddenly a violent argument broke out, followed by a scuffle where a knife was produced. Things looked very ugly until Pierre (one of the senior ratings) was able to calm things down. Not long afterwards some of our 'guests' were taken away by the British military. My two good friends explained to me that these were supporters of the Vichy government and had been taken to a holding camp in Liverpool with a view to eventual repatriation. Gilles and Andre were followers of General Charles de Gaulle and his Free French forces. I remained in contact with them when they served on a French minesweeper, but lost touch with them when I later joined the Royal Navy.

I am greatly indebted to my two friends for the insights they gave me into French culture and the French Navy. It was through them, for example, that I learned of the huge French submarine the 'Surcouf' (which carried a seaplane in a hangar abaft the conning tower) and why July 3rd had

Members of the *Surcouf* crew during their stay at Barmouth

Free French at Barmouth

been such a turning point in Franco-British relations. It was not until after the war had ended that the truth about Winston Churchill's fatal decision to forcibly seize or destroy all French naval ships not under British control was revealed. This had a devastating effect upon future relationships between Britain and France, of which few people were aware at the time. Thanks to my school French I had at least had a peep 'behind the curtain.'

Epilogue

To mark the consecration of the new Coventry Cathedral in May 1962, the composer Benjamin Britten was commissioned to compose the *War Requiem*. The original fourteenth-century cathedral had been destroyed by bombing during WWII.

Britten was delighted by the commission, which gave him complete freedom in deciding the type of music to compose. He chose to set the traditional Latin Mass for the Dead interwoven with nine poems by Wilfred Owen, the famous poet who was killed in action on 4 November 1918, a week before the armistice was signed.

The work was adjudged to be one of the most poignant classical pieces of the twentieth century. Britten dedicated it to four individuals: Pier Dunkerley, David Gill, Michael Halliday, and Roger Burney of the submarine *Surcouf*.

On leaving Barmouth, crew members of the *Surcouf* gave Mr and Mrs Owen small photographs inscribed on the rear with their gratitude and names. Some of these are reproduced below.

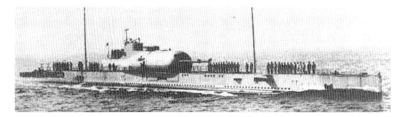

Photograph of the *Surcouf* at sea

Photographs courtesy of Tom Owen

Military Awards
WWII

Brigadier Charles Hilary Vaughan (Pritchard), DSO, and also recipient of the Greek 'Commander of the Order of King George I with Cross Swords'

F/ Lieut RAF J. Bradley, MM, for service in Crete and also recipient of the Greek government DSM

Captain William Jones, OBE, for service on Arctic convoys

Major Tillman, MC with Bar (WWI), DSO (WWII)

Major Humphrey Lloyd Jones, MC, for service in Algeria/Tripoli

Major Desmond Owen, MC, Penmaen Isaf, Dolgellau

Major Dafydd Wyn Jones Williams, MC, for service in North Africa

Major William Hall, MC, Bontddu, for service in France

Another recipient of a military decoration was Howel Eric Jones, who as a youngster lived at Llechwedd Isaf, Cwm Teigl, Llan Ffestiniog. Eric joined the Royal Navy Coastal Command and served on motor torpedo boats (MTBs). In August 1944, his flotilla was based at Arromanches, France. On 20 August, his flotilla was involved in a skirmish with German E-boats and R-boats at the mouth of the River Seine near Le Havre. Eric was part of a three-man gun crew operating a six-pounder. In the course of the action, his two mates were killed, while the boat was severely damaged and had to be towed back to base. Eric was awarded the Distinguished Service Medal for his part in the action, but unfortunately he did not receive his medal from King George VI as he was away on official business.

Another recipient of the military British Empire Medal was

Flight Sergeant Dewi Jones from Llan Ffestiniog. The award was announced on 14 June 1945, but the award citation has not survived. The following Barmouth people also received awards:

Miss Phyllis Hartley, BEM (Mil.)

L/Seaman Berridge, DSM, for service at Dunkirk

Sergeant Neville Jessop, MM, for service on the Anzio Beach Head, Italy

Bombardier J. Shone, MM, for outstanding bravery in Malaya fighting against the Japanese

Unfortunately, an appeal in the local press for information on recipients of gallantry awards during WWII has been very disappointing, and due to a lack of information, this list may be incomplete.

Er Coffadwriaeth (Remembrance): 1939–45

Mewn Angof Ni Chânt Fod
Lest we Forget

Gweddi o Goffadwriaeth

gan y Parchedig Dewi Morris, Porthmadog

Ein Tad nefol a sanctaidd, carem ddiolch i Ti am y cyfle a gawsom i gofio am y rhai a aberthodd eu bywydau dros eu gwlad.

Diolch ein bod wedi gallu rhannu profiadau arbennig, dwys a dwfn, a chofio am y rhai sydd wedi cerdded llwybr anodd, peryglus a chreulon.

Carem gyflwyno i'th ofal rai yn eu profedigaeth a'u hiraeth. Carem ddiolch am y profiad – er ei fod yn un dwys – o allu mynd yn ôl mewn atgofion a hanes, gan gydnabod:

'Araf iawn ŷm ni i ddysgu,
Amyneddgar iawn wyt Ti.'

Diolch ein Tad dy fod yn noddfa a nerth, ac yn gymorth hawdd dy gael bob amser. Yr wyt Ti wedi cynnal, ac yn dal i gynnal, teuluoedd lawer yn eu trallod a'u hiraeth.

O Dduw, arwain ni i heddwch a chyfiawnder.

Rho inni dy dangnefedd, cadw ein calonnau a'n meddyliau yn Iesu Grist ein Harglwydd; a nerth yr Ysbryd Glân a drigo yn ein plith yn awr a hyd byth.

Amen

Lest we Forget

by the Rev. Patrick Slattery, Dolgellau

Lord God, we remember how you created this planet on which we live by bringing order out of chaos. You created the Garden of Eden in all its beauty and saw it was good. You created humans so they could enjoy the benefits and beauty of this world. You gave to us free will to enable us to live and love and become stewards of this beautiful world. We remember how we have failed you by neglecting our responsibilities and becoming destructive beings. We have become obsessed with power and greed and have become destructive beings. This has caused so much unnecessary suffering and loss of lives.

We remember all those who have given their lives to safeguard others in some of the most horrendous acts of man's inhumanity to man caused by times of war. They gave their lives to secure our future. Many perished and have no memorial. We need to remember them in our hearts.

The futility of war has made us aware how vulnerable we are in this age of weapons of mass destruction. We must remember that war is what happens when language fails; there are no winners in war, so there is no purpose to it. The futility of war has made us aware how vulnerable we are in this age of weapons of mass destruction. Help us to remember how foolish we have been, Lord.

Teach us, good Lord, to work together as the nations of this earth to secure peace and justice for all the peoples of this world.

O God of love, our Prince of Peace, make us, we pray, people to work for worldwide peace.

A Prayer for the Fallen

by Les Darbyshire

Almighty, and everlasting God, who art always more ready to hear than we are to pray and are wont to give more than we desire or deserve.

We beseech you, O Lord, in this our prayer of Remembrance, to open our hearts and mind and be mindful of the supreme sacrifice of one's dear brothers and sisters in conflict of war.

We remember all those killed in the war, servicemen and women and civilians who believed that their cause was just and were willing to sacrifice their lives for their beliefs. They also believed that their actions would bring everlasting peace and goodwill to all men. We honour their memories.

We pray for those who needlessly died whilst solely following their daily occupations. We remember them.

Grant us peace, O Lord, let us remember the dedication of the fallen and remember the chaos and destruction and aftermath of war so that we, who remain, can build a world worthy of the ideals in which they believed in.

Let us pray for humanity
May God hold them in peace
May Love flow over the Earth and cleanse us all
This Day and Always. Amen.

War Memorials

The Circular Tour of Remembrance

The reader is invited to join a photo tour of the war memorials in the area.

The tour starts at the Memorial Hospital, Blaenau Ffestiniog and The Oakeley Quarry Memorial at Rhiw then moves on to Maentwrog, Penrhyndeudraeth, Llandecwyn, Talsarnau, Harlech, Llanbedr, Dyffryn Ardudwy, Barmouth, Bontddu, Arthog, Llwyngwril, Tywyn and Aberdyfi before veering back towards Blaenau via Corris, Dolgellau, Trawsfynydd and Llan Ffestiniog.

Please pause and reflect at each print, remembering the words:

A Prayer for the Fallen
They shall not grow old, as we that are left grow old:
Age shall not weary them, nor the years condemn.
At the going down of the sun and in the morning
We will remember them.

R. L. Binyon
1914

Blaenau Ffestiniog War Memorial Hospital

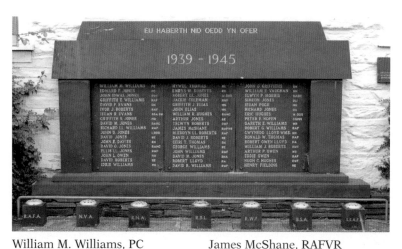

William M. Williams, PC

Edward F. Jones, PC

John Idwal Jones, RWF

Griffith E. Williams, RAF

David P. Evans, RN

Ivor J. Roberts, RAF

Ieuan R. Evans, SBA, RN

Griffith S. Jones, MN

David M. Jones, RASC

Richard Ll. Williams, RWF

John D. Jones, I. GDS

David Jones, RE

John E. Davies, RN

David O. Jones, RAMC

Ellis Ll. Jones, RWF

John L. Owen, MN

David Roberts, RE

Idris Williams, MN

Hywel Thomas, RE

Emrys W. Roberts, RN

Robert Ll. Jones, W. GDS

Jackie Coleman, RWF

Griffith J. Elias, MN

John Elias, MN

William R. Hughes, RAMC

Arthur Jones, RE

Tecwyn Roberts, RWF

James McShane, RAFVR

Bleddyn Ll. Roberts, RAF

David J. Roberts, RE

Ceiri T. Thomas, RN

George Williams, RE

John Williams, RWF

David M. Jones, RHA

Robert Lloyd, RA

David R. Williams, RWF

John O. Griffiths, RN

William E. Vaughan, RN

Elwyn P. Morris, RAOC

Simeon Jones, DLI

Ieuan Pugh, MN

Richard Jones, RN

Eric Hughes, W. GDS

Peter E. Hopen, COMM

Gareth E. Williams, WR

Robert G. Williams, RAF

Gwynedd Lloyd Williams, RN

Ronald W. Thomas, RAF

Robert Owen Lloyd, RA

William J. Roberts, RWF

Arthur P. Owen, WR

Eddie Owen, RAF

Hugh C. Hughes, RWF

Henry Fielding, RE

Rhiw

Roll of Honour
Employees of The Oakeley Slate Quarries Co. Ltd.
1914–1919
(No WWII Casualties inscribed thereon)

Maentwrog

Maentwrog
(No WWII Casualties inscribed thereon)

Penrhyndeudraeth

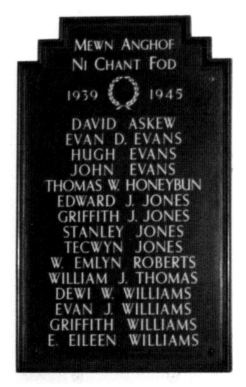

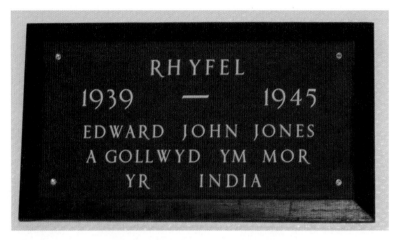

RHYFEL
1939 — 1945
EDWARD JOHN JONES
A GOLLWYD YM MOR
YR INDIA

[Edward John Jones lost at sea in the Indian Ocean]

Llandecwyn

(No WWII Casualties
inscribed thereon)

Talsarnau

Y Rhyfel Mawr 1939–45

Sgt. Ag. R. G. Williams, Derwydd
Cpl. D. B. Maybury, 3, Bryn St
Q.M. R. H. Griffith, Bryntirion
'Mewn angof ni chânt fod'

353

Harlech

1939–1945

Hugh C. Edwards, Pencerrig
Colin J. Griffith, Tregwylan
Clarence G. Hammond, St Davids Hotel
Robert Ll. Lewis, Bryntirion
Ivor Lloyd, 1, Ael-y-Bryn
Robert D. Lloyd, Gwyndy Bach
Emlyn Roberts, 4, Rock Terrace
John Roberts, Isgaer
Owen Roberts, Grogan
Meirion Thomas, 2, Porkington Place
John H. Williams, Isallt

'They were a wall unto us both
by night and day and we were not hurt'
1 Samuel XXV

Llanbedr

Yn y Rhyfel Mawr 1939–1945

Flt/s T. Chadwick, Glyndŵr
Cpl. R. Ll. Jones, Gellibant
Pte. Rt. P. Jones, Brynmoel
Sgt. T. R. Jones, Morfa Mawr
Flt/s P. Lawson, Tynwern
L/s A. C. Stringer, Craig Artro

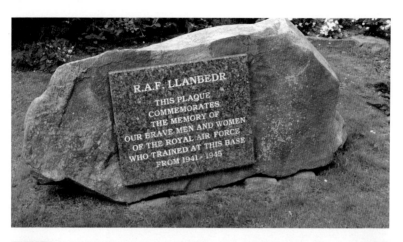

Er Cof annwyl am Corporal Barney Dylan Warburton,
Explosive Ordinance Disposal Royal Engineers 'Llys Brithyll',
Llanbedr, fu farw trwy ddamwain drychinebus yn 27 oed tra'n
gwasanaethu fel cennad hedd dros y Cenhedloedd Unedig.
Stari Vitez, Bosnia, 19 Mawrth 1994.

(Cpl Warburton, Royal Engineers, Bomb Disposal Unit, was
killed in a landmine explosion whilst serving with the UN
Peacekeeping Force in Bosnia)

Dyffryn Ardudwy

Hefyd am y bechgyn a gollwyd yn Rhyfel 1939–1945

Richard Jones
Llewelyn Lewis
William Lowe
Robert Idris Williams

Barmouth

Mewn anghof ni chânt fod
1939–1945

Bernard Bestwick, Harbour View, RH
Kenneth Ellis, Garth, RWF
Edward Field, Tainewyddion, RNVR
Hywel Griffiths, Gibraltar Tce., RNVR
Richard Hughes, Drill y Gar, RAFVR
Evan Jones, Midland Flats, PC
R. Emrys Jones, Maypole House, RAF
Keith Lanman, Lawrenny Lodge, RNVR
Idris Lewis, Beach House, RAFVR
Arthur Ll. Lewis, Llwyn Celyn, IA

E. Einion Morris, Glan-glasfor, WG
Orthin Vaughan Owen, Epworth Villa, RAFVR
Owen Parry, Rose Hill, RNVR
David Prewer, Glanmawddach, RAFVR
F. A. Price, Enfield, SAF
E. A. W. Read, Park Road, RASC
Humphrey Roberts, Fronderw, RAF
Rowland Rowlands, Goronwy Tce, RNVR
Bryan Thomas, Cumberland Hse, RAFVR
Eryl Hughes Williams, The Rectory, RNVR

Bontddu

Pilot Officer Arthur James Fitchett
51st Squadron Bomber Command
25. June 1943.

Arthog

World War
1939–1945

William T. Lewis, Arthog
Trevor Rees, Fairbourne
Charles F. Finlay, Arthog
John Ll. Rees, Arthog

Llwyngwril

1939–1945

Plt/Off C. de G. Findlay
Sgt/Ob J. M. Iliff
Sgt W. T. Lewis
Fl/Lt J. Ll. Rees
F/Sgn-Lr T. L. Rees
F/Sgt D. H. Stinchcombe
Sgt/Plt J. C. Ward

Also
Maj. R. N. Cartside
Fus. D. Lloyd
A.C.1. J. Thomas

Tywyn
St Cadfan's Parish Church

Also in memory of those from this parish who laid down their lives in the Second World War 1939–1945

Thomas William Challoner
David Lewis Davies
Edward Owen Davies
Lewis Davies
William Thos. Patrick Davies
David Alderson Edwards
John Henry Evans
David Richard Griffiths
William John Jarman
Edward Glyndwr Jones

Emyr William Jones
David Francis Lloyd
Archibald Dudley Middleton
Matthew Frank Morris
Claud Mehew Owen
Robert Graham Roberts
William Ifor Roberts
John Cuthbert Stivey
Eileen Williams

Mr David Lloyd George on opening the Institute said: 'I declare this building open as a memorial to the gallant lads from the town who laid down their lives for the liberty and rights of mankind.'

'Institute Opened', *Cambrian News*, 5 November 1926.

Tywyn War Memorial Hospital

Tywyn
Challoner, T.W. P/O
Davies, D. L. Tpr
Davies, E. O. Pte
Davies, L. Sig
Davies, W. T. P. F/Sgt
Edwards, D. A. Sgt
Evans, J. H. Pte
Jarman, W. J. Sgt
Jones, E. G. Pte
Lloyd, D. F. Spr
Middleton, A. Fus
Morris, M. F. Sgt
Roberts, R. G. P/O
Roberts, W. I. Sgt
Stivey, J. C. O/HMS
Williams, E. E. L.WRNS

Bryncrug
Griffiths, D. R. Gnr
Jones, E. W. Gnr
Owen, C. M. Surg. L/T

Llwyngwril
Iliff, J. M. F/Sgt
Lloyd, D. Fus
Stinchcombe, D. F/Sgt
Ward, J. C. F/Sgt

Pennal
Jones, S. Gnr
Lewis, I. G. Pte
Wynne, H. Gnr

Abergynolwyn
Davies, H. E. Sgt
Ellis, O. M. L/Bdr
Owen, J. AC/2
Pugh, R. E. Pte

Aberdyfi
Arthur, C. A. Capt
Clare, S. Sgt
Dain, J. R. Major
Davies, O. L. Fus
Evans, L. Capt
Green, H. C. Dvr
Hayler, J. M. Bdr
Laddy, M. Cmdo
Lloyd, J. C. Sgt
Parry, J. V. Cdt
Rees, J. L. F/Lt
Shortland, W. O. Sgt
Smith, J. Sgt

Bryn Paderau War Memorial

Er Coffadwriaeth
In Rememberance
1939–1945

We shall remember them
Yn angof ni chânt fod

Towyn

T. W. Challoner P. O.
D. L. Davies Tpr.
E. O. Davies Pte.
L. Davies Sig.
W. T. P. Davies F/Sgt.
D. A. Edwards Sgt.
J. H. Evans Pte.
W. J. Jarman Sgt.
E. G. Jones Pte.
D. F. Lloyd Spr.
A. Middleton Fus.
M. F. Morris Sgt.
R. G. Roberts P. O.
W. I. Roberts Sgt.
J. C. Stivey O/HMS.
E. E. Williams L.WRNS.

Bryncrug

D. R. Griffiths Gnr.
E. W. Jones Gnr.
C. M. Owen Surg. L. T.

Aberdovey

C. A. Arthur Capt.
S. Clare Sgt
J. R. Dain Major
O. L. Davies Fus.
L. Evans Capt.
H. C. Green Dvr.
J. M. Hayler Bdr.
M. Laddy Cmdo
J. C. Lloyd Sgt
J. V. Parry Cdt
J. L. Rees F. Lt
W. O. Shortland Sgt
J. Smith Sgt

Pennal

S. Jones Gnr
I. G. Lewis Pte.
H. Wynne Gnr

Abergynolwyn

H. E. Davies Sgt
O. M. Ellis L.Bdr.
J. Owen A.C2.
R. E. Pugh Pte.

Llwyngwril

J. M. Iliff F. Sgt
D. Lloyd Fus.
D. Stinchcombe F. Sgt
J. C. Ward F. Sgt

Aberdyfi

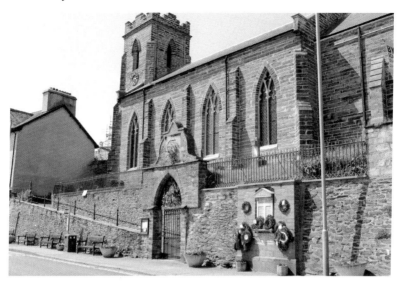

World War 1939–1945
Aberdovey Roll of Honour

Capt. C. Austin Arthur, SWB
Commando Max Laddie, 10th.CU
Sgt Seymour Clare, RAF
Sgt J. C. Lloyd, RAF
Major J. R. Dain, RLR
Cadet J. Vincent Parry, MN
Fus. Owen Leslie Davies, RWF
Fl/Lt John Rees, RAF
Capt. Linus Evans, RWF
Sgt Wilfred O. Shortland, RAF
Tpr Harry C. Green, RAC
Sgt Jack Smith, RTR
Gnr John M. Hayler, RA
Lt David M. De. R. Winser, RAMC

Lest we forget

Aberdyfi – Penhelig

Corris

Rhyfel   1939–1945

Ivor T. Griffiths   Alfred J. Lake

Charles D. Jones   Glynne Parsons

Daniel S. Jones   Alun Thomas

William R. Jones   Harold Thomas

John C. Thomas

'Mewn Angof Ni Chânt Fod'

369

Dolgellau

Hefyd o'r Dref Hon 1939–1945	Hefyd o'r Cylch Cyfagos 1939–1945
Evan Emrys Davies	Alexis A. Aladin
Gwilym Grey Evans	Mary R. Bennett
Robert Ellis Hughes	Evan Williams Edwards
Fred Jones	William Henry Ellis
Ivor Wyn Jones	Lewis Evans
Dewi Cynfal Lewis	Richard Griffiths
Edward Lewis	Einion Jones
Eric Hall Lewis	Malcolm David Owen
Arthur Maelor Owen	Samuel Fred Pickvance
Meirion Pugh	Ivor Wyn Pugh
Emlyn Roberts	Joseph Idris Rowlands
Thomas Bodley Scott	Charles Alexander Wynne-Jones
Thomas Owen Tippett	Ronald Wynne-Jones

Trawsfynydd

Rhyfel 1939–1945
Arthur Jones
John Ellis
Richard Griffiths
E. Thomas Roberts

Yr eildro, mynnai'r heldrin – yn aberth
Ein meibion i'r ddrycin,
Er eu rhoi parha eu rhin
I guro yng nghalon gwerin

H. W. J

371

Llan Ffestiniog

Dafydd Cynfal Davies, 3 Belle Vue
David Wyn Davies, 1 Bryn Tirion
Christmas Hughes, 2 Tan-y-Bryn
Robert Owen Jones, Bryn House
Eric Lloyd Owen, 21 Tyn-y-Maes

Yr eildro, mynnai'r heldrin – yn aberth
Ein meibion i'r ddrycin;
Er eu rhoi parha eu rhin
I guro yng nghalon gwerin

Trawsfynydd   H. W. J.

Beddargraff Kohima

'Pan ddychwelwch gartref dywedwch hyn amdanom ni:
Mai er mwyn eich yfory chwi rhoddasom ein heddiw ni'.

Kohima Epitaph

'When You Go Home, Tell Them Of Us And Say,
For Your Tomorrow, We Gave Our Today'

Acknowledgements

IT IS WITH much pleasure that I give thanks to all those who have helped in the formation of this book and the very many well-wishers who encouraged me to continue with the project.

As in all cases, mention must be made of the individuals who contributed to the text and photographs. It is worth mentioning that in all cases their work has been given freely, and this includes all expenses incurred. The aim was to record the events of the period so that future generations can be made aware of the significant part played by our local community during WWII.

Special thanks to ...

Emeritus Professor Gwyn Thomas, Bangor, for the Rhagair / Foreword and also his support and guidance.

David and Carys Wynne-Hughes, Llangefni, for their immeasurable support, guidance, proofreading, photographs, and editing the chapter on the memorials.

Carys for her excellent research work.

Hugh and Ann Roberts, Henddol, Barmouth, for their support and guidance and the use of Hugh's web photographs: www.flickr.com/photos/abermaw

Also to:

Sir Meurig Rees, Tywyn

Cllr Megan Reynolds, Aberdyfi

Dr David Craik, Harlech & Worcester

Capt. David F. C. Clayton, M. Litt (Oxon), Barrister, RN (Rt'd), Barmouth

The late Cllr J. Iscoed Williams, MBE, Trawsfynydd

Brian Paul, Penrhyndeudraeth

Tommy Owen, Barmouth

Ieu Thomas, Bryncrug

Jane Evans, Aberhosan

Eleanor Owen, Dyffryn Ardudwy

Robert Wyn Jones, Barmouth

Peter Crabtree, Llanbedr

The late Nia Cooke (née Williams), Cardiff

Gwyneth Edwards, Barmouth

The late John Norman Davies, Llangefni

Mr & Mrs Eric Jarman, Barmouth

Robert Ifor Roberts, Singen, Germany

Gareth Tudor Jones, Pwllheli

Paddy Middleton, Northumbria

Michael Jones, Llandeiniolen

Aled Jones, Chester

Edwin Lloyd, Arthog

Gilly Smith, Cardiff

The late Emrys Evans, Blaenau Ffestiniog

Ian Corps, Barmouth

Millicent Edwards, Dyffryn Ardudwy

Nigel Hughes Jones, Rishton, Blackburn

Timothy & Helen Hughes Jones, Blaenau Ffestiniog

The late Walter Pugh, Barmouth

Howard Spier, *AJR Journal*

David Partridge, Botany Bay, Australia

John Meirion Richards, Llwyngwril

Elizabeth Porter, Barmouth

Terwyn Tomos, Tywyn

Ms Linzee Duncan of (www.archieraf.co.uk)

David Sallery, (www.penmorfa.com)

Pieter Jutte, (www.strijdbewijs.nl)

Cadwalader Williams, Barmouth

Gwyneth Jack, Scotland

Graham & Jacky O'Hanlon, Bontddu

Don James, Barmouth

Parch. Dewi Morris, Porthmadog

Rev. Patrick Slattery, Dolgellau

Steffan ab Owain, Blaenau Ffestiniog

E. Griffiths, Weybridge, Surrey – Image of 'Put & Take Top'

Sailors' Institute, Barmouth

Bonhams Auctions, London

The Cambrian News

The National Art Gallery, London

DMH Computers, Llangefni

Royal Marines Historical Society

Llais Ardudwy

Llafar Bro (including *Rhamant Bro*)

Dail Dysynni

Gwynedd Archives, Caernarfon

National Slate Museum, Llanberis

Ynys Môn Archives, Llangefni

Daily Post

Merioneth Archives, Dolgellau

Royal Air Force Museum

Wikipedia

Ffestiniog Grammar School Magazine, *Blodau'r Grug*

Royal Commission on the Ancient and Historical Monuments of Wales

The author acknowledges and offers grateful thanks to all the Archives' staff for their co-operation and valuable assistance so freely given.

The author found the following books useful for information and references and has quoted from them. Wherever possible, he has been granted permission from relevant authors, and he apologises if he has inadvertently omitted any. For more information, it is recommended that readers consult the following:

Bernard O'Conner, *Mawddach Crescent*

George Psychoundakis, *The Cretan Runner*, trans. Patrick Leigh Fermor

W. Stanley Moss, *Ill Met by Moonlight*

Anthony J. Perrett, *Royal Marines in Wales*

James Leasor, *The Unknown Warrior*

Edward Doylerush, *No Landing Place*, vols 1 & 2

Rees Ivor Jones, *The Military in Tywyn, 1795–1999*

Major Roy Rees, *Age Shall Not Weary Them*

Major Bob Smith, *Khaki Shorts*

Paddy Heazel, *Most Secret: The Hidden History of Orford Ness*

Graham & Jacky O'Hanlon, *Military Mawddach*

It was thought appropriate to include in the book photographs of the various memorials situated in our district. These memorials are varied and also include the memorial hospitals in Blaenau Ffestiniog and Tywyn, the memorial halls in Penrhyndeudraeth and Tywyn, and the Tywyn Memorial Institute. In 1990, a new modern remembrance garden was created in Tywyn; the main monument, in polished granite, takes the form of an upright open book with a large cross as the spine. Sitting on a polished granite plinth, the memorial records the names of those local people who lost their lives in both world wars. Aptly, the garden is called Bryn Paderau ('Hill of Prayers') and invokes an atmosphere of remembrance for all those who fell in defence of their country.

In this book, the emphasis has been on the Second World War, and most of the memorials depict losses from that period. Some memorials have been included where no losses in WWII have been recorded. Some memorial plaques depicting later conflicts have also been included.

These memorials are a reminder of the supreme sacrifice made by these gallant people, and we should not forget that because of them our freedom was assured.